# Footwear Impression Evidence

ELSEVIER SERIES IN
**PRACTICAL ASPECTS OF CRIMINAL
AND FORENSIC INVESTIGATIONS**

VERNON J. GEBERTH, BBA, MPS, FBINA *Series Editor*

**Practical Homicide Investigation: Tactics, Procedures, and Forensic
Techniques, Second Edition**
Vernon J. Geberth

**The Counter-Terrorism Handbook: Tactics, Procedures,
and Techniques**
Frank Bolz, Jr., Kenneth J. Dudonis, and David P. Schulz

**Forensic Pathology**
Dominick J. Di Maio and Vincent J. M. Di Maio

**Interpretation of Bloodstain Evidence at Crime Scenes**
William G. Eckert and Stewart H. James

**Tire Imprint Evidence**
Peter McDonald

**Practical Drug Enforcement: Procedures and Administration**
Michael D. Lyman

**Practical Aspects of Rape Investigation: A
Multidisciplinary Approach**
Robert R. Hazelwood and Ann Wolbert Burgess

**The Sexual Exploitation of Children: A Practical Guide to
Assessment, Investigation, and Intervention**
Seth L. Goldstein

**Gunshot Wounds: Practical Aspects of Firearms, Ballistics, and
Forensic Techniques**
Vincent J. M. Di Maio

**Friction Ridge Skin: Comparison and Identification of Fingerprints**
James F. Cowger

**Footwear Impression Evidence**
William J. Bodziak

# Footwear Impression Evidence

## WILLIAM J. BODZIAK

Supervisory Special Agent
Laboratory Division
Federal Bureau of Investigation
Washington, D.C.

**Elsevier**
New York · Amsterdam · London

Elsevier Science Publishing Co., Inc.
655 Avenue of the Americas, New York, New York 10010

Sole distributors outside the United States and Canada:
Elsevier Science Publishers B.V.
P.O. Box 211, 1000 AE Amsterdam, The Netherlands

© 1990 by Elsevier Science Publishing Co., Inc.

This book has been registered with the Copyright Clearance Center, Inc. For further information please contact the Copyright Clearance Center, Inc. Salem, Massachusetts.

This book is printed on acid-free paper.

Library of Congress Cataloging-in-Publication Data
Bodziak, William J.
    Footwear impression evidence / William J. Bodziak.
      p.    cm.—(Practical aspects of criminal & forensic investigation)
    Includes index.
    ISBN 0-444-01542-6 (alk. paper)
    1. Footprints—Identification.   2. Footwear—Identification.
3. Criminal investigation.    I. Title.    II. Series: Elsevier series
in practical aspects of criminal and forensic investigations.
HV8077.5.F6B63      1990
363.2′562—dc20
                                                    90-43976
                                                        CIP

Current printing (last digit):

10  9  8  7  6  5  4  3  2  1

Manufactured in the United States of America

*This book is dedicated
in loving memory
of my father*

# Contents

## Section III
## THE INTERPRETATION AND EXAMINATION OF FOOTWEAR IMPRESSION EVIDENCE

# Preface

Shoes are fascinating items of clothing. They are made in a variety of ways and in thousands of designs. In turn, each design is made in many distinguishable sizes. As the outsole wears, their design and other characteristics steadily change. They acquire cuts, scratches, nicks, and other characteristics of a random nature. These traits serve to give them a tremendous degree of individuality. As they track through soil, snow, sand, residue, and other materials, supporting the weight of their wearer, they impress their distinct and individual features on or into the surfaces over which they pass.

Items of footwear and their impressions that remain at the crime scene offer sound, reliable, and demonstrative evidence of a person's presence. Yet, despite the fact that footwear impressions are present at most crime scenes, they still constitute only a small fragment of the physical evidence that crime scene technicians collect and that investigators and prosecutors use in the proof of facts. In searching for some explanations as to why footwear impression evidence hasn't received greater emphasis, my experience and tenure in this area since 1973 has led to certain observations and deductions.

First, in the development and growth of laboratories throughout the world, the responsibilities for the examination of footwear impression evidence have historically fallen to several different disciplines. Some laboratories designated their fingerprint examiners to examine this evidence, reasoning that a "footprint" and a fingerprint examination must be alike. This, in addition to the convenience that most laboratories already employed fingerprint examiners, resulted in footwear impression examinations becoming part of many latent fingerprint examiners' responsibility. Likewise, some laboratories designated their documents examiners to examine the footwear impressions. Their reasoning was that a "shoe print," like a rubber stamp examination, was clearly the same as a document printing examination. Other laboratories designated their toolmark and firearms examiners to examine footwear evidence, likening the three-dimensional impressions to a tool mark. Even laboratory examiners designated as criminalists, microscopists, trace analysts, and chemists have, in certain instances, been assigned the responsibility of footwear impression evidence.

As a result of this treatment of footwear impression evidence as an "occasional examination" that could be conveniently handled by persons in other disciplines, that evidence, during the further development of laboratories and the growth in recent years in the forensic sciences, has failed to be given the necessary emphasis and attention that is deserved and needed. Fingerprint examiners, document examiners, toolmark examiners, and the like, who spent the overwhelming majority of their time in their respective primary forensic disciplines, could not dedicate the necessary time and resources toward the examination of footwear impression evidence. Likewise, the topic of footwear impression evidence was rarely discussed at forensic science meetings of those groups and was rarely published in their respective journals.

This second rate treatment of footwear impression evidence by laboratory and crime scene personnel spilled over into the investigative and judicial areas as well. Footwear impression evidence was seldom looked for at crime scenes and when found, was seldom examined and utilized to its fullest extent. Consequently, investigators and prosecutors rarely had reason to understand and appreciate the full importance of that physical evidence and failed to utilize it in the proof of facts of their case.

Fortunately, this is changing. In recent years there have been numerous seminars, published articles, and presentations covering the collection and examination of footwear impression evidence. Footwear impression evidence is not only being utilized with increasing frequency in the United States, but also by law enforcement agencies in England, Canada, Australia, India, Japan, Germany, Holland, Finland, New Zealand, and by virtually every country that utilizes forensic examinations.

At the same time, changes in technology have assisted in helping to retrieve this type of evidence from the crime scene. The improvement, development, and availability of the electrostatic lifting device and quality gelatin footprint lifters; the use of dental stone casting materials, better film and camera technology, and the increased application of both old and new enhancement techniques and materials have greatly contributed toward the successful detection and utilization of footwear impression evidence.

In addition, recent years have witnessed dramatic world changes in the footwear industry. Literally thousands of shoe designs, each available in many sizes, are available to the consumer nowadays. The shoes people wear are also more likely to have synthetic outsoles. Those outsoles, in turn, are more likely to acquire detectable characteristics and to leave traces of their impressions at the crime scene.

In order to fully utilize this evidence, footwear examiners need to be knowledgable and practiced in all the facets related to this evidence, including the proper methods of detecting and retrieving footwear impressions at the crime scene, the photography and enhancement of those impressions, the manufacturing of footwear, and the evaluation of footwear evidence being examined. Any weak link concerning the discovery, retrieval, examination, and proper utilization as evidence in court will adversely affect the usefulness and success of this evidence. For that reason, it is also crucial that examiners be actively involved in passing this knowledge along to their colleagues, including crime scene technicians, investigators, and prosecutors. Today's footwear examiner cannot be satisfied to know that footwear impressions were found at only a small fraction of their crime scenes when common sense dictates that more are present.

I am aware of a few laboratories that in recent years have finally given due emphasis to footwear evidence. They have insisted that their crime scene technicians preserve the crime scene and aggressively search for footwear impressions. And, to their surprise, they found that they were detecting many more impressions than before. Their examiners have since conducted more examinations that have not only given them more experience but have allowed them to justify and dedicate more time toward casework and training to this area. As a result more cases have been solved and more court trials were won due to the contribution that evidence made.

Since first being assigned to the FBI laboratory in 1973, I steadily accumulated casework experience, reference materials, photographs, and other information concerning footwear impression evidence. That effort intensified in 1982 and thereafter when I began participating in seminars hosted by other forensic laboratories, interacted with other footwear examiners, and began organizing footwear impression seminars and classes at the FBI Academy in Quantico, Virginia. The result was a large accumulation of information concerning the materials and procedures that were essential in locating and collecting footwear impression evidence at the crime scene as well as the comparison of a suspect's shoes with the questioned impression evidence. Drawing upon that information and experience, I have written this book. I hope its contents will provide the necessary information and incentive to those in the law enforcement community to become more aware of and to better utilize footwear impression evidence.

# Acknowledgments

To my wife Shirley and to my children, Bill, Leslie, and Chuck, I would like to extend my sincere and loving thanks for their help, support, and understanding during the many nights and weekends that I spent writing this book.

I would also like to offer my appreciation to the following individuals in the FBI Laboratory who contributed considerable time and assistance in the preparation of this book; in particular, to Danny L. Keen, Richard R. Thomas, William W. Magle, William H. Peters, Dawn D. Hester, and James C. Burggraff for their outstanding forensic photography; to William L. Wempe and the personnel of the Photographic Processing Unit for their photographic support and assistance; to Kathleen W. Johnson for her outstanding artwork; to Colleen Wade and Cindy Poyer, forensic librarians, who offered invaluable assistance in locating many of the items in the bibliography; to Sharon D. Clayborne for her much needed assistance; to Unit Chiefs James E. Lile and Gerald B. Richards for their support and encouragement and for their technical review, to Cynthia Ann Turcea, James Gerhart, John F. Paulisick of the FBI Laboratory and to Ernest D. Hamm of the Florida Department of Law Enforcement.

I would like to offer my special thanks and appreciation to Roger T. Castonguay, former Assistant Director of the FBI laboratory, for his support of this project at its onset and to John W. Hicks, current Assistant Director of the FBI laboratory, for his continued support.

# Awareness, Detection, and Treatment of Footwear Impression Evidence

# 1

Wherever he steps, whatever he touches, whatever he leaves even unconsciously, will serve as silent witness against him. Not only his fingerprints or his footprints, but his hair, the fibers from his clothes, the glass he breaks, the tool marks he leaves, the paint he scratches, the blood or semen he deposits or collects—all of these and more bear mute witness against him. This is evidence that does not forget. It is not confused by the excitement of the moment. It is not absent because human witnesses are. It cannot perjure itself. It cannot be wholly absent. Only its interpretation can err. Only human failure to find it, study and understand it, can diminish its value.

*Crime Investigation,* second edition, Paul L. Kirk (deceased), edited by John I. Thornton (1974), p. 2.

## The Importance of Footwear Impression Evidence

### Impression Evidence

Impression evidence can be generally defined as *objects or materials which have retained the characteristics of other objects or materials which have been impressed against them.*

Of the many forms of impression evidence, the most common forms encountered in forensic work include fingerprints, palm prints, footwear impressions, tire impressions, and bite marks. Other forms of impression evidence include glove prints, bare footprints, socked foot impressions, lip impressions, ear impressions, and contusion and abrasion pattern injuries.

### Footwear Impressions: A Valuable Form of Physical Evidence

Crimes involve people and places. Persons committing a crime leave footwear impressions en route to, at, and exiting the crime scene. As a form of physical evidence, these impressions can provide an important link between the criminal and the crime scene. Footwear impression evidence unfortunately has been neglected to the extent that it is used in only a small percentage of cases. Neglect of this evidence is not forgivable, but there are some reasons that may help account for it.

The location of footwear impression evidence, primarily on ground surfaces, makes it sometimes difficult or inconvenient to find, particularly if the impressions are latent or nearly invisible. Specialized lighting and techniques are often required, along with an aggressive effort to find the impressions. Crime scene technicians may have little or no experience in searching for those types of impressions, and may consider the search too time consuming and cumbersome. This perception is understandable, as many crime scene technicians are unfamiliar with the best techniques or are unequipped to use them. In addition, the footwear impressions of the subject may be mixed with those of other persons such as paramedics and investigators, who may have arrived at the scene ahead of the crime scene technician. The fact that there may be footwear impressions in addition to those of the suspect does not necessarily mean that the suspect's were destroyed, yet many technicians are discouraged by such tracked areas.

Footwear impression evidence has been frequently undervalued by investigators, attorneys, and the courts due to their limited knowledge of it. I still get asked by investigators the common questions, "Can you compare a footwear impression with a shoe?" and "Is it possible to positively identify a footwear impression with a shoe?" And it is not uncommon, in cases where a positive identification is made, to have the prosecuting attorney ask, "Can you *really* say that that shoe positively made that impression?"

The long-term effect of this misunderstanding of footwear evidence has been a further discouragement and deterrent for the crime scene officer to look for footwear impressions. Additionally, because much of the footwear evidence is latent or nearly invisible, the crime scene technician may erroneously feel that it is not present or, by not thoroughly looking, may even rationalize its believed nonexistence.

The crime scene technician and/or investigator must be aware of the full importance of footwear impressions as physical evidence. When securing the crime scene area, they must avoid the destruction of all forms of evidence, including footwear impressions. Before beginning the crime scene search, careful thought should be given to what occurred at the crime scene, how footwear impression evidence could contribute to the proof of facts, and what areas of the crime scene might contain footwear impression evidence. Then the *footwear impressions should be looked for aggressively and carefully.* What is not looked for will not be found!

## Frequency of Footwear Impressions

Each time a person takes a step, their footwear is impressed against the ground surface and can cause a deformation of the ground surface or result in the transfer of trace materials and residue between the ground and the shoe. Although not all of the impressions will be visible or detectable, the chances are excellent that some will be.

If a crime had occurred in an area where the ground was soft, such as a sandy beach or a soft dirt road, no one would contest the common-sense deduction that footwear impressions would be present. It would be simply impossible for the subject to step in those areas without leaving many footwear impressions in the soft surface. If that same crime were to have taken place at another location with a different surface, one would not assume the presence of footwear impressions. However, the subject's shoes would have impressed themselves against the ground's surface just as many times. There would also be an excellent chance that one or more of those impressions could be located and retrieved.

Today, everyone accepts the potential for the presence of latent fingerprints at a crime scene. Unfortunately, it is often not recognized that there is an equal chance that a latent footwear impression could be present as well. The average investigator could list many possible reasons why fingerprints would be left at a crime scene and their probable locations. The same investigators are not usually as knowledgeable about footwear impressions. Yet with every step that is taken, whether on soil, snow, concrete, a tile floor, carpeting, glass, a wooden window sill, a piece of paper, a bank counter, or one of many other objects and materials, a representation of the characteristics of the shoe outsole can be impressed against and retained by that surface, in either a visible or a latent form.

## Durability of Footwear Impressions

Footwear impressions are either permanent or can be permanently recorded. With few exceptions, footwear impressions at crime scenes are of sufficient durability to allow for their discovery, retrieval, recording, and examination. In fact, their permanence in some cases is surprising.

## Positive Identification of Footwear

In many instances, footwear impressions can be *positively identified* as having been made by a specific shoe. This identification is based on random characteristics that the shoe has acquired and is as strong as the identification of fingerprints, tool marks, or handwriting.

In other instances, the characteristics transferred in a footwear impression may not be sufficient to positively identify with a specific shoe. However, the detail that is present may still help in the proof of facts. The size and design characteristics of the shoes alone, as explained in later chapters, are so numerous and diverse that any specific size and design of shoe, without regard to wear or other unique characteristics, will be owned by only a very small fraction of one percent of the general population. Additional factors, like mold characteristics and wear, although still not sufficient to enable positive identification, can further reduce the number of other shoes that could have made the impression.

## Information Provided by Footwear Impressions

Footwear impressions can reveal, in many cases, the type, make, description, and approximate or precise size of the footwear that made them. This information can assist in identifying a suspect. In addition, the location of footwear impressions at the scene can often help to reconstruct the crime. The presence, characteristics, and condition of the impressions can assist in determining the number of suspects involved, their path through and away from the crime scene, their involvement in the crime, and the events that occurred during the crime. Footwear impressions at crime scenes can also be used to corroborate or refute information provided by other witnesses.

## Walking Gait Measurements

Many criminology texts and articles written on footwear impressions have outlined methods for recording information relating to a person's gait. These features include the relative angle of each foot, the distance between each step, and other measurements related to the position and placement of the foot during normal walking. It has been my experience that footwear impressions left at crime scenes rarely, if ever, offer the necessary succession of impressions to make use of this type of information. Even in the rare case where a sufficient number of succeeding impressions might appear to represent the ordinary gait of the perpetrator, there is no way of knowing if these impressions were, in fact, the result of normal walking or if the subject was running, walking fast, or otherwise acting in a way that would alter his or her gait. Without this knowledge, gait measurements might be erroneously evaluated.

The observed gait characteristics, when they are present on exterior surfaces, are used successfully in the tracking of individuals. Expert trackers, like those with the U.S. Border Patrol (Kearney J, 1983), use gait information along with other tracking signs when tracking illegal immigrants, missing children, and criminals. Tracking is the best application of this type of information, since the gait characteristics of a person are not individual identifying ones but are class characteristics of a group of persons sharing a gait pattern. In tracking a person, gait information is used in combination with other footwear characteristics, to help distinguish one person from others whose paths may have crossed the same area.

The gait information present at crime scenes, particularly from impressions on confined interior surfaces, would have little value in independently establishing the identity of a subject.

## Substrates for Footwear Impressions

Several things can occur when a shoe makes contact with the ground. They include the creation of static charges, the deformation of the surface, and the transfer of residue or trace materials between the shoe and the surface.

### Creation of Static Charges

When a shoe is impressed against a surface, it can create an electrostatic charge on that surface (Davis RJ, 1988). This can be demonstrated by taking a clean, dry shoe and stepping on a hard, flat surface, such as a tile floor. If several light puffs of black powder or toner are then applied to the area, the powder or toner will be attracted to the residual static charge left by the impression, and a visual image will result (Figure 1.1). Likewise, if the clean, dry shoe were used to step on carpeting, an application of small polystyrene beads would result in the visualization of the impression because the beads are attracted to the residual charge created by the impression. Unfortunately, the residual static charge does not last long and is not demonstrable in high humidity or damp environments. Static charges, in part, account for the strong adherence of residue, dust, and other trace materials that are transferred from the shoe to the surface.

### Deformation of the Surface

If the ground surface is soft and yields to pressure exerted by the shoe, it will deform, either temporarily or permanently, and may acquire the characteristics of the shoe. If the surface is snow, sand, soil, or similar material, the impression will be a three-dimensional, permanent one. If the surface is resilient, such as carpet, grass, or skin, the deformation caused by the impression will be temporary, although some permanent

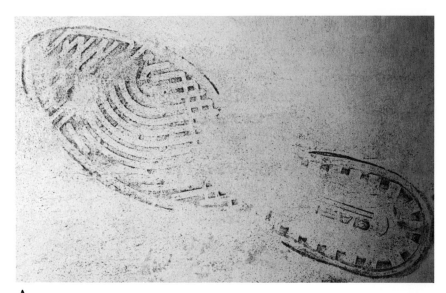

**A**
**1.1**   A footwear impression in a dry environment will create a static charge, which can be visualized by applying a fine powder or toner across the surface. (A) This impression was a latent static charge on a floor over which several puffs of blower fingerprint powder were applied. The powder adherred mainly to the charged areas of the footwear impression. (B) A piece of paper was stepped on with clean shoes. No impressions were visible on the paper before processing with physical developer.

two-dimensional marks or damage, such as stains, contusions, or the transfer of residue, may occur in conjunction with these impressions.

One interesting method of showing footwear impressions on resilient carpeting involves the use of holography to record the outline of the impression (Bradford WR, 1976). The carpet, in the area stepped on, is crushed and, over a period of time, slowly returns to its original shape. The holograph, as a result of minute movements of the carpet's fibers between two separate exposures, is able to visualize the general shape of the footwear impression. This method of detection is, of course, not practical or possible at crime scenes.

## Transfer of Trace or Residue Materials

With many two-dimensional impressions, there is a transfer of trace materials or residue between the footwear and the surface. An impression that results when a shoe deposits material onto a surface is a

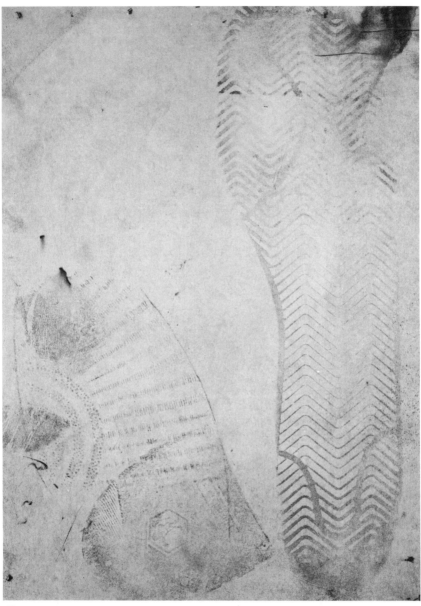

**B**

positive impression, one in which the residue visually represents the areas of the outsole that actually came in contact with the ground surface. The impressions in Figures 1.1 and 1.2 are examples of positive impressions. Positive impressions constitute the most common form of two-dimensional impressions. A negative impression, one in which the

**1.2**   A piece of glass containing a residue impression. This impression shows up light in color since it is a positive residue impression and reflects more light than the darker background.

residue visually represents the areas of the outsole that did *not* come in contact with the surface, is produced when a shoe removes residue from a surface. Figure 1.3 provides examples of negative impressions. Negative impressions occur less frequently than positive impressions.

Two-dimensional impressions can occur when the shoes are wet or dry and can occur on a large variety of receiving surfaces. Some examples of the many possibilities are discussed.

*Clean dry shoes on dry surfaces.* Nonleather outsoles or heels are composed of compounds such as rubber, polyurethane, polyvinyl chloride, and ethyl vinyl acetate. Trace materials from these compounds bleed through the outsole and can be deposited on or into the surface in trace quantities. Therefore, a shoe with a perfectly clean outsole, even a brand new shoe, can still leave a trace of its impression on paper items, pieces of glass, and polished surfaces by depositing trace materials from the outsoles. Figure 1.1B shows the developed latent footwear impressions on paper that was treated with physical developer. It is one example of how clean, dry shoes can leave

1.3 (A) A piece of glass with a film on it which was stepped on at a crime scene. The film, which can consist of dirt, residue and a number of other things was removed in the area where the clean shoe made contact with it. When photographed with a dark background, the impressioned area shows up dark. (B) An impression resulting from a clean shoe stepping on a residue covered cabinet and resulting in a negative impression.

A

B

latent impressions that can later be developed through chemical enhancement.

Clean footwear can also leave impressions in the film that is left on surfaces by the accumulation of waxes, oils, or dirt. This is seen most frequently on nonporous and polished surfaces. Flooring, glass, and counter tops often contain a film of wax residue or dirt and therefore are good candidates for retaining impressions. To illustrate this, a worn but clean, dry shoe was used to step on a piece of glass. Figure 1.3A depicts the resulting impression. The glass had a film of accumulated material on it, and the shoe lifted that film off in the areas of contact, leaving a negative impression. The glass was photographed with oblique light and a black background. The negative impression therefore appears dark, since the areas of the glass that were touched by the shoe and had the film removed now allow the black background to show through. Figure 1.3B also depicts a negative impression, which resulted when a shoe stepped on a cabinet that contained a heavy coating of accumulated dust and residue. The dust and residue adhered to the portion of the shoe outsole that made contact with the cabinet and was removed with the shoe, leaving a light image in those areas.

Clean, dry shoes can leave depressions on carpeting, though many types of carpeting are not suitable for retaining footwear impressions. Some carpeting, particularly if it has been recently vacuumed, will retain footwear impressions for a sufficient amount of time and can reveal the shape and dimensions of the footwear, and occasionally some design information. If impressions in carpet are located, they can be photographed with oblique lighting and then further treated with the electrostatic lifting device. They can also furnish information concerning the movement of the subject and the possible location of other footwear impressions.

From this discussion, it can be seen that it is very possible for a suspect whose shoes are dry and free of residue or other materials to leave two-dimensional impressions of excellent quality as she or he travels through the crime scene.

Impressions made by clean, dry shoes are usually hard to detect. They should be searched for carefully and thoroughly with the proper lighting in areas where the subject would possibly have walked across broken glass, paper, waxed or polished surfaces, or surfaces containing a fine film or residue. Papers that have been strewn around or dropped on the floor, and those that are otherwise located where the suspect may have stepped, should also be closely examined. Paper items that have been stepped on should be candidates for electrostatic and chemical processing.

A recently developed device known as an Intensified Ultraviolet Viewer (Hammamatsu Corporation, Bridgewater, NJ) can be used with a shortwave light source to enable the visual detection and photography of latent impressions made by rubber shoes that have tracked across *highly reflective* polished or waxed surfaces. The system uses reflected shortwave ultraviolet light to visualize the otherwise latent impressions. The attachment of a camera to the intensified viewer provides the means to permanently record those impressions.

*Dry residue impressions.* When shoes track across a dirty surface, they will acquire a coating of accumulated residue. If they then track onto a relatively clean surface, residue in the form of footwear impressions is deposited, even though those impressions, because of their trace quantity and lack of contrast with the surface, might not be visible.

Shoes pick up whatever loose residue and dust may be on the surface they cross. As long as they remain in contact with the same surface, there will probably not be any *visible* residue impressions left, because any residue deposited by the shoe cannot be distinguished from the existing residue on that surface. When the shoe crosses a relatively cleaner surface, the reverse takes place, and the shoe deposits that residue onto the cleaner surface. Eventually, if the footwear continues to track across clean surface, all of the residue will be lost from the surface of the shoe. Whenever there are areas that are relatively clean or dirty in contrast to each other, i.e., a dirty outside surface next to a relatively clean inside surface, there is an excellent potential for a transfer of residue or dust to be left in the form of both visible and latent footwear impressions.

Dry residue impressions, because of their lack of contrast with the surface, are difficult to locate and very often go undiscovered. A bright floodlight used to direct an oblique light across the surface, and the electrostatic lifting device, discussed later in this book, are excellent devices for finding and recovering dry residue impressions. Figure 1.4A shows a tile floor containing an impression which is rendered invisible in the normal surrounding room light. Figure 1.4B depicts a strong oblique light source in the darkened room being used to locate the same residue impression on the tile floor. A similar dry residue impression on a carpeted surface may not be visible even with oblique light; however, electrostatic processing of the carpet would both lift and reveal that impression.

Items such as floors, paper, glass, boxes, and other surfaces that may have been stepped on should always be considered as potentially bearing residue footwear impressions. Figure 1.2 depicts a piece of glass containing a dry residue impression. This impression is light colored, as opposed to that in Figure 1.3A. It is a deposition of residue on the glass by the raised areas of the outsole and is therefore a positive impression. Figure 1.5 shows a piece of paper with a partial impression in blood and a very faint impression in residue. An electrostatic lift of the paper revealed two impressions in residue. The light color of the paper had

A

**1.4 (A)** An area of flooring, pictured under normal indoor overhead lighting, does not reveal any footwear impressions. **(B)** By darkening the room and using a strong oblique light source held close to the ground, several footwear impressions become visible.

B

obscured part of one residue impression and all of the second residue impression. Other examples of how the electrostatic lifter can both enhance impressions that contrast poorly with the substrate as well as reveal latent impressions are given in Chapter 4.

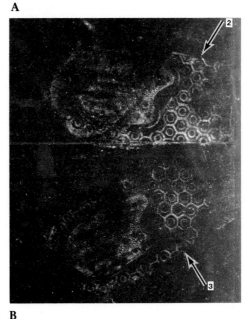

**1.5** **(A)** A piece of paper bearing (1) a bloody footwear impression and (2) a very light and partial residue impression. **(B)** An electrostatic lift of the paper not only enhanced the residue impression (2) but revealed a second residue impression next to it (3).

*Wet impressions.* Impressions made when a clean shoe outsole is wet or damp constitute a different type of impression. Most of these impressions dry before they are found, but must still be considered as impressions of wet origin for the purposes of retrieval. When there is

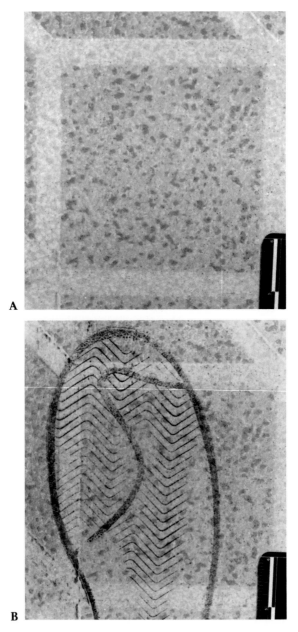

**1.6** **(A)** A latent impression resulted from a wet shoe stepping on a waxed or polished surface. The quality of the impression will vary with the waxed surface, the moisture on the shoe, the type of outsole and other factors. **(B)** This impression was enhanced by dusting with black fingerprint powder.

rain, heavy dew, or snow on the ground, most of the impressions, particularly at the point of entry, will be wet impressions. If a wet outsole should come in contact with a clean surface, such as a waxed floor, counter top, or desk top, it can leave a watermark or disturbance in the waxed or polished surface. Like dry residue impressions, wet impressions of clean shoes are often difficult to see and photograph. Since they are nothing more than disturbances in the wax or film of a polished surface without the presence of transferred residue, they are sometimes latent or can be seen only from an angle. Wet impressions on a waxed or polished surface can be enhanced with fingerprint powder, after which they can be photographed and then lifted with an adhesive or gelatin lifter of contrasting color. It is not uncommon for this type of impression to be located accidentally while an area is being dusted for fingerprints. A classic example is when a waxed counter top in a bank is stepped on by a vaulting bank robber whose shoes have remained damp from the snow or rain outside. Figure 1.6 depicts an impression of this type that has been enhanced with silver fingerprint powder. Crime scenes having large, clean, waxed surfaces or polished floors that may have been walked on by suspects having damp shoes, whether dampened by rain, snow, or dew, can contain numerous footwear impressions of value. In such a scenario, the crime scene technician might consider processing the entire floor with fingerprint powder of contrasting color, using a feather brush.

Impressions can also occur when the outsole is wet and contains residue or tracks over a dirty surface. Impressions of wet origin that contain residue or are made on dirty surfaces are usually more difficult to lift and the results are more unpredictable. In some cases they cannot be successfully lifted. Other impressions, especially those on smooth, nonporous surfaces, will not adhere well to the surface and can become very fragile when they dry out. It is often possible to recognize impressions of wet origin based on certain features of the impression itself, such as water stains and smears. If impressions of wet origin on dirty surfaces must be lifted, commercial gelatin lifting materials offer the best method. The gelatin lift can be allowed to remain for 10 to 20 minutes on the impression before it is removed. This will sometimes re-humidify the impression and allow for a better lift. Figure 1.7 shows a wet residue impression.

*Impressions in other materials.* Impressions will result when a shoe tracks through oil, grease, blood, and other similar materials. These types of impressions are usually more visible and easier to detect than the types discussed above, but they can occur as latent impressions as well.

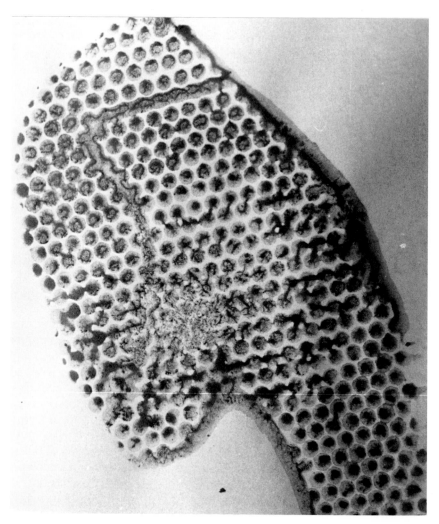

**1.7** A wet residue impression on a porous surface. Characteristics in the impression, such as stippling and beading of the water/residue mixture, indicate that it is of wet origin.

## Finding Footwear Impressions at the Scene of a Crime

### Why Footwear Impressions Are Overlooked

All crime scenes should be approached with the expectation that they contain footwear impressions. *Investigators and crime scene technicians should be aggressive in their search for such impressions.* Lack of success in finding footwear impressions at a crime scene is often due to one or more of the following:

1. Not believing that visible and/or latent footwear impressions will be found at the crime scene and not aggressively looking for them.
2. Incomplete searches of the scene, possibly due to the inability to determine the exact points of entry and exit. Searches may also be incomplete because of lack of proper knowledge of the ways footwear impressions can occur and how they can be found.
3. Arrival at the scene after other persons have trampled over the impression evidence and failure to look for footwear impressions in those areas. Allowing unauthorized personnel (all persons other than the crime scene technicians) to walk through the crime scene area.
4. The combination of shoe and surface characteristics not being conducive to the production of footwear impression evidence.
5. The impressions having been intentionally destroyed by the subjects. This is an unlikely possibility except in cases involving the cleanup of blood impressions.
6. Weather destroying exterior impressions.

Figure 1.8 is a diagram showing the likelihood of finding footwear impressions on various surfaces under different circumstances. As can be seen, the likelihood for an item of footwear to leave either a visible or a detectable latent impression exists in most situations. Those marked "very likely" will occur in almost every instance. Those marked "likely" will usually occur to some degree. Those marked "unlikely" indicate situations in which a footwear impression is still possible, but in most instances will not occur.

## Specific Areas to Check for Footwear Impression Evidence

Footwear impressions can be found anywhere in and around the crime scene. Areas where *special attention* to footwear impression evidence should be given include:

*The actual point of occurrence of the crime.* The point of occurrence is the specific area where the crime was committed. In homicides, rapes, assaults, and other crimes against a person, there is often a struggle or extra activity that results in many footwear impressions in the specific area where the crime took place. There can be impressions left in the victim's blood, impressions on the victim's clothing and body resulting from the victim being kicked, and impressions on items knocked to the floor during the struggle. In burglaries, there may be items such as safe insulation, paper, or other debris on the floor as a result of the crime that will retain impressions of footwear.

*The point of entry.* The point of entry is the location where the subject entered an interior area. If a window that has been pried

### Likelihood of Detectable Footwear Impressions Occurring on DIFFERENT TWO-DIMENSIONAL SHOE/SURFACE COMBINATIONS

| SURFACE | Damp or Wet Shoes | Shoe with blood, grease, oil, etc. | Dry Shoes with Dust or Residue | Clean Dry Shoe (no dust or residue) |
|---|---|---|---|---|
| CARPET | unlikely | very likely | likely | unlikely |
| DIRTY FLOOR with accumulation of dust, dirt, or residue | likely | very likely | unlikely | unlikely |
| RELATIVELY CLEAN, but unwaxed floor | likely | very likely | very likely | unlikely |
| CLEAN WAXED Tile or Wood Floor | likely | very likely | very likely | likely |
| WAXED Bank Counter, Desk Top, etc. | likely | very likely | very likely | likely |
| GLASS | very likely | very likely | very likely | likely |
| KICKED IN DOOR | very likely | very likely | very likely | likely |
| PAPER, CARDBOARD, etc. | very likely | very likely | very likely | likely |

**1.8**    The likelihood of two-dimensional footwear impressions of value for examination purposes being left on various surfaces is greater than you might expect. Those combinations marked "very likely" reflect an almost certain occurrence of a footwear impression. Those marked "likely" reflect a reasonable chance of a footwear impression. Those marked "unlikely" reflect a situation where it is not likely, but still possible to have a footwear impression occur.

open or broken, a door that has been kicked in, or a similarly obvious point of forced entry can be found, the area where the subject would have walked before and after entering the scene can be specifically defined. Forced entries, because of the unnatural way in which the subject entered and because of the greater likelihood of stepping on objects, debris, or broken glass, usually provide a greater chance for finding footwear impressions than crime scenes where the point of entry was a common one, such as the front door. The search for impressions should include the exterior surfaces, such as flower beds, back porches, and other areas immediately outside the point of entry.

*The route through the crime area.* Depending on the nature of the crime and the successful discovery of the point of entry, the point of occurrence, and the point of exit, the route the subject took through the crime scene may or may not be apparent. Anywhere the route is apparent should be thoroughly searched for impressions, particularly if that route passes through dusty or dirty surfaces, such as an unfinished basement floor or a dusty back porch.

*The point of exit and other exterior areas.* Exit routes from the crime scene may be harder to determine. Impressions in soft exterior ground surfaces that lead away from the general scene may contribute to reconstruction of the direction in which the subject fled. Crime scenes adjacent to or surrounded by soft ground surfaces should be immediately sealed off and carefully searched. The location of footwear impressions in exterior areas left by the suspect while fleeing the scene can result in the discovery of additional evidence, such as discarded weapons and tire tread impressions. In many crimes, the subject will hide outside and observe the area prior to committing the crime. It is therefore not uncommon to find footwear impressions just outside a crime scene near trees, bushes, or other obstructions behind which the subject hid. Exterior surfaces that are snow-covered or that consist of soft soil or sand, if properly preserved and searched, can provide extensive footwear evidence.

*Near other footwear impressions.* When any footwear impression is located, it provides an important clue to the possible location of other footwear impressions.

## General Crime Scene Procedures

In order to help assure better success in the search for footwear impression evidence, the following suggestions are made and should be implemented in the current crime scene procedure:

1. Seal the scene. *Do not allow anyone, including other law enforcement personnel, into the general crime scene area, except when it is necessary to tend to victims.* This should include broad exterior areas where the subject may have left impressions either before or after the crime. When the actual crime scene search begins, only those conducting that search should walk through the scene.

2. If it is the scene of a homicide, remember that valuable impressions are often located around and beneath the victim's body.

3. Prior to the crime scene search, determine what crime has taken place, the point of occurrence and the points of entry and exit, if possible, and whatever other details of the crime are known. Based on this knowledge, try to reconstruct what occurred during the crime. Consider what physical conditions are present both inside and outside the scene that are particularly good for retaining footwear impressions. Look for the type of footwear impression evidence that the conditions and surfaces would warrant wherever the subject may have stepped. If weather is a factor, first tend to those impressions that could be destroyed or deteriorate.

4. Be especially aware of impressions that, due to their partial or latent nature, may be difficult to detect. Realize that partial impressions and other impressions that might initially look to be of limited value are as easily examined and identified as full impressions.

5. Photograph and then recover the footwear impression evidence.

### Methods of Searching

Search for the impressions in one small area or room at one time. A methodical visual search with existing light should be made first. It should be possible to detect the obvious and most visible footwear impressions, such as those in blood, grease, or other visible residue. To assist in locating footwear impressions that are not easily detected in normal lighting, the area being searched should be darkened. A bright, oblique light source held just off of and parallel to the ground, as shown in Figure 1.4, should be used to search for residue or dust impressions that are not visible in normal room light. A portable flood light is most effective; however, a bright flashlight will also work well. The oblique light works best for detecting impressions on smooth surfaces like tile or wood flooring. Impressions on carpeting or other rough or porous surfaces may still be invisible, even with the oblique light. The electrostatic lifting device can be used to search those areas for dry residue impressions.

Very often, investigators neglect to search certain areas of the crime scene because they have been walked over by investigators, paramedics, or other individuals. It should be emphasized that although the area that contains the suspect's impressions may have been walked on, the impressions themselves have not necessarily been tracked over. The chances of all of the subject's impressions being partially or completely obliterated by crime scene personnel is unlikely. If an impression was tracked over, part of that impression would probably still be intact and would be just as valuable as any other partial impression.

## Hypothetical Crime Scene

Figure 1.9 is a diagram of a hypothetical crime scene. It provides a few examples of how a person could leave footwear impressions at various locations in a scene. Although it is unlikely that all of those impressions would be left at a single scene, it is *not* unlikely that several of them could be found at a single crime scene.

In the example shown in Figure 1.9, the first impressions left (1) were those retained in the soil behind some shrubbery. Criminals commonly stalk or observe the scene or the victim prior to the crime, and therefore impressions in soft exterior surfaces where the subject stood, walked, or hid can often be found.

En route to the point of entry, the subject walked across wet, dew-covered grass. The subject then broke into the house through a glass window. As the subject stepped through the window onto a desk, a footwear impression was left on a piece of the broken glass from the window (2) by one of the damp shoes and also on the desktop itself (3), which has a waxed surface. No impressions were left on the carpet in that room by the damp but clean shoes. As the subject walked through the next room, which has a dry but dirty floor, the shoes accumulated the dry residue. The subject then kicked in a door (4) and left a dry residue impression on it. Further steps into the next room on the clean tile floor left additional residue footwear impressions for the first few steps, (5) until the shoes no longer contained residue. These impressions would probably only be detected with a strong oblique light or the electrostatic lifting device. The fact that one room is dirty and the next clean, combined with the known point of entry, should suggest to the crime scene technician that footwear impression evidence is likely to exist in those areas.

Next, the subject moved through the carpeted room with clean shoes. On this particular carpeting, no permanent impressions of value were left. As the subject moved part way into the kitchen onto the clean tile floor, no impressions were left. At this point, the homicide was committed. During the scuffle, some papers were knocked to the floor. One shoe stepped entirely in a pool of blood and left a series of tracked blood impressions over the next few steps (6). The toe of the other shoe stepped only partially in the blood. It left a partial blood impression on the paper (7) and then tracked several partial blood impressions across the tile floor. The position of the toe area of the impression on the paper indicates that the remaining area of the shoe also stepped on the paper. The paper is therefore a candidate for chemical processing to develop the remaining latent impression on the paper. Upon entering the garage, the subject stepped in an oil stain with one shoe and subsequently tracked impressions in oil (8). After the subject left the garage, some additional impressions were made outside in the soft flower bed, and these indicate the direction in which the subject fled (9).

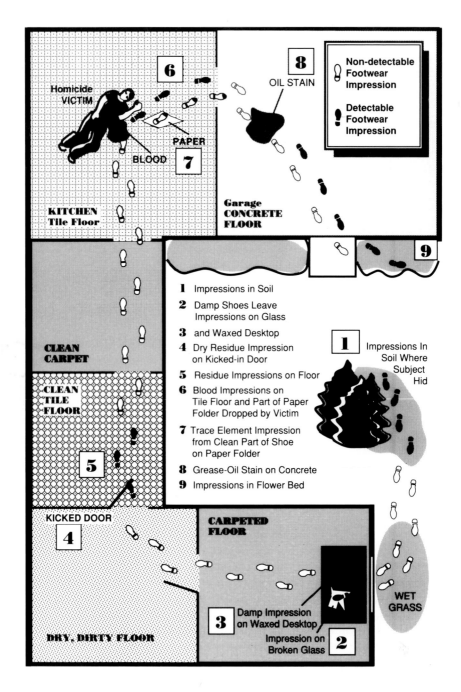

**1.9** A hypothetical crime scene illustrates some of the many ways in which footwear impressions can occur at a crime scene.

## General Treatment of Detected Footwear Impressions

Once detected, footwear impressions should be handled as listed below. The succeeding chapters on photography, casting, lifting, and enhancement will provide additional information regarding the procedures, methods, and materials for those techniques.

> *Take general crime scene photographs.* They provide a recording of the original appearance and location of the impressions.
>
> *Take "examination quality" photographs.* These are close-up photographs that record the necessary detail for a scientific comparison with the suspect's shoes.
>
> *Make notes and crime scene sketches.* They note the exact whereabouts and circumstances surrounding the footwear impressions and coordinate the photographs, casts, and lifts with the scene.
>
> *Remove the impressioned item from the scene.* The impressioned item should be preserved and transmitted to the laboratory if at all possible, even if it means cutting out carpeting, flooring, etc. *If the impressioned item cannot be physically removed from the scene, then*
>
> *Cast the impression* if it is three-dimensional.
>
> *Lift the impression.* If the impression cannot be lifted, attempt to enhance the impression at the scene and, if successful, rephotograph it.

**1.10**   General instructions for the treatment of footwear impression evidence at crime scenes.

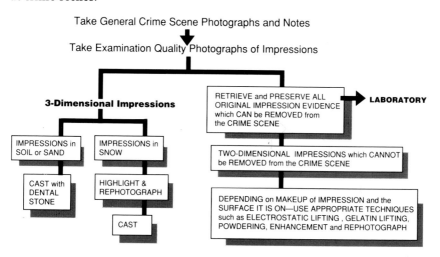

Never cover an impression with tape to preserve it. This will only serve to obliterate it and make subsequent enhancement impossible.

Figure 1.10 is an outline that provides general instructions for the treatment of footwear impressions at a crime scene.

# Photography of Footwear Impressions

2

Photography at crime scenes is an unsurpassed means of illustrating items of evidence and their relationship to each other and their physical surroundings. Photography accomplishes this more efficiently and with more detail than any sketch or verbal description could ever hope to achieve. In addition to providing a pictorial documentation of the crime scene, photographs assist in the overall investigation. They are often used to support and verify testimony of witnesses and to assist in the evaluation of evidence. In some cases, photographs are a critical factor in determining the guilt or innocence of a suspect.

There are two separate types of photography that are used to record information at a crime scene—*general crime scene* photography and *examination quality* photography. General crime scene photographs of a particular area or object are normally taken from three distances: (1) long-range photographs that show the overall scene, (2) midrange photographs that show a closer view of a certain area, and (3) close-up photographs that concentrate on a particular area or object as it relates to its immediate surroundings (Figure 2.1, A-C). The second type of photography at crime scenes involves taking examination quality photographs of a specific area or object. Examination quality photographs are taken close enough to fill the frame with the area or object being photographed and capture the maximum amount of detail, thus enabling later analysis or examination (Figure 2.1D).

## General Crime Scene Photography and Footwear Impression Evidence

General crime scene photography can present a broad range of photographic problems. The scenes and various items that need to be photo-

A

B

**2.1** Relating the footwear impression to the scene is best done by placing markers or numbers next to the impressions. The long-range, medium-range, and close-range general crime scene photographs (**A** through **C**) provide a "zoom-in" effect on the footwear impression. A series of examination quality photographs, one of which is depicted in **D**, completes the photographic docu-

C

D

mentation of that evidence and provides highly detailed, quality photographs suitable for a scientific comparison with a known shoe of a suspect. The particular photograph depicted in **D** was taken using the natural oblique light of the sun. Additional photographs with that light blocked out and using oblique light from a flash should also be taken (see Figure 2.15(C)).

graphed vary immensely from one crime scene to another. More in-depth information concerning general crime scene photography should be obtained from other sources, if needed. In this chapter, only the aspects of general crime scene photography as they relate to footwear impression evidence will be addressed.

## Camera and Film Choices for General Crime Scene Photography

The camera used for the general crime scene photographs should be capable of conveniently taking the full range of distant and medium- and close-range photographs. A 35-mm or $2\frac{1}{4}$-inch negative format camera with an assortment of lenses is suitable. Color film should be used, since it gives a better and more natural representation of the crime scene. Color films having an ISO of 200 or 400 are usually the preferred film choices for general crime scene photography because they are more flexible under a variety of lighting conditions. Films having an ISO of 100 would also be suitable if the scene has sufficient natural lighting; however, photography in areas having poor natural lighting and that must rely on a flash may result in short depth of illumination with ISO 100 film. For instance, a dimly lit room photographed with ISO 100 film and an electronic flash may not be sufficiently illuminated to result in a good exposure of the far end of the room.

Consideration should seriously be given to using two separate cameras, one for general crime scene photographs and one for examination quality photographs. On many occasions, the wrong lens and/or wrong film is used to make examination quality photographs of footwear impressions because the same camera was being shared and was also being used for general crime scene photographs. By having separate cameras, there will be no conflict in the use of the lenses and films during the crime scene processing. Although the same camera could be used for both, it is more efficient, more practical, and more professional to have separate cameras.

## Relating the Footwear Impression to the Scene

A system for relating the footwear impressions in the general crime scene photographs to the crime scene sketches, notes, and examination quality photographs should be used. An easy way to photographically record and document footwear impressions is to place a numbered cone or marker next to each impression.

Figure 2.1 shows an example of how this simple technique can be used to make a permanent and accurate record of the footwear impressions at the crime scene. The long-range, medium-range, and close-range photographs (Figure 2.1A-C) provide a "zoom-in" effect that documents precisely which footwear impressions were found at what locations. A series of examination quality photographs (like the example in Figure 2.1D) with corresponding numbers on labels in the photographs are then taken. The examination quality photographs provide the greater detail necessary for use in the examination of the impressions.

This method will not only assist the crime scene officer's documentation of the crime scene but will make easier the recollection of the circumstances surrounding the impressions and can be very effective in re-creating the scene in court. Any crime scene sketches or notes that are prepared and any examination quality photographs that are taken later should use the same respective numbers. This will enable cross-referencing of all photographs with lifts or casts of each impression. It will also permit anyone to view a particular impression in any general crime scene photograph and refer to that same impression in the crime scene sketch and notes, as well as in the examination quality photographs.

The photographs, crime scene sketches, and notes should contain sufficient information concerning the relationship of the footwear impressions to one another to assist in the reconstruction of the crime. If general crime scene photographs have been taken without labeling or numbering the impressions, it may be difficult or impossible for an examiner to relate a cast or lift to photographs of the same impression. Without labels, it is also very difficult for the investigator to later recollect the specific location in a crime scene area that a particular impression came from.

## Examination Quality Photographs of Footwear Impressions

Examination quality photographs, sometimes called evidence photographs, are those taken so as to record the maximum amount of detail in the impression. The detail is necessary so that these photographs can be used in scientific comparisons with known shoes. They should be clearly distinguished from the general scene photographs, which are taken *only* to show the location and general features of the impressions and which therefore *do not* show much detail within the impression itself.

To ensure that examination quality photographs of impressions provide the footwear examiner with the maximum amount of detail and the minimum amount of distortion, they must be taken in a certain, prescribed way. Consideration should be given to the type of camera, film, lighting, and other factors, as discussed below.

*Selecting the Right Camera*

There are three different camera sizes that are commonly used for examination quality photographs. Those cameras hold the 4 × 5-inch, the 2¼-inch, and the 35-mm negative sizes (Figure 2.2).

Before selecting the type of camera to be used for examination quality photographs, it should be understood that the original negatives will have to be enlarged from two to 20 or more times, depending on the negative size and the area the impression occupies on the negative. During the enlargement process, film grain, camera movement, or focus problems will be magnified and will drastically restrict the use of the photograph in a detailed comparison.

Figure 2.3 illustrates the relative size of the 35-mm, 2¼-inch and 4 × 5-inch negatives compared with the actual size of the footwear impression. Referring to that illustration, it is easy to visualize how many times each negative would have to be enlarged before it would reach the natural size of the footwear impression. The 35-mm negative would have to be enlarged 10 times, the 2¼-inch negative would have to be enlarged 5½ times, and the 4 × 5-inch negative would have to be

**2.2**   Three of the most commonly used cameras for both crime scene and examination quality photographs are (1) the 4 × 5-inch camera, (2) the 2¼-inch camera, which uses 120 roll film, and (3) the 35-mm camera, which uses 35-mm roll film.

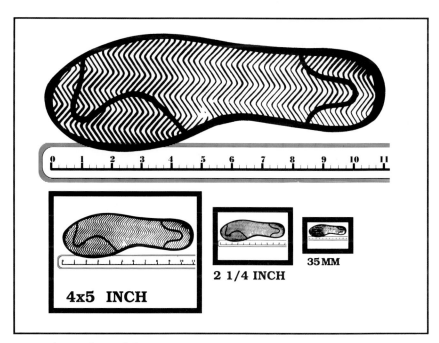

**2.3** Relationships of the image size on 4 × 5-inch, 2¼-inch and 35-mm negatives to the natural size of the impression. Because the image size is smaller on the 35-mm negative, it will require greater enlargement than a 2¼-inch or 4 × 5-inch negative to make a natural-size print.

enlarged 2½ times in order to bring the impression up to natural size. These calculations presume that the negative areas were fully used, meaning that the footwear impression images filled most of the space on the negatives. If the impression images represented a smaller portion of those negatives, they would have to be enlarged even more.

Cameras having larger negative sizes are therefore better suited for examination quality photographs. Unfortunately, cameras having large negative formats are not used by as many crime scene photographers as are smaller cameras, due to cost, convenience, and personal choice.

The 4 × 5-inch camera is the largest negative format camera that is normally used at a crime scene. Although 4 × 5-inch film packs exist, most film used is 4 × 5-inch single-sheet film. The size and weight of this camera make it more cumbersome, and a photographer having considerable experience with this type of camera is usually required in order to take full advantage of its capabilities. The amount of photographic information that can be recorded on a 4 × 5-inch negative camera exceeds that for the 2¼-inch and 35-mm cameras because of the larger negative size.

The $2\frac{1}{4}$-inch negative format cameras have replaced the 4 × 5-inch cameras of many crime scene photographers. They still have a relatively large negative format, but are more versatile and easier to use because roll film is used instead of hand-loaded sheet film. Some $2\frac{1}{4}$-inch cameras (Figure 2.3) have excellent lens assortments and operate with through-the-lens focusing and metering in the same manner as a 35-mm camera.

The 35-mm camera is the camera most commonly used at crime scenes for several reasons. It is usually less expensive than the 4 × 5-inch and $2\frac{1}{4}$-inch format cameras. It is easier to train personnel to use, especially since many have 35-mm cameras of their own. It is used by many investigators who take crime scene photographs because their departments lack a designated crime scene photographer. The negative size of the 35-mm camera is much smaller than that of the $2\frac{1}{4}$-inch and 4 × 5-inch cameras. Even if the image size of a footwear impression fills the majority of the negative, the negative will require being enlarged 10 or more times before a natural-size photographic print can be made. This requires the photographer using a 35-mm camera to take as perfect a picture as possible and leaves virtually no room for error. Slight focus problems, the use of grainy film, or any slight movement of the camera will be magnified when the enlarged, natural-size prints are made. It should be emphasized that in order to take examination quality photographs with a 35-mm camera and obtain quality evidence photographs that capture the minute detail present in the impressions, the instructions provided in this chapter must be strictly adhered to.

If a 35-mm camera is used, it should be equipped with a 50-mm macro lens in order to provide a normal lens and camera relationship. The macro lens will also enable close-up photography, if necessary. A wide-angle or telephoto lens should never be used for examination quality photographs. *The 35-mm camera should not be the fixed-lens variety with built-in auto-flash and auto-focus features.* The 35-mm camera used for evidence photography must have a removable lens and should permit manual focusing. In addition, the flash must be removable and usable on a 6-foot extension cord attached to and synchronized with the camera.

Figure 2.4 shows a properly equipped, manual-focus 35-mm camera mounted on a tripod. The camera is equipped with a 50-mm macro lens, a focus adapter, a cable shutter release, an electronic flash, and a 6-foot flash extension cord, and is loaded with a fine-grained ISO 100 black-and-white film. Equipped in this manner and properly used, the 35-mm camera can be used to take examination quality photographs.

Cameras that have a smaller negative format such as the 110 format cameras or disk cameras are *not* suited or intended for this type of photography.

**2.4** A 35-mm camera properly equipped to take examination quality photographs. Included are a 50-mm macro lens, fine-grained film, a cable shutter release, a focus aid, an electronic flash, a 6-foot flash extension cord, an inverted tripod, and a scale.

## Choosing the Proper Film

Examination quality photographs require the use of fine-grained films. Black-and-white film has some advantages over color film that make it better suited for most examination quality photography. Black-and-white film can be processed for its finest grain structure. Additionally, with black-and-white film, contrast can be enhanced or reduced when processing and printing. With color film, this cannot be done to the same extent. Currently, one of the best black-and-white films available is Kodak T-Max 100. This film does not require special processing. Other films, such as Kodak Tech Pan, although an excellent film for examination quality photographs, requires a special processing and may be too contrasty if processed in normal developers. The major film companies have law enforcement representatives who can be consulted regarding their best current films for this type of photography.

In the past, the use of color film has been discouraged for examination quality photographs, especially those intended to show fine detail after considerable enlargement. In some instances, fine-grained color film has been used for examination quality photographs to supplement black-and-white photographs. Examples of this would include contusion impressions on a body, impressions in blood and impressions in other materials that might be different in color, but not in tone, from their background. In those situations, color photographs *in addition* to the black-and-white photographs are encouraged and may enable the footwear examiner to better interpret the information present in those impressions. Kodak Ektar 25, Ektar 125, or VR 100 are suitable color films for supplemental color photography.

Unfortunately, many departments have adopted policies of using only one film, either color *or* black-and-white, for all purposes. This film is almost always a color film that is suitable for the general crime photography but that is not always the best film for examination quality photographs. If *only* color film can be used, then quality color films such as Kodak Ektar 25 or Ektar 125 films or other quality color films having an ISO of 125 or less are also acceptable.

Instant films, those that provide an instant print at the scene, should not be used for examination quality photographs. Their resolution is not as good as the better conventional film choices, and they usually do not have negatives. Slide film should also not be used for impression photography.

## Choosing and Using a Scale

*The importance of using a scale.* Two of the most common mistakes made in taking examination quality photographs are not using a scale and using an improper scale. A scale should *always* be used when making examination quality photographs of evidence so that a reference of size is present. When enlargements are made for examination purposes, they can be enlarged to a natural size only by referring to that scale. The term "natural size" as used here means that the photographic enlargement is sized so that one inch or millimeter on the scale in the enlarged photograph equals one true inch or millimeter. This should not be confused with the photographic term of "one to one" (1:1). In a 1:1 photograph, the size of the image on the negative is the actual life size of the object being photographed. Thus a 1:1 photographic contact print will always be natural size, but a natural-size print is not always from a 1:1 photograph. Although this may sound trivial, it is mentioned here for two reasons. First, in the case of footwear impressions, which usually are in the 10- to 13-inch range, it would be necessary to have a camera with a negative of that size before it would be possible to take a 1:1 photograph. Since it is not practical to have cameras with that negative format size at a crime scene, the use of a ruler or other acceptable scale in the photograph must be used so the photograph can be accurately enlarged to a natural size. Second, there has been a recent tendency to use the terms 1:1 and natural size interchangeably, and it is appropriate here to restate the difference between them.

Many years ago, there were stories that some courts might not accept photographs of footwear impressions that depicted a ruler or other scale next to the impression. Apparently, the rationale of their thinking was that only photographs of the impressions as they naturally appeared and were first seen at the crime scene should be used in court. Although this could never be verified, even if it were true, it doesn't justify the mistake of not using a scale for the examination quality photographs. Unfortunately, as a precaution against this potential obstacle in court, some crime scene schools and photographic classes temporarily taught their students to take photographs alternately with and without a scale. Several of the older articles on the topic of footwear impression evidence also recommended that only every other photograph of an impression should contain a scale. Although in theory, two subsequent photographs of equal quality, one having a scale and the other not, could be taken by an expert photographer, this rarely proves to be the case in real-life practice at crime scenes. In addition, this requirement would automatically double the number of photographs that otherwise would have to be taken. The bottom line on this issue is that an examination quality photograph without a scale is of limited value to an examiner, so why take it? *Always use a scale!* If court photographs are needed without the scale in them, then photographic prints with the scale cropped out can be used. Also remember that the close-up general crime scene photographs can be used in court as a record of where that impression was found and how it appeared when first discovered.

*The best type of scale.* Over the years, I have seen many items in photographs that have been placed next to footwear impressions for use as a scale. In addition to the countless varieties of rulers, other items such as coins, pens, pencils, business cards, 3 × 5-inch cards, keys, flashlights, and shoes have been placed beside the impressions being photographed with the hope that those photographs could then be enlarged to a natural size by using those objects as a scale.

Frequently the question arises "What is the best scale to use when photographing impression evidence?" Before answering that question, it is necessary to understand what qualities are needed in a scale, why they are needed, and how easily and accurately different scales can be used in the photographic printing process.

Based on years of experience in examining, photographing, and printing photographic enlargements of impression evidence, certain qualities of scales have been recognized as essential. These qualities are best assembled in the form of a linear scale such as a ruler.

*Length of the scale.* The scale used should extend the full length of the impression and, in the case of a small, partial impression, it should be a minimum of 6 inches long. By having this length, the position of the scale can be better checked to see if it is even with and on the same plane as the impressed surface. This length is also important when natural-size photographic prints are being made. It is far easier to be accurate when making a natural-size photographic print using the reference marks on a scale 6 to 12 inches in length than it is to use reference marks on a scale that is only 1 or 2 inches long. Realizing that it is sometimes difficult in a darkroom to line up the scales precisely, consider this: If the person making the photographic enlargement is $\frac{1}{32}$ inch off when using a 1-inch scale, then for a 12-inch footwear impression, the total error will be twelve times that amount, or $\frac{3}{8}$ inch. If a 12-inch scale is used instead, and the person making the enlargement is $\frac{1}{32}$ inch off for the full 12-inch scale, the total error would be only that same $\frac{1}{32}$ inch. Using the full 12-inch scale in the darkroom simply makes it much easier to be accurate. Of course, it is possible to print accurate enlargements with the smaller scale, but it is far more difficult and more prone to error.

*Aids in checking perspective.* Perspective problems can occur if the film plane is not parallel to the impression. Photographs of impressions that are taken in the correct manner should not have any significant perspective problems. Since the examiner is frequently not the photographer, something should be present in the photograph that will confirm that the perspective is correct. Whereas pronounced perspective problems are usually very apparent in a photographed impression, minor perspective problems are harder to identify without aids. In the case of a ruler, certain features, if present, can provide assistance in detecting and/or correcting perspective problems.

The first is a right angle. A right-angled ruler is a better instrument for the determination and possible correction of any perspective problems than a straight ruler. It is also particularly valuable for those two-dimensional impressions that seem to disappear when the camera is positioned over the impression yet seem to show up well when viewed and photographed at an angle. In those cases, it might be necessary to intentionally take the photograph out of perspective and then to correct that perspective later on. If a right-angled ruler is available, it should be used whenever the ruler can be placed evenly and on the same plane as the questioned impression. This would include most two-dimensional impressions and some three-dimensional impressions. Precautions should be taken when using a right-angled ruler to assure that the ruler does not cross over the top of the impression.

The second feature that provides assistance in detecting and/or correcting perspective problems is a circle. Circles that are viewed straight on will appear round. If they are viewed at an angle, they will appear elliptical. Thus, any ruler, straight or right-angled, with circles on it, can offer some additional assistance in both detecting and correcting perspective.

*Surface qualities of scales.* Whether a straight or right-angled ruler, the scale should have a nonreflective surface with contrasting numerals and markings. This will make them more distinct and readable under the variety of lighting and exposures that will be encountered. The contrasting scale should be finely divided into increments of $\frac{1}{32}$ inch or into millimeters.

A variety of rulers is available in nonreflective colors, i.e., black numerals on a white background, black numerals on a gray background, white on gray, and so forth. The nonreflective surface is necessary to prevent unwanted reflections of light into the lens of the camera, which in turn could interfere with both the overall exposure of the impression and the legibility of the scale in that area.

One way to place a nonreflective matte surface on any reflective ruler is to spray the ruler with a photographic matte spray. This will dull the reflective surface and can transform a highly reflective metal or plastic ruler into a usable nonreflective scale.

*Physical characteristics of scales.* The ruler should be both flat and thin. The thickness of the ruler should be ideally no greater than $\frac{1}{32}$ inch. Flatness is needed for several reasons. The ruler must be placed on the same plane as the impression. A thick ruler simply cannot be placed on the same plane as an impression on a hard surface such as a tile floor. A $\frac{1}{4}$-inch thick ruler next to a bloody footwear impression on a tile floor, when enlarged so that 12 inches on the ruler equals 12 inches on the photographic print, will have an error factor of approximately $\frac{1}{8}$ inch per

12 inches. With a $\frac{1}{32}$-inch-thick flat ruler, the error is negligible. In a three-dimensional impression in sand, soil, or snow, where the ruler must be set into the adjacent surface so that it is on the same plane as the bottom of the impression, thickness is not a factor, since the ruler can be set into the ground until the top surface bearing the scale is on the proper plane.

The ruler must be rigid in order to assure that it is not sagging or twisting. It is also important that the ruler be totally flat as opposed to a curved, flimsy, beveled, or sculptured ruler. The flatness assures uniformity of the scale markings and also prevents a misreading of the ruler during the enlargement process, as might happen if the scale markings vary from high spots to low spots. Rulers that have the scale angled on their beveled or sculptured edges are *not* desirable.

*Scale comparisons.* Figures 2.5 and 2.6 show a comparison of several scales and the advantages and disadvantages of each. The choices listed represent those that are frequently encountered in casework. It is unfortunate that so many of the poorer scales are still used. There seem to be a couple of primary reasons why the better scales are not used: The photographer may be unaware of what constitutes the proper scale, or the proper scale may not be on hand at the crime scene when it is needed.

Cloth measuring tapes, sculptured plastic rulers, and metal retractable tapes all have shortcomings when it comes to meeting the criteria of being flat and rigid. Coins, pens, pencils and similar "scales of desperation," even if submitted along with the film to be used as a reference of size, prove to be difficult to use accurately in the darkroom during the enlargement process and, in some instances, may permit only photographic prints that are approximately natural size.

Another scale that is commonly used is a paper scale or paper evidence tag bearing the department's name. These are fine for identifying the photographer or the impression being photographed, but their use as scales is very limited. Paper scales are very seldom more than 2 inches in length, which is a problem in itself. In addition, they are usually bent or have corners that curl up. This causes inaccuracies when they are the only scales to rely on during the enlargement process. I have also witnessed, on a number of occasions, the practice of making photocopies of paper scales because the supply had run out. Since most photocopying processes do not reproduce items in their precise actual size, scales that have been copied are more than likely inaccurate. Photocopies of previously photocopied scales would further compound this problem. Paper scales with adhesive backings, which are for one-time use only, are acceptable in certain situations as long as their accuracy is checked and they cannot be stretched. Even then, they would be useful

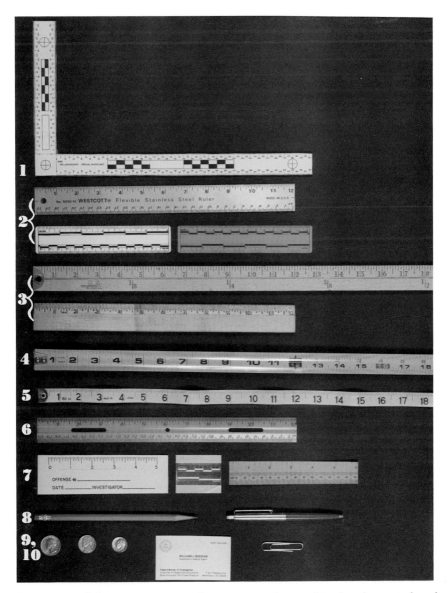

**2.5**   Some of the many proper and improper scales used in the photography of impression evidence.

only if the impression was on a hard, flat surface. They would not yield good results on an uneven surface or one that the adhesive material would not stick to, as in the case of impressions in soil or on very dusty surfaces.

## QUALITIES IN SCALES

as they relate to the Photography of Footwear Impressions

| CHOICES | | Does it have a finely divided scale? | Can it be placed evenly on the same plane as 2-D impression? | Can it easily be placed on the same plane as 3-D impression? | Is it straight and rigid? | Will the scale photograph well under various lighting conditions? | Is it easy to prepare natural size photographic prints using this scale? | Does it provide a means of checking and correcting perspective distortion? |
|---|---|---|---|---|---|---|---|---|
| 1 | Thin, Rigid Ruler 9-12 inches long, with 90° right angle; Non-reflective surface and finely divided scale | yes | yes | yes | yes | yes | yes | yes |
| 2 | Thin, Rigid Ruler 6-12" long, Non-reflective surface, finely divided scale | yes | yes | yes | yes | yes | yes | some |
| 3 | Yardstick or 12" thick Brown Wooden Ruler with Black Numerals | yes | no | some | yes | yes | some | no |
| 4 | Metal Retractable Tape Ruler | yes | no | no | no | no | no | no |
| 5 | Cloth Measuring Tape | yes | no | no | no | some | no | no |
| 6 | Colored or Clear Sculptured Plastic Ruler | yes | no | no | yes | no | no | no |
| 7 | Paper Label with Scale | yes | not if curled | no | no | yes | no | no |
| 8 | Pens, Pencils | no | no | no | yes | no | no | no |
| 9 | Coins | no | yes | no | yes | yes | no | yes |
| 10 | Miscellaneous Objects such as Business Cards, Paper Clips, Etc. | no | some | some | some | some | no | no |

**2.6** Comparison of the qualities of the scales pictured in Figure 2.5.

## Labels or Evidence Tags

In conjunction with the markers that are used in the general crime scene photographs, a label should be placed next to the impression containing the same number or other appropriate identifying data (Figure 2.1D). In cases where there are several impressions, especially if they are at different locations, it is difficult for the photographer to remember where each of the photographed impressions came from, or the sequence they were in. By labeling or marking the impressions in each photograph with the same numbers used for the general scene photographs, sketches, notes, lifts, and casts, the photographer will be precisely documenting where a particular photographed impression came from. This will also make it easier for the examiner to collectively examine all of the photographs taken of each impression, as well as any lifts or casts of that impression. The label can be placed either on or next to the ruler.

## Tripods

It is very important, when taking examination quality photographs, to *always* use a tripod. The tripod assists in the proper positioning of the camera and provides a steady base that helps prevent movement of the camera during exposure. In order to avoid a perspective problem when photographing an impression, it is imperative that the film plane in the camera be parallel to the plane of the impression. Some tripods come with levels built in them. These are very helpful when the impressions are on level surfaces; however, caution should be taken in presuming that the impressions themselves are on level surfaces and in putting too much faith in the tripod level. If the impression is not on a level surface, the camera will have to be carefully adjusted on the tripod to keep the film parallel to the impression. This can best be accomplished by visually checking the camera position from two or three sides and making any necessary adjustments. The tripod enables the photographer to do this in the most accurate and efficient manner by holding the camera in a fixed position after it has been properly adjusted.

The type of tripod best suited for impression photography is one that can hold the camera in an inverted position (Figure 2.4). With a tripod of this type it is possible to literally hang the camera directly above the impression, where it can be adjusted so that the film plane is parallel to the plane of the impression and where there is no interference from the legs of the tripod. Tripods that cannot be inverted may be more awkward but can still be successfully used. The tripod also leaves the photographer's hands free for other tasks, which is useful when trying to simultaneously position the light source and activate the shutter. When using a tripod, *always* use a cable shutter release to reduce the chance of movement during exposure. If for some reason a cable shutter release is not available, the self-timer that is standard on many cameras can be used to release the shutter. If the timer is used, it should be cocked before focusing the camera, and caution should be used when activating the shutter release mechanism so the camera is not moved out of focus.

Trying to hold the camera in your hands may seem quick and convenient, but it is a poor method of taking examination quality photographs. Reliance on one's senses to place the film plane parallel to that of the impression combined with the continuous movement of the camera held in one's hands will affect perspective and focus and are likely to result in poor photographs. Figure 2.7 demonstrates correct and incorrect methods of positioning the camera over an impression.

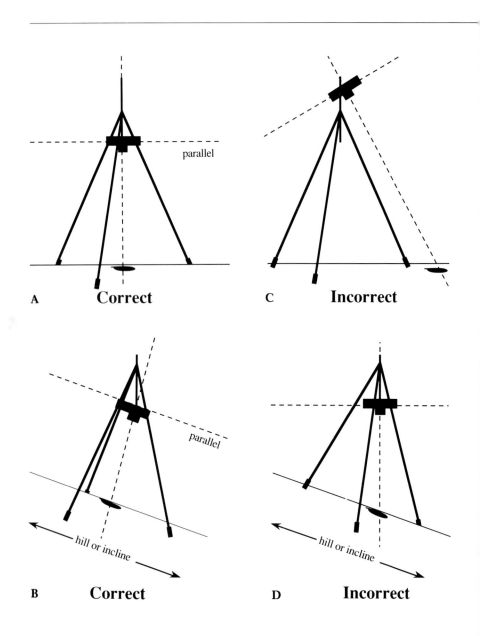

A    **Correct**                          C    **Incorrect**

B    **Correct**                          D    **Incorrect**

## Lighting

There are many types of lighting that can be used when photographing impressions at crime scenes. Some photographs can be taken with natural lighting, while others must use artificial lighting from either a flood light or a camera flash.

E **Incorrect**

**2.7** Correct and incorrect tripod setups. (**A**) On a level surface, the camera should be placed on a tripod with the film plane parallel to the impression. (**B**) If the surface is on an incline, the camera should be angled so that the film plane is still parallel to the impression. **C** depicts an incorrect position of the camera on the tripod, since the camera is mounted at an angle and the film plane is *not* parallel to the impression. **D** also depicts an incorrect position of the camera, which is on an incline with the camera pointed straight down and not with the film parallel to the impression. (**E**) This example, also incorrect, represents the result of taking a photograph without using a tripod. Persons taking photographs in this manner will seldom succeed in getting the film plane parallel to the impression and will also have difficulty avoiding movement of the camera and keeping the picture in focus.

*Natural or ambient light.* Ambient light is the available or existing light that naturally surrounds the impression. Impressions that show up well under the existing light should be photographed first using that light source. The "through-the-lens" meter may be all that is needed to get a proper exposure. If the camera is not equipped with a built-in meter, then a light meter can be used instead. It should be emphasized that although ambient light may indeed produce a seemingly good photograph, *more than one method should always be employed.* It is always desirable to take additional photographs using a second light source, such as an oblique light source, which may provide improved detail and contrast over the photographs taken with existing lighting.

*Reflected light.* Sometimes a detailed impression can be seen well by the human eye in the ambient light that surrounds it, but additional light is needed for the impression to record well on film. A flood lamp or camera flash reflected off of the ceiling or other surface or directed at the impression at a 45-degree angle from at least 5 feet away can increase the light surrounding the impression in the same manner as the existing ambient light and allow a better exposure to be made.

In other situations, the impression can be seen with the reflected ambient light, such as from a window or overhead light fixture, but the impression is only visible when viewed from an angle. When viewed through the lens of a camera placed directly over the impression, it is no longer visible. One possible way to photograph an impression of this type is to use the reflected ambient light and photograph the impression at the angle from which it is most visible. A rectangular ruler or a right-angled ruler, such as the one shown in Figure 2.5, *must* be positioned around the impression so that the perspective problems that will exist in the photograph can later be corrected. It is difficult to take detailed photographs of impressions of this type, since the camera usually needs to be some distance away from the impression. Impressions such as these can and, hopefully, will be retrieved, enhanced, or lifted after photography.

*Oblique light.* More often than not, an impression, although visible and photographable with ambient or reflected lighting, does not allow its maximum detail to be recorded with that lighting. By using oblique light, a greater amount of contrast and detail can be perceived in the photograph.

To obtain oblique lighting, the source is positioned at a low angle of incidence relative to the surface being photographed. Oblique lighting is also commonly referred to as "side lighting."

Oblique light, in the instance of deep three-dimensional impressions,

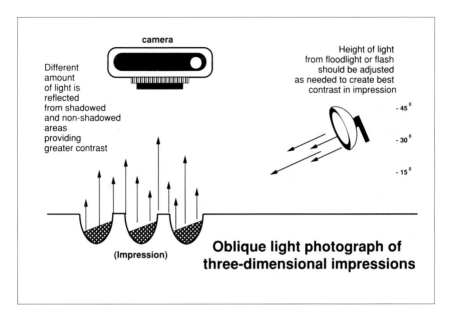

**2.8**   Oblique light photography of three-dimensional impressions.

creates shadowing between the high and low areas of the impression, which in turn provides a greater amount of contrast between those areas in the photograph. As a result, the shape and contours within the impression will be better revealed. In the instance of impressions in soil, sand, or snow, the best angle for the oblique light will vary with the depth of the impression. The deeper the impression, the higher above the ground the oblique light will need to be positioned. In more shallow impressions, the oblique light will need to be positioned closer to the ground (Figure 2.8).

For two-dimensional impressions, such as those in dust or residue, the oblique light is usually more effective at a very low angle, sometimes literally positioned on the ground and just grazing the impression. This will cause the light to be reflected off the dust or residue particles and up into the camera lens (Figure 2.9).

Any experienced footwear examiner will agree that the failure to properly use oblique light is one of the most serious mistakes encountered in the photography of footwear impression evidence. *Oblique light should always be used when photographing three-dimensional impressions and for most two-dimensional impressions, particularly those in dust or residue.* The illustrations in Figures 2.10 and 2.11 display the difference in results between using and not using oblique lighting.

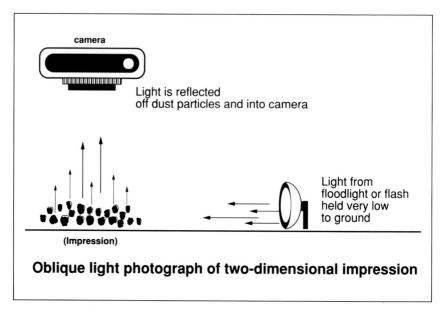

camera

Light is reflected
off dust particles and into camera

Light from
floodlight or flash
held very low
to ground

(Impression)

**Oblique light photograph of two-dimensional impression**

**2.9**  Oblique light photography of two-dimensional impressions.

*Using oblique light with three-dimensional impressions.* The examination quality photographs of *all* three-dimensional impressions should include a series of photographs taken with an oblique light source.

First, determine the optimal height for the oblique light source. To do this, use a flood light, flash light, or other bright light source, and shine it across the impression. Vary the height of the oblique light source from the ground up to about 45 degrees until you find the position that seems to show the impression best. Remember that the photographic reason for using oblique light in a three-dimensional impression is to improve the contrast in the photograph by shadowing the low areas in the impression while illuminating the high areas. If the impression is shallow, the oblique light source must remain in a fairly low position or it will result in illumination of the low areas of the impression as well. If the impression is deep, the oblique light must be raised higher or too much of the impression will be shadowed.

Figure 2.11 shows four photographs of the same impression. Figure 2.11A was taken with existing overhead lighting and no oblique lighting. As a result, the contrast is very poor. Parts B, C, and D of Figure 2.11 were taken with the oblique lighting at 10, 25, and 45 degrees, respectively. The position of the flash at 10 degrees and 25 degrees, for this particular impression, provided better contrast than with the flash in a position of 45 degrees or with existing overhead lighting.

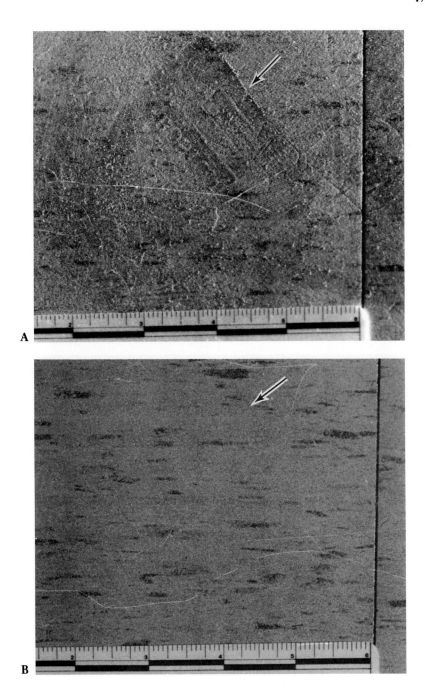

**2.10**  Photographs of a heel impression in dust (**A**) with and (**B**) without oblique light. The heel impression is not visible unless oblique lighting parallel to the surface is used.

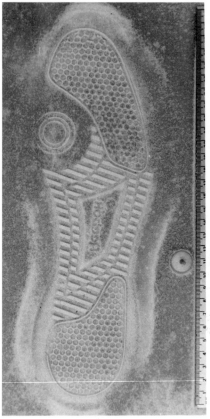

**A**                                        **B**

**2.11** Four photographs of the same impression with the light at different heights. The use of an oblique light source at the proper height is of great importance when photographing three-dimensional impressions. (**A**) was taken with existing overhead lighting and no oblique light. (**B**) was taken with oblique

Once the desired height of the oblique light has been determined, the camera flash can be held in that same position when photographing the impression. Always leave approximately 5 feet between the light source and the impression to allow for an even distribution of light. If the camera is equipped with a flash but does not have an extension cord that enables the flash to be positioned at the proper height and distance, it will be impossible to take proper photographs using oblique lighting. Even when the camera is equipped with an extension cord, poor photographs can result when a tripod is not used and the camera is held by hand. It is virtually impossible for anyone to hold a flash 5 feet from an impression and still hold the camera directly over the impression.

C                                    D

light at 10 degrees. (C) was taken with oblique light at 25 degrees. (D) was taken with oblique light at 45 degrees. The small golf spotter, used as a light source indicator is located between the ruler and the impression and provides a reference to the direction and approximate angle of the light.

Many extension cords for 35-mm cameras are only 3 feet in length, so it may be necessary to connect two extension cords together in order to get a 6 foot cord.

The importance of positioning the flash at a distance of 5 feet from the impression and aiming it evenly across the impression should be emphasized. If the flash or light source is positioned or aimed wrong, uneven lighting can occur. Examples would be: light reflecting off the impression and back into the camera lens, resulting in a bright, washed out, and possibly overexposed area of the photograph; and too much light on the side of the exposure closer to the light source and too little light on the side farther away from the light source.

A

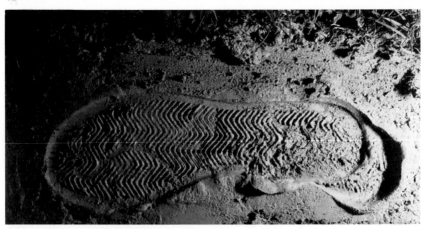

**B**
**2.12** The oblique light source should be at least 5 feet from the impression and should be a flood light or an electronic flash. (A) is an exposure made with a flashlight, which provided uneven and inadequate light. (B) is an exposure made using an electronic flash held too close to the impression and aimed at the heel of the impression instead of evenly across the surface. As a result, the picture is overexposed at the heel end and underexposed at the toe.

Some examples of uneven lighting are shown in Figure 2.12. Figure 2.12A was obtained using a flashlight as an oblique light source. Figure 2.12B resulted when an electronic flash was improperly aimed toward the ground on the near side of the impression instead of evenly across it.

When photographing three-dimensional impressions, particularly those that are deep, the shadowed areas can be partially recovered by reflecting some light back into those areas. This technique is known as "fill lighting" and is accomplished simply by placing a piece of white chartboard at the part of the impression farthest from the oblique light source so it will reflect some of the light back down into the impression, thus filling in the dark, shadowed areas with some light.

If desired, the use of an inverted thumb tack or golf spotter, as shown in Figure 2.11, can be included in the photograph to show the direction of the shadow cast by the oblique light source. This method of using a light source indicator was first suggested by Hamm (1982). Its purpose is to enable the examiner to recreate the same shadow effect in the known impression as was in the questioned impression.

Golf spotters, thumbtacks, and other items, when used as light source indicators, can help the examiner interpret and re-create the direction of light and are recommended as such. They are not recommended for use as scales. Although there may be ways to mathematically calculate the depth of an impression by the length of the shadow cast by a light source indicator of known height, this may not be as certain or as easy as it sounds for most photographers. Errors could be caused in photographs of impressions on sloping or uneven ground. For instance, there would be no reasonable way for an investigator or examiner to know whether the entire crime scene is on a 5-degree slope. Also, the surface is often uneven within and around the impression, where the light source indicator must be placed. In addition, a circular golf spotter or thumbtack is not the object preferred by most darkroom photographers for accurately enlarging photographs to natural size.

*Using oblique light with two-dimensional impressions.* Two-dimensional impressions in dust or residue should also be photographed using oblique light. Since two-dimensional impressions are enhanced by light being reflected off the dust particles and into the camera, the light source in those cases almost always works best resting on or near the surface. The distance of the flash or flood light source should be approximately 5 feet from the impression. Most flood lamps or bulb flash units, because of their size, cannot be placed as close to the ground as necessary. The electronic flash can be placed flat on the ground and can be placed on the manual setting. The difference of 5 degrees or so between the angle at which a flat electronic flash and a more bulky light source can be positioned can make a great deal of difference in the resulting photographs.

When using an oblique light source that is positioned close to the impressioned surface, it will usually be necessary to open the f-stop on the camera four to five times more than the setting that might otherwise be predicted.

*Number of exposures.* Whether photographing a two-dimensional or three-dimensional impression, several exposures of each impression should be taken. Varying the f-stop settings to obtain lighter and darker

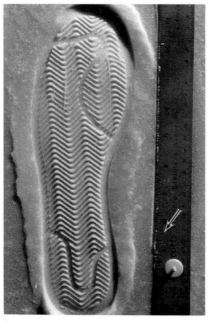    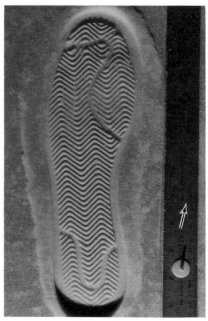

A                                    B

images is called bracketing the exposures. Since it is difficult to accurately calculate or guess the proper f-stop and exposure time in any
oblique light situation, particularly in crime scene situations, bracketing exposures will help ensure that some photographs have been made
with the proper exposure. The use of a light meter can help provide an
estimate of the exposure and f-stop setting. The focus should be
checked before each exposure.

The oblique light source should then be moved to two more positions
around the impression, and several additional exposures should be
made at each position, again varying the f-stop and checking the focus
for each exposure. The three positions should be at least 100 degrees
apart. For example, three suitable positions at which to place a light
source might be 30 degrees, 130 degrees, and 230 degrees on a circle
around an impression. This procedure is depicted in Figure 2.13, along
with photographs with the light source taken in different positions. By
moving the light source to at least three different positions around the
impression, shadows will be cast in three-dimensional impressions or
light will be reflected off the dust or residue in two-dimensional impressions from three different angles. The combination of the photographs
taken with the light source in three different positions will collectively

**2.13** The oblique light source should be placed in three different positions at least 100 degrees apart. In this example, **(A)** is at 70 degrees, **(B)** is at 190 degrees, and **(C)** is at 290 degrees. The varied positions will collectively capture more detail than photographs from one position alone. The examples shown in **(A)**, **(B)**, and **(C)** are summarized in **(D)**.

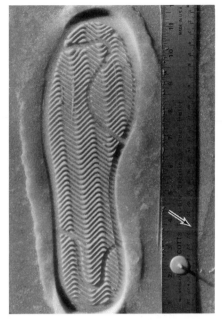

C

D

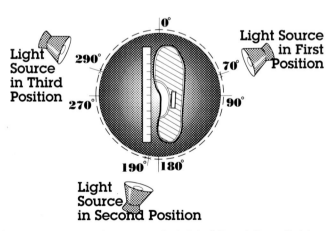

After determining the proper height of the oblique light source, photograph with the light source in three different positions with at least 100 degrees separation.

depict far more detail and information from the impression than photographs with lighting from one side alone.

Although examination quality photography at the crime scene does not sound like an easy task, once the procedure is established, it can be *easily* and *successfully* undertaken by a conscientious photographer. By taking many photographs of each impression and varying the lighting and aperture settings in accordance with the above instructions, there is a greater likelihood of capturing the maximum detail in each impression. *Film is cheap in comparison to your time, the total cost of the investigation, and the seriousness of the crime.*

*Special problems with oblique light.* When using oblique light in situations where there is a great deal of ambient light, such as is often the case outside on a bright cloudy day or a sunny day, it will be necessary to shield the impression in some way from the bright ambient light source. The light can be shielded in a number of ways, such as using a piece of cardboard or an umbrella, or by draping a black cloth over and around the tripod. Anything that will block out some of the bright light and allow the camera to react more to the oblique light than to the ambient light will improve the resulting photographs.

Figure 2.14 shows a simple way of achieving this. After the camera has been set up on the tripod, a black cloth is draped around the sides of the tripod, to make a tent. This will block out a considerable portion of the bright ambient light and will allow for a picture of greater contrast to be taken with the oblique light. Figure 2.15 shows the difference this procedure can make. Figure 2.15A is an impression photographed with the existing sunlight. Figure 2.15B was taken with an oblique light source and the existing natural sunlight, but no sun screen. In Figure 2.15C, an oblique light source has been used with a sun screen.

Occasionally the indented areas that have been shadowed by oblique light will appear raised instead of indented. By turning the photograph 180 degrees, the indented areas will appear indented. If several persons were to view the photograph, some might see certain areas indented, while the others might see the same areas raised. This phenomenon is referred to as the "inversion effect," which is merely an optical illusion (Figure 2.16). I have not experienced any problems associated with this phenomenon while examining photographs of impressions.

## Focusing the Camera

It is hard to imagine that anyone who knows how to use a camera and does so on a regular basis would take photographs that were out of focus; however, poor focus is one of the most common mistakes en-

**2.14** When the ambient (existing) light is too intense, such as on a sunny or bright hazy day, a piece of black cloth can be used as a sun screen by draping it around the tripod. This will block out much of the ambient light and will allow the oblique light from the electronic flash to be more effectively used. The oblique light from the flash can be directed into the open side of the tent, as viewed here.

A

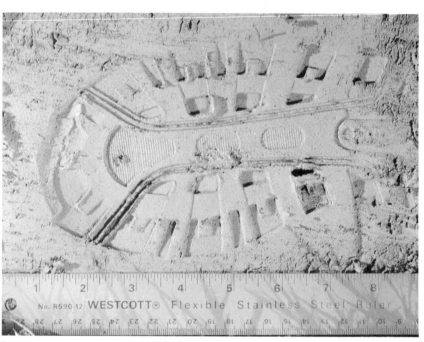

B

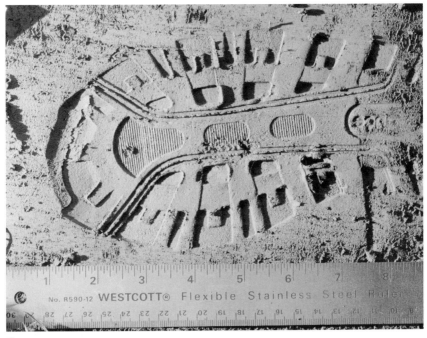

C

**2.15** Impression photographed (**A**) with existing sunlight which happened to be at a low angle and no sun screen, (**B**) with existing sunlight combined with oblique flash but no sun screen, and (**C**) with an oblique flash and sun screen. The combined oblique light and sun screen (**C**) provides greater contrast and therefore greater detail.

countered in photographs of impression evidence. One reason for this is obviously simple carelessness. Another reason is that the camera has been focused on the ruler or label instead of on the impression. Although both the ruler and the impression should theoretically be on the same plane, there will always be minor differences. *The impression and not the ruler or label should always be the object of focusing.*

Out-of-focus pictures can also occur when the film plane is not parallel to the surface of an uneven impression, causing part of the impression to be out of focus when another part is in focus.

If the camera is hand held, it stands to reason that the photographer, bending over an impression, trying to fill the frame with the impression and scale, checking that the exposure and lighting are correct, and then focusing the camera, is going to have many out of focus photographs due to unintentional movements caused by attention to many tasks. If the camera is positioned properly on a tripod, this is less likely to

**A**

**B**

**2.16** The inversion effect is an optical illusion that is frequently encountered in photographs using oblique light. Indented areas of a photograph will appear raised when viewed one way but appear depressed when inverted.

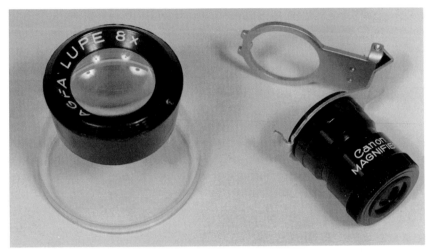

**A**

**B**

**2.17** Magnifiers that can assist in focusing a camera, including one that can be used on the ground glass screen of some cameras and another that attaches to the eyepiece of the 35-mm camera. These devices are shown in **A** and again, as used on the cameras, in **B**.

happen but still does, due frequently to unintentionally bumping the tripod or the settling of the tripod legs into the soft ground. Since there are many ways to lose focus, the last thing that should be done before every exposure is to focus or refocus the camera.

There are a couple of devices that make the process of focusing much easier and may assure better results for some. Those devices (Figure 2.17) are the focus loop and the macro focuser. The focus loop is a hand-held magnifier that can be placed against the ground lens screen of the camera. It is commonly used with the 4 × 5-inch camera. For cameras that focus through the lens, the macro focuser attaches to the eyepiece of the camera and provides a magnified view of the focusing screen.

Examination quality photographs, because they are concerned with minute detail and because they will be enlarged many times, need to be in perfect focus, not just approximate focus. Focus aids may assist the photographer in accomplishing this, but *the focus still must be checked prior to each exposure.*

A shutter cable release should be used to ensure that the camera stays in focus during the actual exposure. Some cameras have a self-timer that permits the shutter to be released several seconds after touching the shutter release button on the camera; however, this still necessitates touching the camera, which could knock the camera out of focus. The shutter release cable gives the photographer complete control and can release the shutter without risking movement of the tripod or camera.

## Procedure Checklist for Examination Quality Photographs

The following is a quick checklist for taking examination quality photographs:

1. Position a proper scale next to and on the same plane as the impression. Place a label in the picture to identify which impression you are photographing.
2. Use a proper camera and lens. Load the camera with fine-grained film having an ISO of 125 or less. Check the ISO setting on the camera. Attach a cable shutter release.
3. Place the camera on a tripod and position it over the impression so that the frame is filled with the impression and ruler. Make sure the film plane is parallel to the impression's surface.
4. Determine what lighting will be used. In most cases, oblique light should be used.
5. When oblique lighting is used, the flash should be at least 5 feet from the impression. Determine the height of the light that is best for each impression. Take several photographs with the light held at that height in each of three different positions, at least 100 degrees apart. Block out any bright ambient light, if necessary, to maximize the benefit of the oblique light.
6. Check the f-stop, shutter speed, and flash synchronization.
7. Focus the camera on the impression prior to each exposure. Use a focus aid if needed. Use the cable shutter release to prevent movement of the camera during exposure.
8. Bracket the exposures at each position of the light source.

## Photographic Equipment Kit Checklist

Having a photographic kit prepared in advance will help in the proper photographic treatment of the evidence. Below is a list of items that should be included in a crime scene kit to cover general crime scene photographs and examination quality photographs:

Camera(s) with manual focus and interchangeable lenses

Normal macro lens (for examination quality photographs)

Wide-angle lens (for general crime scene photographs)

Cable shutter release

Electronic flash

Flash extension cords (two 3-foot cords or one 6-foot cord)

Light meter (for incident light as well as flash)

Device for checking focus (focus loop or macro focuser)

Tripod (preferably the invertible type)

Proper fine-grained films (black-and-white *and* color)

Suitable straight ruler(s) for use as scales

Right-angled or rectangular rulers

Labels and writing instruments

Numbered markers for general scene photography

White chartboard for back fill lighting

Black cloth or screen for ambient light shield

Lens filters

# Casting Three-Dimensional Footwear Impressions

3

Many years ago, the casting process was the predominant method for retrieving three-dimensional footwear impression evidence. Although at that time the impressions were also photographed, the bulky and primitive photographic equipment, combined with slower films, made photography more difficult, less available, less convenient, and often less successful than casting. Most of the older literature on casting footwear impressions advocated the use of plaster of Paris. The proper casting procedure required the use of about 5 pounds of plaster of Paris for the average footwear impression. This translated into an inconvenient, messy procedure, especially if several casts were needed. In addition, because the plaster of Paris was not sufficiently hard, the detail necessary for positive identification was often eroded away when the cast was cleaned.

During the last 20 to 30 years, with the wider availability of improved photographic equipment and faster films, photographing footwear impression evidence has become easier and more convenient, and therefore more popular, than casting. Improved photographic capabilities now permit the capturing of detail that was often lost with the old photographic equipment or during the cleaning of the soft plaster of Paris casts. As a result, the practice of casting footwear impressions declined in favor of photography. Very few footwear impressions were cast, and if they were, plaster of Paris was usually used.

Fortunately, in recent years, there has been a renewed emphasis on casting. With newer and better quality dental stone casting materials and more simplified methods, casting footwear impressions is not only easier, but more convenient and successful than the casting methods of the past.

This chapter will address the currently recommended methods and materials for casting and will explain why a three-dimensional impression should always be cast in addition to being photographed.

## Introduction to Casting

### Definitions

Three-dimensional footwear impressions are those that have depth in addition to length and width. They are most commonly found outdoors in soil, sand, and snow. They can range from very shallow to several inches deep. Due to the various textures and compositions of soil, sand, and snow, the degree of detail that can be transferred from the footwear and that can then be retained in the impression will vary tremendously. The detail in some of these impressions may be very coarse and may not even reflect the gross characteristics of size and design. Other impressions may reflect unbelievably clear, accurately sized, and even microscopic detail transferred from the footwear that made them.

Casting, in the simplest of definitions, is the filling of a three-dimensional form. In the case of forensic footwear impression evidence, casting may be defined as *the filling of a three-dimensional footwear impression with a material that will take on and retain the characteristics left in that impression by the footwear.*

### The Importance of Casting

Whereas photography is worthwhile and absolutely necessary, casts offer an opportunity to capture additional qualities that may be present in three-dimensional footwear impressions but that are not usually revealed as well or at all with photography.

A cast is an actual life-size molding of the impression. It reveals every characteristic including the unevenness of the surface and the variance in the depth of the impression. It is capable of reproducing all the detail present in an impression, including microscopic detail, which can later be closely examined in the laboratory. There are no focus problems or lighting problems, as is often the case with photography. Additionally, there are no size problems. Modern casting materials have excellent dimensional stability. A dental stone cast is, for all practical purposes, the true size of the impression it filled. Because the cast is a positive likeness of the footwear that made the impression, it can be compared directly with the known footwear. In the courtroom, the cast provides a tangible piece of evidence that is easily displayed and understood by the jury.

Articles written on the methods of retrieving three-dimensional impressions have always supported casting. None that I am aware of have stated that casting was unnecessary. Nearly 50 years ago, an article in the *FBI Law Enforcement Bulletin* stated, "Casts are considered superior to photography since they reproduce all three dimensions of the impression and thus permit a more detailed examination than could be made from a photograph" (1945). More recently, DeHaan (1982) asserted that "useful information is more often found in the cast than in the average photograph."

A similar opinion is expressed by Mansfield (1970): "For impressions outside, the . . . cast provides better evidence than the photograph because of its perspective depth." In their book, *An Introduction to Criminalistics*, O'Hara and Osterburg (1949) state, "By far the best means of studying an impression in mud, snow, or other surfaces is that of the . . . cast. Quite frequently, a properly made cast will offer much more information to the eye than the impression itself." Finally, Cassidy (1980) comments, "The number of accidental characteristics recorded in the three-dimensional impression will surprise you."

My own experiences have demonstrated that casts of footwear impressions are extremely valuable as a means of retrieving the maximum amount of detail from an impression and that they provide the examiner with far more information than do photographs alone.

## Benefits of Casts over Photographs

Both photography and casting provide a great deal of information about an impression, but each can also supply some information that the other may not. As summarized in Figure 3.1, *photography and casting supplement one another and together can provide the maximum information about an impression to the examiner.*

As an illustration of how a cast may provide information not easily obtained from a photograph, Figure 3.2 depicts the mechanics of a common scenario in three-dimensional impressions, that of an impression being made in a soft, yielding surface. As the heel strikes the surface (Figure 3.2A), some of the surface material is pushed forward into a mound. As the impression continues, the shoe will roll over the mound (Figure 3.2B) and push off the other side to complete the impression (Figure 3.2C). This can be easily demonstrated by walking in soft sand, first very slowly, and then gradually faster. The faster the walk, the harder the heel will strike and the deeper it will dig into the sand. The deeper the heel goes, the greater the amount of sand that will mound up. The resulting impression will not be a level or flat impression.

When photographs are taken of this impression, two problems will immediately arise. First, it will not be possible to place a ruler on the same plane as the entire impression. The impression's varied depth will

● "Photography and casting supplement one another to give the maximum amount of information about an impression to the examiner"

| Examination Quality Photographs | Casting |
|---|---|
| ■ Show impression as it was at the crime scene along with any rocks, sticks or other debris which may be in, around or part of the impression | ■ Gives Life-like and actual-size molding of the original impression including uneven surfaces and depths |
| ■ Show the condition and detail of the impression | ■ Gives reproduction of microscopic characteristics |
| ■ In some instances, such as with impressions in extremely coarse surfaces, photographs may represent the impression better than a cast | ■ In deep impressions, gives reproduction of characteristics of the sides of outsoles and midsoles of the shoe which are usually not re-produced in photographs |
| | ■ No focus or scale problems |
| ■ Back up casting | ■ Provides tangible 3—dimensional evidence |
| | ■ Backs up photography |

**3.1** Photography and casting supplement one another.

**3.2** A typical three-dimensional impression in a soft, yielding surface. The heel strikes the surface and pushes the soil forward (**A**). As the step continues, the shoe rolls over the mound of soil (**B**) and then pushes off (**C**). The resulting impression has an uneven surface and appears shorter in a photograph than the shoe that made it (**D**).

A

HEEL STRIKE

SOIL PUSHED FORWARD INTO MOUND

SLIPPAGE

SOFT YIELDING SURFACE

**B**

**C**

**D**

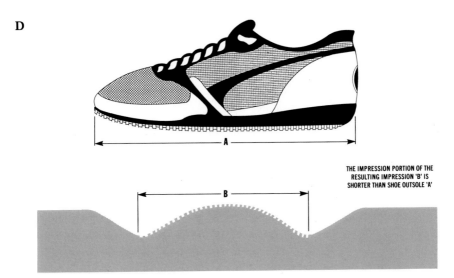

SHOE BENDS OVER MOUND OF SOIL

PUSH OFF WITH TOE

SLIPPING SOIL PUSHED BACK

A

THE IMPRESSION PORTION OF THE RESULTING IMPRESSION 'B' IS SHORTER THAN SHOE OUTSOLE 'A'

B

therefore affect both the scale factor and the ability to have the film plane parallel to the full impression. Second, photographs of the impression would depict the length of the impression as dimension B in Figure 3.2D, which is shorter than the actual outsole of the shoe that made it, as represented by dimension A in Figure 3.2D. A cast of the impression will help to account for this unevenness and will assist greatly in the overall comparison and evaluation.

Figure 3.3 depicts a second type of three-dimensional impression, i.e., that made by a relatively even strike of the footwear on a more firm surface. The impression is shallow and any unevenness would be negligible. Photographs of this impression would be in agreement with the size characteristics of a cast of this impression. But even in such a simple impression as this, the more minute characteristics, no matter how well intentioned the photographer, are often not reproduced photographically. Figure 3.4 illustrates one possible reason why. The majority of significant detail and identifying characteristics on the bottom surface of a shoe outsole are there because these areas touch the ground most frequently. Thus, the areas with the most important detail are represented in the deepest areas of the three-dimensional impression, and some of the microscopic characteristics that can be used to identify a suspect's shoe are often shaded out instead of enhanced by the shadow of an oblique light. If the impression is photographed with the oblique light source in three or four different positions, it may be possible to capture the detail of those minute characteristics—but only for certain if the crime scene photographer knows those characteristics are there and positions the oblique lighting properly. Unfortunately, the crime

**3.3**   An even impression in a firm surface.

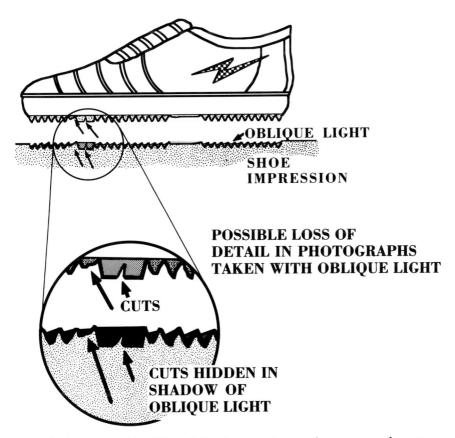

**OBLIQUE LIGHT**

**SHOE IMPRESSION**

**POSSIBLE LOSS OF DETAIL IN PHOTOGRAPHS TAKEN WITH OBLIQUE LIGHT**

**CUTS**

**CUTS HIDDEN IN SHADOW OF OBLIQUE LIGHT**

**3.4**  Shadows caused by oblique light photography can obscure some characteristics in the impression.

scene technician does not see that amount of detail in the impression at the crime scene, nor is it possible to examine each impression at the scene.

No matter how well intentioned the photographer may be, all of the characteristics in an impression cannot be photographically retrieved. In fact, in the actual practice of photography at crime scenes, much of this minute detail may be lost. Casting is a way of ensuring that this detail is preserved. An illustration of this fine detail can be seen in Figure 3.5, which depicts a very enlarged portion of a small segment of a cast of an impression and the corresponding area on the shoe that made the impression. Once this detail is retained in a cast, any segment of the cast can be photographed in the lab with appropriate lighting to further enhance the detail.

**A**

**B**

**3.5** Photograph of a very enlarged area of a cast **(A)** and shoe **(B)** showing microscopic detail reproduced in the cast.

## Choice of Casting Material

A search of the literature on casting footwear impressions reveals that many casting materials have been used at one time or another, with varying degrees of success. For a long while, the most commonly used and written about material was plaster of Paris. Other materials used have included various silicones, moulages, paraffin wax, alginates, die stones, and dental stones.

The silicone-based materials are expensive, do not adequately release the material in which the impression was made, and are sometimes too viscous to flow properly into the impression. Although certain impressions, such as those in heavy clay soils, could probably be cast with low-viscosity silicone materials, the silicone would not rival better choices.

Paraffin wax is not suitable for a number of reasons. It is inconvenient to use because of the time it takes to melt the necessary $1\frac{1}{2}$ pounds needed for an impression. It is expensive, and it is not readily found in the quantities that would be needed for frequent use. Additionally, paraffin wax does not always reproduce the degree of detail that other materials do on the large variety of surfaces on which casting materials are used.

Moulages are hard, plasticlike materials that must be heated in a double-boiler until they melt. The hot liquid is then poured into an impressioned area. When it cools, it hardens and can be removed. The detail it renders for footwear impressions is not as good as that obtained with gypsum products, and the procedure is lengthy.

In the past, plaster of Paris was the most commonly used casting material. *It is no longer regarded as a desirable material for use in the casting of footwear impressions.* Although plaster of Paris, a gypsum product, has the ability to reproduce fine detail, its weakness for footwear casting lies in its lack of hardness. Because it is soft, it is very difficult and in fact, in most instances, impossible to clean a plaster of Paris cast without serious loss of the very detail one was trying to reproduce and preserve. It has also become apparent that plaster of Paris is inconsistent in its quality. My experiences have shown that, on a single occasion, one plaster of Paris cast may turn out chalky, while another may turn out soft and wet and resistant to drying. These inconsistencies are possibly due to shelf-life problems and the fact that plaster comes in so many different forms and qualities. The *RCMP Gazette* reported, "Many casts fail through the use of a poor grade or old plaster, which does not set properly" (1965).

Dental stones and die stones are a slightly different form of gypsum than plasters. They have been used very successfully in recent years as casting materials for footwear impressions. The *FBI Law Enforcement*

*Bulletin* advises, "It is now recommended that only dental stone be used for casting impressions" (1986).

## Qualities Casting Materials Should Have

To be suitable for casting footwear impressions, considering the needs of both the person making the cast and the person who will examine it, certain criteria need to be met. The casting material

1. Should be capable of reproducing very fine detail,
2. Should have the viscosity necessary to flow evenly into the impression but not be absorbed into it,
3. Should be able to be cleaned without loss of detail and should release itself from the material in which the impression was made,
4. Should be reasonable in cost,
5. Should be easily obtainable in a consistent form and quality,
6. Should be easy to mix and use, even under adverse conditions,
7. Should set in a reasonable amount of time, be durable, and have dimensional stability,
8. Should not require special equipment or complex procedures, and
9. Should not have a limited shelf life.

As can be observed in Figure 3.6, dental stones meet all of the requirements necessary to be good casting materials. They are easy to use and mix. They require only a couple of pounds of material to cast a full-size footwear impression. They are hard, durable, and easy to clean without any loss of detail. They are inexpensive, readily available, and do not have shelf-life problems.

Figure 3.7 depicts an enlarged portion of a cast of an impression made by a new shoe in clay soil. Half the cast was made using dental stone, while the other half was made using plaster of Paris. The cast was allowed to dry for 4 days and was then carefully cleaned. The plaster cast, being softer, lost considerable detail during the cleaning process. The detail on the dental stone cast remained sharp and intact after cleaning.

Only dental stones or die stones should be used for casting footwear impressions. Nevertheless, plaster of Paris has been used for so long that it has been difficult to convey to all crime scene technicians the reasons and the need for the change to dental stone. The following discussion provides some additional comparisons of the plasters and stones.

## Stones Versus Plasters

Plaster of Paris, dental plaster, dental stones, and die stones are all obtained from the mineral gypsum. Gypsum is the dihydrate form of calcium sulfate ($CaSO_4 \cdot 2H_2O$). The reaction converting gypsum to

## COMPARISON of MATERIALS
### for CASTING 3-DIMENSIONAL FOOTWEAR IMPRESSIONS

| | PLASTER of PARIS | DENTAL STONE | SILICONE | PARRAFIN |
|---|---|---|---|---|
| Shelf Life and Quality | UNCERTAIN | EXCELLENT | EXCELLENT | EXCELLENT |
| Cost per Pound | ABOUT THE SAME FOR BOTH | | EXPENSIVE | EXPENSIVE |
| Ability to Reproduce Fine Detail | YES | YES | ON SOME SURFACES | ON SOME SURFACES |
| Hardness and Durability | SOFT | EXCELLENT | EXCELLENT | VERY GOOD |
| Ability to be Cleaned without Loss of Detail | POOR—because of softness, cannot chemically clean or immerse in water without serious loss of detail | EXCELLENT—can clean by immersing in potassium sulfate solution. with soft brush | With use on SOME SURFACES and with release agent | With USE ON SOME surfaces |
| Positive Identifications with Known Shoes | FEW—because of loss of detail in cleaning | MANY | POSSIBLE, BUT NOT LIKELY— | |
| Amount of Material and Water Needed for Footwear Impression | About 5 Pounds of Plaster of Paris And 90 oz. of Water | 2 lbs of Dental Stone and 12 oz. of water | About 1 1/2 to 2 lbs. of Silicone | About 1 1/2 to 2 lbs. of Melted Parrafin |
| Reinforcement Material Needed? | YES—Needed to prevent cast from breaking | NO—Not Needed | NO—Not Needed | NO—Not Needed |
| Form Around Impression Needed? | YES—Needed for thickness so that reinforcement material can be placed within it | NO—Not needed for strength—only if necessary to restrict flow of Casting Material | NO—Not needed for strength—only if necessary to restrict flow of Casting Material | NO—Not needed for strength—only if necessary to restrict flow of Casting Material |
| Ease of Use | Messy and cumbersome because of quantity that must be used | Easy and not messy—particularly if Zip-lock bags are used | Hard to mix well with catalyst at crime scene & is messy | Time consuming, cumbersome and messy |
| Popularity among Crime Scene Persons, Once Used | NOT POPULAR | POPULAR | NOT POPULAR for 3-D Impressions | NOT POPULAR |

3.6  Comparison of materials for casting three-dimensional footwear impressions.

**3.7**   A cast of an impression in clay soil made by a new shoe. Half the cast was made with buff-colored dental stone (the darker side) and the other half, with plaster of Paris. The cast was dried thoroughly and then cleaned. Note how the plaster of Paris portion looks washed out, contains brush marks, and has not retained the crisp, sharp detail of the shoe. The dental stone portion has retained all of the original detail.

plaster with loss of water is reversible, so the addition of water to plaster will result once again in gypsum.

$$CaSO_4 \cdot 2H_2O + heat \rightarrow CaSO_4 \cdot \tfrac{1}{2}H_2O + 1\tfrac{1}{2}H_2O \uparrow$$
$$\quad\text{gypsum} \qquad\qquad\qquad \text{plaster}$$

$$CaSO_4 \cdot \tfrac{1}{2}H_2O + 1\tfrac{1}{2}H_2O \rightarrow CaSO_4 \cdot 2H_2O + heat$$
$$\quad\text{plaster} \qquad\qquad\qquad \text{gypsum}$$

*Plaster of Paris* is produced by simply heating the crushed gypsum in an open oven at a temperature of around 120°C. This product is called $\beta$-calcium sulfate hemihydrate. The powder produced consists of irregularly shaped, porous particles.

*Dental stone* is produced by heating the gypsum mineral in an autoclave under pressure and in the presence of steam. The powder produced by this method contains particles that are more uniform in shape and more dense than the plaster particles. The hemihydrate produced this way is referred to as $\alpha$-calcium sulfate hemihydrate.

An improved *die stone* is produced when the gypsum is boiled in another chemical, such as a 30% calcium chloride solution, after which it is washed, dried, and ground to a fine particle size. This powder is even more dense than the dental stone or plaster.

Although the stones are chemically identical to the plasters, and all will form gypsum when mixed with water, the different manner in which they are manufactured produces different sizes, shapes, and densities of crystals. This results in other important differences between the plasters and the stones. Some plasters, including dental plasters, with their larger particle size, require approximately 70 parts water by weight per 100 parts plaster, whereas stones, with a smaller particle size, only require 22 to 32 parts water by weight per 100 parts stone. Plasters usually have a dry compression strength or hardness of approximately 1,200 to 2,000 psi, whereas the stones' compression strength ranges from 8,000 to 15,000 psi. Thus, die stone and dental stone are both harder and more durable than the plasters.

With regard to the casting of footwear impressions, the smaller particle size (and therefore superior hardness), strength, and durability make the stones far better than the plasters. The increased strength of the stones means that it is no longer necessary to pour a thick cast, shored up with a form and filled with reinforcement material. With stones, $1\frac{1}{2}$ to 2 pounds of casting material will easily fill a footwear impression. This, combined with the reduced water requirements, means that 2 pounds of stone casting material will require only 10 to 12 ounces of water. As will be discussed later, the dental stone can easily be stored in a zip-lock bag to which water can be added when needed.

Additionally, the dental stone and die stone casts can be cleaned without loss of detail. Brennan (1983) reports that dental stone and die stone are best cleaned in a saturated solution of potassium sulfate for approximately 1 hour. During this procedure, degassing of the cast will take place, resulting in streams of air bubbles being released from within the cast, which assists in loosening clinging soil. This procedure will not work with the plasters because immersion of plaster casts in the solution will soften them and result in erosion and loss of detail.

## Methods of Casting with Dental Stone

### Supplies to Have Available

A major reason why casts are often not made at crime scenes is simply that no casting materials are on hand when needed. Obtaining the necessary casting materials and supplies beforehand and having them readily available is essential. It is not convenient, practical, or good planning to have to hastily look for casting supplies while trying to conduct other matters of importance at the crime scene. The following materials should be obtained and kept available:

1. Dental stone or die stone, either in bulk form or premeasured into several zip-lock bags (2 pounds per bag)
2. Water
3. Form material (for use on uneven surfaces)
4. Spoon or flat stick (optional, for bulk mixing)
5. Rubber mixing bowl (optional, for bulk mixing)

Figure 3.8 shows the few items needed to prepare a quality cast of a footwear impression. In most instances, only dental stone in a zip-lock bag and water are needed.

In light of the uncertain shelf life and the aforementioned disadvantages of plasters, the use of any remaining plaster materials should be discouraged. Old supplies of plaster casting materials should be discarded. Dental stone and die stone are readily available from local dental supply houses. If local sources are not available, dental stone and die stone can be easily ordered and shipped through the mail from several national suppliers. Although the actual prices by weight of plaster of Paris and dental stone are essentially the same, forms and reinforcement materials are not needed with dental stone and only 2 pounds of dental stone are needed per impression compared to 5 pounds of plaster of Paris, so dental stone is less expensive to use for casting.

## Preparing the Footwear Impression for Casting

Many impressions need little if any preparation prior to casting with dental stone. One specific instruction that has received much attention in the literature has been clearing the impressioned areas of any debris. It should be emphasized that *in no instance* should an attempt be made to remove any debris that is part of the impression or that was there when the impression was made. When footwear impressions are made over rocks, sticks, or other debris, excellent reproduction or detail is still very possible and probably exists immediately adjacent to these items. Any attempt to try to remove such debris, which may now be imbedded in the impression, will almost certainly interfere with and ruin that part of the impression. Furthermore, because those items were between the shoe and the ground when the impression was made, their removal will in no way reveal any useful impression beneath them. If a loose leaf or twig has managed to fall into the impression *after* it was made, then it can be carefully removed. It would seem, however, that this would be an infrequent occurrence.

**3.8** Dental stone and water are all that are normally needed to make a cast.

## When Forms Are Not Used

Old literature and techniques always advised using a form because all casting was done with plaster of Paris. The form was required simply because the plaster cast had to be approximately 2 inches thick to provide room enough to place reinforcement material within it. Most footwear impressions that are cast with dental stone *will not* require a form. If the impression is on a relatively level surface, the casting material can be carefully poured, allowing the material to flow into and

**A**

**3.9** A pancake dental stone cast poured over an area filled with footwear impressions (**A**). The cast, after cleaning (**B**). The side of a pancake cast that has retained detail left from the side of the shoe (**C**). Note the lettering from the brand name and the sidewall stitching indicated by the arrows.

overflow out of the impression. The end result will look somewhat like a pancake. A pancake cast is pictured in Figure 3.9A and B. It is important that the entire impressed area be filled with casting material, particularly in deeper impressions. Significant detail is sometimes transferred from the midsole and the sides of the shoe and is retained in the impression. Figure 3.9C depicts the edge of a pancake cast of an impression that has retained detail from the side of the shoe. Once the casting material has overflowed, any additional material left in the bag can be slowly poured over the center of the cast to allow that portion of the cast to build up its thickness.

*Using a Form*

In some instances, an impression may be on a slope or may be deep on one end and shallow on the other. A partial form can be used to control the flow of the casting material on one side. The partial form can range from a short semicircle to an elongated horseshoe shape on the low side of the impression, positioned so the thickness builds up on that side

**B**

**C**

first and directs the flow of the casting material back toward the impression. Form material can consist of premade forms, aluminum flashing, strips of chartboard, or other suitable material.

In those cases where a partial or full form must be used to contain the dental stone mixture, care should be taken in the placement of the form

**3.10**  A partial form used to retain the casting material over the area of a footwear impression on a slight hill. Note how the dental stone is poured onto the ground on the uphill side of the impression, thus allowing the dental stone to flow into the impression. Casting material should never be poured directly on the impression.

around the impression. At least $1\frac{1}{2}$ to 2 inches of space should be left between the edges of the footwear impression and the form material. This will not only allow an area onto which the casting material can be poured, but it will also reduce the possibility of distortion of the adjacent ground that in turn would disturb the edges of the impression. The form material itself should rest evenly on or in the ground so that the casting material will not seep or flow beneath it. It may be necessary to gently press the form material into the ground or, once the form is in place, fill any gaps that may remain between the form and the ground by placing some loose soil on the outside edges of the form. Figure 3.10 illustrates the proper use of a partial form to contain the dental stone mixture in an impression that is on a slight slope.

## Fixatives

Throughout the footwear literature, there have been numerous "recipes" recommended for preparing the impression with a fixative or spray prior to casting. For example, "If the surface containing the print consists of dust or sand, we should first apply a clear plastic or lacquer coating as a fixative using a spray applicator" (Samen CC, 1972).

More than 30 years ago, the *Ohio Law Enforcement Training Bulletin* directed, "Spray ordinary white shellac, thinned with wood alcohol, into the print. . . . Allow the first coat to harden ten to fifteen minutes. . . . Apply the second coat of shellac. . . . Allow to harden" (1959). Similarly, in 1951, the *FBI Law Enforcement Bulletin* recommended, "Impressions in sand, loose soil, and snow must be strengthened with a plastic spray, shellac, or other quick dry fixative. . . . The spray should be directed over the impression rather than directly at it" (1951). More recently, Cassidy (1980) advocated a different technique:

> The impression should now be covered with some form of release agent to allow the dirt to come away from the cast with ease. Various agents from frying pan sprays to oil can be used for this purpose. However, from tests conducted I have found baby powder to be an excellent release agent. . . . The talc should be drifted over the impression using a small atomizer or aerosol can plus a deflector card.

There also have been references that implied that fixatives or sprays are of no benefit or may possibly harm the impression: "The last item that can and should be eliminated from the casting kit are the fixative and release agents. . . . Damage to an impression is as likely to occur when the release and fixatives are used as when they are not" (Vandiver JV, 1980). The same author also states, "Tests without a fixative and with a clear fixative pointed out that neither . . . helped produce a better cast" (Vandiver JV, 1981).

Many of the recommended methods for "fixing" an impression, particularly with shellacs and sprays, were used in conjunction with plaster of Paris and were intended, according to the authors' directions, to build up a protective layer or shell over which the plaster was poured. This was undoubtedly being done, not because plaster would harm the impression, but rather to provide a protective layer that would prevent the detail from being lost when the soft plaster cast was cleaned. This "protective shield" is not necessary with dental stone.

Experience has shown that spraying any fixative over a dry impression, such as one in dry sand or loose, dry soil, does not have any effect on the retention of detail in a dental stone cast. Improper use of fixatives in large quantities might even obscure or fill in minute detail.

Light talcs or very fine powders, so fine that they would not obscure even the most microscopic characteristics, are occasionally used to provide a "cleaner" cast. A very light dusting of the talc or powder over the impression will prevent some of the soil from adhering to the cast. The dusting should be so light that it is hardly visible. The talc or powder should not be applied so heavily that it builds up on the surface of the impression. Casts of impressions that have been treated this way will release most, if not all, of the soil when they are lifted. With the use of dental stone and the ability to clean a dental stone cast thoroughly and without any loss of detail, as will be explained later, the use of fixative materials is a personal choice more than a requirement.

## Mixing Dental Stone

*Reclosable bag method.* Reclosable plastic bags (such as Ziplock) are now being recommended as a means of storing premeasured amounts of dental stone powder. A zip-lock bag measuring approximately 8 × 12 inches can easily store 2 pounds of dental stone powder. When the time comes to make a cast, the zip-lock bag containing the dental stone powder can be used as a mixing container. With premeasured zip-lock bags on hand, casting impressions at the crime scene will involve only the addition of a few ounces of water. The bag can be used to both mix and pour the dental stone mixture. Those who have tried this method have found it to be a quick, clean, and convenient method of casting.

Dental stone, like other gypsum materials, is usually sold in quantities of 25, 50, or 100 pounds. Carrying containers of this size around at a crime scene is both awkward and inconvenient. Once a quantity of 8 × 12-inch plastic bags has been obtained, the larger containers of dental stone can be quickly divided into 2-pound portions. The weighing of those portions needs only to be estimated. An easy way to accomplish this is to first weigh out 2 pounds of dental stone powder and add it to a zip-lock bag. Hold the bag at the top, and use a permanent marker to mark the level of the powder in the bag. Then pour the powder out of the bag, and use the empty bag as a reference for marking other bags. By placing other bags over the measured bag and marking them in the same spot, the level to which the dental stone must be added can be closely approximated. In this way, it is very easy to mark and fill a quantity of zip-lock bags with approximately 2 pounds of dental stone in each. Once the bags are filled, they can be laid on one side and flattened to remove the excess air. The bags should then be zipped closed. The bags will keep the casting material dry and will be convenient to use when needed. It is a good idea to prepare these bags of dental stone powder in advance. The dental stone will then have a chance to settle, which will reduce the amount of air in the resulting cast. As Vandiver (1980) states,

> The reason for the traditional method of adding plaster to water is to reduce the amount of trapped air in the final mixture. . . . What we

previously overlooked, though, is that most of the air is introduced by the traditional methods of preparing plaster. . . . Premeasured bags of *dental stone* allow the contents to settle and air escape long before water is added.

When the time comes to prepare a cast, the zip-lock bag of dental stone is ready and convenient. To reach the necessary viscosity, dental stone requires about 6 ounces of water per pound. Die stone will require even less water. For a 2-pound bag of dental stone, approximately 10 to 12 ounces of water must be added. This can be conveniently done by using a 12-ounce beverage can or other measure. Since the exact amount of casting material will vary slightly from bag to bag, and the powder-to-water ratio will vary slightly from one brand of dental stone or die stone to another, the following procedure is recommended. Pour about two thirds of the estimated water needed into the bag. Zip the bag closed, and mix the casting material by massaging and gently squeezing the bag. If the mixture is too thick, add a small amount of water and continue to mix the material. Make sure that all the material in the corners of the bag is mixed. If too much water is accidentally added, simply add a small amount of dental stone from another bag. The proper viscosity should be that of pancake batter or thick cream. The mixture should not be watery nor should it be so thick that it will not flow into an impression. When the water and dental stone are completely mixed and the proper viscosity is reached, the casting material is ready to be poured. This is easily accomplished by simply unzipping the bag and, holding it at ground level next to the edge of the impression, carefully pouring the material into the impression.

Once tried, the zip-lock bag method proves to be a very popular one and provides a convenient, clean, and rapid way of preparing a quality cast. If more than one cast is being prepared, the person doing the casting can solicit the help of another individual to assist in the mixing portion of this process. If the impressions are extremely large and deep, it may be desirable to mix a larger amount of dental stone in a small bucket or rubber container rather than using several bags.

*Mixing dental stone in a bucket.* If a large quantity of dental stone is to be mixed at one time in a bucket, an estimate of the quantity of material should be made. If there are six full footwear impressions, you can figure on 12 pounds of dental stone and 72 ounces of water (6 ounces per pound). The ratio needs only to be approximate. The water should first be added to the bucket, and then the dental stone should be added to the water and allowed to settle and soak for about 2 minutes. The mixture should then be stirred thoroughly. Add more dental stone or water to adjust the viscosity of the mixture to pancake batter consistency. Once the material is thoroughly mixed and is at the proper viscosity, the material can be poured into the impressioned area.

*Pouring the Casting Material*

Whether a form is used or not and whether the casting material is mixed in zip-lock bags or in buckets, the procedure and precautions for pouring the casting material into the impressioned area are the same. Casting material has sufficient weight and volume to easily erode and destroy valuable detail if it is carelessly poured directly onto the impression. This is especially true in the case of fragile soil and sand impressions. When pouring the casting material from the zip-lock bags, the bag should be placed next to the impression so that the casting material does not cascade onto the impression but instead falls on the adjacent ground, after which it will flow into the impression.

When pouring the material from a bucket into the impression, a flat stick or a spoon should be held over an area to the side of the impression. The casting material can be poured from the bucket onto the flat side of the stick or spoon so that the implement will absorb the impact of the dental stone, which will then flow harmlessly into the impression. With impressions that are on a slope or with impressions that have forms around them, the casting material can be poured from the bucket onto the ground next to the impression so that the casting material will naturally flow into the impression (Figure 3.10). Again, it should be emphasized that the entire impression must be filled with casting material until it has overflowed.

Sometimes when mixing large amounts of dental stone in a bucket, the viscosity of the dental stone may be ideal when the first cast is poured, but too viscous by the time the last cast is poured. This is due to settling of the mixture. Making sure the dental stone and water are thoroughly mixed before pouring each impression can help offset settling.

Occasionally, whether the dental stone mixture is in a bucket or a bag, it is not apparent that the mixture is too viscous until it has actually been poured. Of course, then it is too late to change the mixture. The viscous mixture can be maneuvered to flow into the impression simply by taking your finger or a small stick and vibrating it back and forth on the surface of the mixture. This will help the dental stone to relax and flow into the impression. Be careful not to put the stick below the surface of the casting material, as it would damage the impression.

Before the cast completely hardens, it is possible to scratch the date, your initials, and other needed information onto the top of it.

The cast should then be left undisturbed for at least 20 minutes in warm weather. If the temperature is cold, the cast should be allowed to sit considerably longer. Many casts have been destroyed or damaged because they were lifted too soon. When the time has come to lift the cast, care should be taken not to damage it. If the cast has been poured in sand or loose soil, it should lift very easily. Casts poured in heavier soils, such as mud or clay, may require more careful treatment when being lifted.

## Underwater Casting

Impressions that are partially or totally underwater can also be cast. The following instructions should be followed:

Do not attempt to drain away any of the water over the impression area. This is not necessary and will only risk disturbing the impression. If any leaves or twigs are floating over the impression, you may safely remove them, but do not attempt to remove any debris if it is part of or is touching the impression. Movement of any type in the water risks disturbing the impression.

Carefully place a full casting frame around the impression that is large enough to allow 2 inches on all sides of the impression. This allowance will prevent the impression from being distorted or disturbed when the form is pressed into place. The frame should be high enough so that its sides will rise above the water line, permitting it to be put in place without anyone having to reach into the water. A disposable frame made from chartboard or cardboard can be made for this purpose.

Lightly sprinkle or sift dental stone or die stone over the areas of the impression that are underwater until an inch of the casting material covers that area.

Prepare a mixture of dental stone or die stone in a separate container in the same manner as you would for dry impressions, except that the mixture must be slightly thicker. Prepare enough so that it will fill the framed area with a 2-inch thickness of dental stone. Add the mixture to the framed impression by carefully scooping it into that area, allowing it to settle through the water and onto the impression. Make sure the entire bottom surface is eventually covered well with the casting material. The cast should be allowed to set for at least 60 minutes.

Impressions that are only partially underwater, or that have water standing in them, can be cast with the regular casting procedure, using a more viscous mixture. The dental stone mixture will displace the water.

## After the Cast is Poured

### Allowing the Cast to Air Dry

Once removed, the cast will usually have some quantity of soil or sand that is wet and covers the impression side of the cast. *No attempts should be made to clean the cast at this point.* Although the dental stone has set and appears to be hard and dry to the touch, it is *not* completely dry or hardened. The cast should be allowed to air dry at room temperature for at least 48 hours. After the cast is fully dried, it is ready for cleaning by the examiner, for shipping to a laboratory, or for storing. The thoroughly dried cast can safely be stored in a sturdy *paper* bag. It should be noted that casts should *never be placed or stored in plastic bags.* Casts always contain some moisture. The placement of casts in plastic bags traps moisture escaping from the inside of the cast and causes it to condense on the outside of the cast.

## Cleaning Stone Casts

One of the most significant advantages and reasons for using dental stone or die stone over other casting materials is the ability to clean the casts without loss of detail. Cleaning the casts should always be performed in the laboratory, either by or under the supervision of the examiner who will be examining the cast. Newly poured casts should never be cleaned. The cast should always be allowed to air dry for at least 48 hours before cleaning.

Brennan (1983) has determined that an easy and efficient way of cleaning dental and die stone casts is with the use of potassium sulfate. Submerging a dental stone or die stone cast into a saturated solution of potassium sulfate will cause air to be released from the cast. Since this air is released from within the cast, it helps loosen the soil from the surface of the cast. In his research, Brennan has also asserted that this method contributes to the preservation of detail.

To clean a cast in this manner, a container large enough to submerge the cast is needed, along with an ample supply of potassium sulfate. A saturated potassium sulfate solution should be prepared in the container. Carefully, the cast should be fully submerged in the solution at room temperature and allowed to sit for approximately 1 hour. On placing the cast in the solution, streams of bubbles will come from within the cast. After the soil has been softened, a soft bristled brush can be used to help remove it from the surface of the cast. Brushing should be done with the cast still in the solution. The cast should then be thoroughly rinsed with water and allowed to drain and air dry. If a considerable amount of heavy soil is clinging to a cast, it can be soaked first for 30 minutes in the potassium sulfate solution, which should enable the majority of the soil to be removed, and then it can be moved to a clean potassium sulfate solution for the remaining 30 minutes.

## Photographing the Cast

After any cast has been cleaned and prior to examination, it should be photographed. To photograph the cast, use a fine-grained, black-and-white film, such as Kodak T-Max 100, combined with an oblique light source. The use of fill lighting to lighten the shadowed areas is usually beneficial. Photographs of the cast can serve many purposes. Because the detail in the cast is best seen with the use of oblique light, this type of photograph will enable easier study of the total detail present in the cast. The photographs will provide a permanent record of the cast. Notations can be made on them, and the photographs can be used later for presentation of your findings in court.

## Shipping and Storing Casts

Once a cast has been prepared, it will require reasonably careful attention during storage and subsequent shipment to ensure that it is not broken or otherwise mishandled. The cast should be completely dry. It should *never* be stored or shipped in plastic wrapping. When shipping casts, each cast should be individually placed in a thick paper bag. Dry packing material can be used to separate each cast from the others and to afford the necessary protection from breakage. The container should be marked "fragile."

## Casting Footwear Impressions in Snow

In many areas of the country, snow is on the ground for a substantial number of days each year. Footwear impressions in snow often provide investigators with excellent information regarding the number of suspects, the approximate time of the crime, the point of entry and exit, and the direction in which the suspect left the crime scene. As with other footwear impressions, examination quality photographs of impressions in snow should be taken before casts are made. Additional examination quality photographs, with the added highlights provided with Snow Print Wax or other colored spray aerosols, will provide further detail. Figure 3.11A shows an examination quality photograph of an impression in snow. Figure 3.11B shows that same impression after it has been highlighted with a light spray of red Snow Print Wax.

Older methods of casting footwear impressions in snow involved tedious procedures with very limited results. For instance, a 1972 article recommended the following method:

> Shake or dust lightly a thin layer of talc over the impressioned area, followed by a layer of shellac or clear lacquer. This step is repeated a minimum of three times, allowing several minutes between each application. . . . Once the base is dry, shake or dust three thin layers of dry plaster, alternating with a water spray over the original crust (Samen CC, 1972).

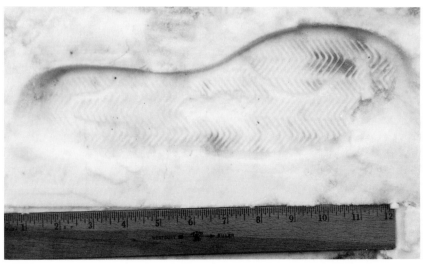

**A**

**B**

**3.11**    An impression in snow (**A**), which is highlighted by spraying the impression at an angle with Snow Print Wax (**B**) and then coated with three or four

Years before that, the *FBI Law Enforcement Bulletin* advised that "a fine layer of talcum powder sprinkled over the surface of a snow impression will serve to insulate the snow from the heat of the setting plaster" (Anonymous, 1951).

**C**

**D**

heavy sprays of Snow Print Wax (**C**). The impression is then filled with a cooled mixture of dental stone (**D**).

## Snow Print Wax

Snow Print Wax offers a quick and easy method for casting footwear impressions in snow (Carlsson K, 1982). This product, originally from Sweden, was introduced in this country around 1983. It is an aerosol spray wax that is available in both bright red and brown. When it is applied to the impression, it will form a wax shell and will preserve the detail in the snow impression. The wax shell is then filled with cooled dental stone to provide a means of lifting the fragile wax shell. The wax does not melt the snow, as some aerosol spray paints do, and therefore appears to be a better medium than spray paint for the highlighting of snow impressions for photography.

This product comes in an aerosol can with instructions on the label. It should not be confused with the snow wax spray used for Christmas decorations. This decorative type of wax aerosol will melt and destroy snow impressions. Snow Print Wax is best utilized in the retrieval of footwear impressions as follows:

Be sure to photograph the snow impression in accordance with the instructions provided in the chapter on photography, making sure that the ruler is on the same plane as the impression as in Figure 3.11A. Next, using Snow Print Wax, lightly spray the footwear impression at an angle so as to highlight the raised areas of the impression but not entirely cover the impression. Be careful not to hold the can so close to the impression so as to allow the blast of the aerosol to damage the impression. Then rephotograph the snow impression in the same manner as before, as shown in Figure 3.11B.

If impressions in snow are treated with colored waxes or paints and are in direct sunlight, the colored materials will absorb heat from the sun and can cause the impression to melt rapidly. For that reason, anytime a snow impression in sun is sprayed, the sun's rays should be blocked from striking the impression until the impression has been cast.

Continue to spray the impression carefully, so as not to destroy the impression with the force of the aerosol. Add two or three generous coats of Snow Print Wax to the impression, attempting to evenly and thoroughly cover the entire impression, as shown in Figure 3.11C. Include any areas on the side of the impression that represent the midsole of the shoe. If any areas are not completely sealed with the wax, the dental stone added later may seep through the holes and undercut the impression. This could ruin the impression altogether or cause the dental stone to harden beneath the impression, thus obstructing its visibility. Based on my experience, it takes at least three and sometimes four heavy applications of Snow Print Wax to provide a sufficiently thick coat over the impression.

When you are satisfied that the impression has been completely covered, allow the wax shell to set for about 10 minutes. While the shell is setting, prepare a 2-pound mixture of dental stone. Using cold water or substituting some snow for the water in the mixture will help reduce the heat generated by the dental stone mixture.

The viscosity of the dental stone should be adjusted to a slightly thicker mixture than normally used. It should be carefully poured into the impression over the wax shell. The slightly thicker mixture helps prevent the dental stone from breaking through the thin areas of the wax shell. If necessary, to help the thick dental stone mixture relax and flow into the shell, slightly agitate the upper surface of the dental stone with a stick. Be careful not to damage the impression (Figure 3.11D).

Cover the cast with a box or sheet of newspaper to help it set more quickly in the cold weather. Allow the cast to sit undisturbed for at least 60 minutes. When the cast is removed, it must be removed carefully to minimize touching the bottom surface. The wax will have retained the detail, but the wax shell will remain soft. Even after drying for 48 hours, the detail in the wax can be rubbed off with a finger. Figure 3.12 shows the finished red wax cast.

One disadvantage of this material lies in the storage and treatment of Snow Print Wax: The label on the Snow Print Wax can states that the can must be at room temperature or it will lose its pressure. It also states that the can may be placed in warm water to bring it back to a working temperature. Once the cans are subjected to freezing conditions, such as may be encountered if they are stored in a car during a cold winter, it has been my experience that the aerosol may not work as well or at all. In addition, the aerosol spray nozzle often "spits" or sprays unevenly if cold or improperly stored. The manufacturer has helped in this regard by providing three nozzles with each can. It may be wise to keep only a portion of the supply of this product inside the crime scene vehicle, with the remainder being stored safely indoors where it will always remain at room temperature. That way, if there is ever a

**3.12** The cast made using the Snow Print Wax procedure shown in Figure 3.11.

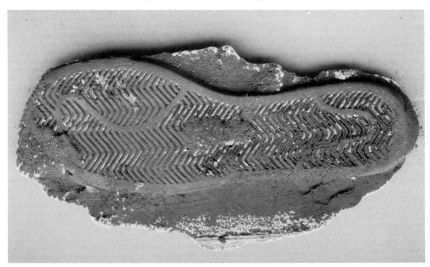

problem with the spraying, the material that has been stored in a warm environment would be available.

Casts made using Snow Print Wax are very fragile. The wax shell that contains the detail is soft and can be rubbed away when it is touched. For that reason, nothing should be allowed to touch the impressioned surface of the cast. Snow Print Wax casts should be photographed as soon as possible to assure that a record of their detail is maintained. In addition, if a Snow Print Wax cast is allowed to sit in the sun, it will possibly melt. I recently had two casts that had been placed in the sun for about 10 minutes where the outside temperature was 62°F. The intense rays of the sun began to melt both casts, one of which is pictured in Figure 3.13. This can be avoided simply through careful storage and handling of the casts.

## Sulfur Casting

Casting footwear impression in snow with sulfur has been practiced in many countries for years. Some of the difficulties encountered with this technique are discussed by Carlsson and Maehly (1976):

> At present, the recommended procedure for securing impressions in snow—at least in Scandinavia—is casting with sulphur. This must be done slightly above the melting point of sulphur (113 degrees) and is tricky to carry out. If the temperature is too high, melting will occur and valuable detail will be destroyed. Even under perfect conditions, some melting takes place and gives a cast with a somewhat porous and unsharp surface. Also, in loose powdery snow, the sulphur sometimes runs through the trail and collects under its surface.

Other authors appear to have experienced no problems with the technique:

> The traditional method of casting snow impressions is with molten sulphur. The sulphur in powder form is heated to approximately 115 degrees Celsius and then the molten mass is rapidly poured into the snow impression where it solidifies, accurately capturing the impression's detail (Cassidy M, 1980).

There are many people who have had good success casting footwear impressions in snow with sulfur, though personally I have had only limited success with sulfur casting. I have been able to recover size and design detail in all cases, but fine detail in only a few. All of the persons I know who have claimed to be satisfied with sulfur casting reside in very cold climates. Perhaps their success with sulfur casting is a result of the type of snow and conditions found in colder climates. If the snow is porous, the sulfur will also retain the texture of the snow crystals and will interfere with the finer detail in the impression.

**3.13** A cast made with Snow Print Wax that was allowed to sit in the sun. Note the melting of the wax shell, which formed a glaze.

Casting with melted sulfur involves (1) the careful melting of a quantity of sulfur, (2) the recooling of the melted sulfur to a temperature just above its crystallization point, and (3) the rapid pouring of the liquid sulfur into the snow impression. As the sulfur comes in contact with the snow, it recrystallizes immediately, retaining the detail of the impression.

To make a sulfur cast, the following materials will be needed:

1. A quantity of crystalline sulfur. Approximately 5 pounds of powdered sulfur will be needed for each impression. Reportedly, sulfur that has been melted and resolidified is better. It may therefore be desirable to buy sulfur that has been processed in this manner or, alternatively, to take some powdered sulfur and melt and resolidify it yourself.
2. A heating plate with a stirring capability. The heating plate offers much safer and more uniform heat than a gas burner. If for some reason, the casts need to be made far from a power source, a gas burner can be used. Appropriate cautions must be used whenever heating sulfur with an open flame heat source.
3. A 1-quart aluminum pot with a handle and a lid. This will be used to heat the sulfur. The lid and handle will come in handy if you need to transport the hot, molten sulfur some distance from the heating source to the impression.
4. A magnetic stirring bar to be used with the heating plate or something that can be used to stir the sulfur.
5. Some strips of chartboard, wood, or metal flashing that can be used to create a pouring channel.

To make a sulfur cast of an impression, a channel must be prepared that will direct the flow of the molten sulfur into the footwear impression. To do this, build up a portion of the snow to a level that is higher than the impression. This, either by itself or with the assistance of some form material, will serve to direct the sulfur into the impression. No other preparation of the impression is needed (Figure 3.14B).

Place the magnetic stirrer in the bottom of the aluminum pot and fill the pot with sulfur. Place it on the electric heating plate and turn the heat on a low to medium setting. Also turn on the stirring mechanism. Sulfur melts at around 115°C; however, if the sulfur should reach 170°C, it will *irreversibly* change into a syrupy, thick brown mass and will be permanently ruined. For that reason, the sulfur must be heated slowly, increasing the temperature a little at a time, and must be stirred constantly. As the sulfur begins to melt, it will take up less room in the container and more sulfur can be added until eventually the proper quantity of melted sulfur is obtained. About 5 pounds of sulfur is required for one impression. Continually stir the sulfur throughout this entire process to avoid the sulfur on the bottom getting too hot.

When all the sulfur has been melted, as shown in Figure 3.14A, the heat source can be removed or turned off. The stirring must continue, to ensure that a uniform temperature remains throughout the liquid sulfur. When the uniform temperature of the sulfur drops to within a few degrees of the crystalline point of 115°C, the sulfur will begin to crystallize around the edges and on the surface. Continue stirring slowly until you see that crystals are still present and are not redissolving, even during the stirring process. At this point, the sulfur is ready for pouring into the impression. A thermometer with an appropriate scale can be used during this entire process to monitor the temperature, if desired.

Pour the entire amount of sulfur into the prepared channel so that it will be directed down the channel and into the impression. The pouring process should be done *quickly and without hesitation*. The sulfur will crystallize immediately as it makes contact with the surface of the impression and will take on the detail in the impression (Figure 3.14C).

Although the recrystallized sulfur will appear hard, the inner areas of the cast will remain hot and soft for some time. The cast should therefore be allowed to sit undisturbed for at least 30 minutes until it is thoroughly cooled. Sulfur casts are very fragile and brittle, so extreme care must be exercised when lifting and handling the cast.

The sulfur cast will provide a representation of the detail in the snow impression, but, as previously mentioned, will also reproduce any texture pattern in the snow. This is shown in Figure 3.15.

### Paraffin Casting

Paraffin wax can also be used to cast a footwear impression in snow; however, it is not a recommended material. The paraffin must be slowly melted and will require at least 1½ pounds for a footwear impression. A black wax crayon can be added to the paraffin to impart color to the cast and provide better contrast. The paraffin must be melted slowly for safety reasons, since rapid melting of paraffin can result in popping or "exploding." The paraffin can be melted in an aluminum pot on a heating plate (Figure 3.16A). A channel must be prepared, as for the sulfur cast, to guide the melted paraffin into the impression (Figure 3.16B).

When the paraffin completely melts, the heat should be turned off, and the paraffin should be stirred occasionally as it cools back down to its melting point. As the cooling paraffin approaches that temperature, a wax skin will begin forming on the surface, which will redissolve with stirring. When it cools a little more, it will be harder for the skin to dissolve. The paraffin is then ready to be poured into the channel. Up to this point, the time required and general procedures for melting the paraffin are very similar to those for sulfur.

When the paraffin is poured into the impression, it will form a shell where it makes contact with the colder snow impression. The rapid cooling can cause air entrapment between the wax and the impression. This trapped air can interfere with the detail in the impression, and an accurate recording will not be reproduced in those areas. In addition,

**A**

**B**

**3.14** The procedure for making a sulfur cast involves (**A**) melting the sulfur, (**B**) preparing a channel to direct the sulfur into the impression, and (**C**) pouring the sulfur into the channel, allowing it to flow into the impressioned area.

C

**3.15** A sulfur cast obtained using the procedure shown in Figure 3.14.

**A**

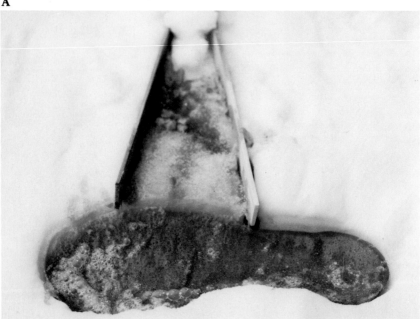

**B**

**3.16**  The procedure for making a paraffin cast involves (**A**) melting the paraffin and (**B**) pouring it into a prepared channel that directs the paraffin into the impression.

the paraffin in the interior parts of the cast that are not in direct contact with the snow will remain very hot. The hot paraffin will keep the hardened portion next to the impression soft, which, combined with the weight of the paraffin, can result in distortion, twisting, and bending of the cast. Both the air entrapment and twisting can be seen in Figure 3.17.

**3.17** A paraffin cast. Note the twisting of the cast (**A**), which has resulted from the sagging of the warm, soft paraffin under its own weight. Also note the spaces formed by trapped air (**B**).

**A**

**B**

For these reasons, and due to the length of the procedure, paraffin is not recommended as a good casting material for snow impressions.

## Auto Spray Primer with Dental Stone

Another method of highlighting and casting snow impressions has been recommended by some (Johnson R, 1983; Wolfe JR and Beheim CW, 1989). This technique involves the use of gray auto spray primer that comes in aerosol cans and is used to prime cars before painting. The sandable primers seem to work better. The application of a gray primer to the impression's surface, if in direct sunlight, will cause the impression to melt rapidly. This will occur even in subzero temperatures. To avoid this, a piece of chartboard or another makeshift screen should be placed in a position to shield the impression from the sun prior to using this method.

The impression is first lightly sprayed with the gray primer to highlight it, as was previously demonstrated with Snow Print Wax. At that point, additional examination quality photographs of the highlighted impression should be taken. No further application of the primer should be made. The primer should only be used to lightly color the surface of the impression as needed to highlight it, but not to coat it in the manner that Snow Print Wax was used. The impression should now be filled with a mixture of chilled dental stone. To obtain this mixture, prepare a 5% to 10% solution of potassium sulfate in water. Then add snow to the water to make a slurry of icy water. Use this icy potassium sulfate solution to mix with the dental stone. The addition of potassium sulfate with the water will not only accelerate the setting of the cast but will reduce the freezing point of the mixture well below 32°F. In subfreezing temperatures, the use of dental stone without potassium sulfate would possibly allow the casting mixture to freeze before setting. The cast would also take an extremely long time to set. The potassium sulfate mixture can reduce the freezing point considerably, thus allowing the cast to set before freezing occurs. The finished cast will have the color of the gray primer. A cast obtained with this procedure is shown in Figure 3.18.

## Summary of Snow Casting

Snow varies because of differences in temperature and other variables that accompany snow. Snow can be dry or wet, powdered or well packed, fresh or remelted.

The choice of Snow Print Wax, sulfur, or gray primer with cooled dental stone for casting snow impressions should be based on one's personal experience with each method, as well as the snow conditions and temperatures existing at a particular crime scene.

**3.18** A gray auto body primer/cooled dental stone cast (courtesy of Alaska Scientific Crime Detection Laboratory).

## The Importance of Casting All Three-Dimensional Impressions

The question often arises as to whether it is necessary to cast every footwear impression located at the crime scene. There are many good arguments that support casting all impressions. A partial impression, due to the soil composition and the manner in which the soil contacted the surface of the footwear, may leave a more valuable and detailed impression than one that includes the whole surface of the shoe. It is not possible at the crime scene to see all the detail present in each impression, nor would all crime scene technicians be likely to recognize the true value of that detail. Guesswork in picking the best impression at the crime scene might be in error. The crime scene technician, if confronted with ten latent fingerprints at a scene, might surmise that some of those impressions may have sufficient detail to effect an identification and others may not. However, she or he would know that the best place to determine that is in the laboratory and not at the scene. The technician wouldn't lift five of those ten impressions and leave the other five at the crime scene, because of the real possibility that the most valuable impression might be left behind and lost. The same consideration should apply to casting footwear impression evidence.

There may be a few reasons why it is simply not possible or reasonable to cast all of the footwear impressions at a scene, but there are only a few. In most cases, if feasible and conditions permit, *all* footwear impressions should be photographed and cast. In actual practice, not much more time or effort is involved in casting ten impressions than in casting three or four, providing you are properly prepared.

Most shoes, particularly athletic shoes and hiking boots, have rubber outsoles and have sufficient random characteristics such as cuts and nicks on them to make them unique and identifiable. The chances of such shoes leaving three-dimensional impressions that retain sufficient detail to be suitable for identification are excellent. Evidence with the potential to provide such information should never be left at the crime scene. *All* impressions, whether in soil, sand, snow, or even underwater, are suitable for casting. *Casts should always be made of three-dimensional impressions. Evidence that is left at the crime scene is lost forever!*

# Lifting Two-Dimensional Footwear Impressions

# 4

Lifting a footwear impression involves transferring a two-dimensional impression from its original surface to a surface that will provide better contrast. The lift provides not only improved visibility of the impression's features through improved contrast, but also a means of transporting the impression to the laboratory for later examination.

Unfortunately, some impressions may only lift partially, and others may not lift at all. As a result, there is always a risk that impressions may be destroyed during attempts to lift them. *Visible* footwear impressions on items that can be retrieved from the scene and transported to the laboratory *should not be lifted at the scene.* In the laboratory, there will be more time and resources to take forensic photographs and otherwise enhance the impression. Removing the impression from the scene sometimes necessitates cutting out pieces of carpet or flooring; however, the effort is well worth it. Footwear impressions should be lifted *only* when the item bearing the impression *cannot be safely removed* from the scene or *cannot be removed* from the scene at all.

One of the problems long encountered in lifting footwear impressions has been the lack of adequate lifting materials. Most of the lifting materials that have been and still are available are either those primarily developed and used for latent fingerprints or those of the makeshift variety. Materials used successfully for fingerprints are not always as successful or adequate for lifting footwear impressions. The rubber adhesive fingerprint lifters have sufficient tackiness to lift fingerprint powder but not to lift many of the footwear impressions encountered. Clear adhesive lifting tape, also successfully used to transfer dusted fingerprints to contrasting colored paper, is clumsy and difficult to use when trying to lift the larger footwear impressions.

One of the worst lifting materials for footwear impressions is the footprint-size *transparent adhesive* lifter. The effect of the adhesive combined with the lack of contrast usually results in partial or total loss of any original impressions lifted with transparent adhesive lifter. Other footwear impression lifting materials of the makeshift variety include contact paper, clear and colored tapes of all types and sizes, and carbon paper. Fortunately, in recent years, some new products and materials have been specifically developed for lifting footwear impressions, including the electrostatic lifting device and gelatin footprint lifters.

The many materials that a shoe may track through and then redeposit in the form of an impression, combined with the many surfaces that a shoe can impress those materials on, results in a large number of impression/surface combinations. Deposited materials will adhere to different surfaces in a variety of ways. A dry residue impression will not bond well to a smooth, dry surface and therefore can easily be lifted. Add moisture to the residue or add texture to the surface, and the degree of bonding will likely increase. Successful lifting of the impression then becomes more difficult. Impressions that result when a person tracks through oil, grease, blood, or other similar materials usually will penetrate or bond to the surface sufficiently to prevent a quality lift.

It is important to consider the type of surface an impression is on, as well as the materials and conditions surrounding the impression. Recognizing these factors will assist in determining whether an impression can or should be lifted and, if so, the best methods to use. Some of the factors to consider when deciding what methods of lifting or enhancement should be used include the following:

1. The general category of the surface: porous versus nonporous, etc.
2. The specific surface the impression is on: paper, plastic, carpet, fabric, etc.
3. The condition of the surface: dry, wet, damp, clean, or dirty
4. The color of the surface and the impression, i.e., the amount of contrast between the two
5. The presence of any interfering materials such as dirt, dust, or grease which may also be lifted and therefore obscure the impression
6. The relative humidity—high humidity may interfere with electrostatic lifting

There is no way to list or accurately predict what the best method of lifting might be for every possible situation. Crime scene technicians and examiners who are familiar and experienced with the following methods and materials should be able to select the most appropriate choice in those cases *where the original impression cannot be retained* and a lift must be attempted.

## Lifting Impressions Electrostatically

*The Origin of Electrostatic Lifting*

In July, 1970, a 41-year-old police officer named Kato Masao of Shikoku, Japan, realized that dust had been accumulating around the high-voltage areas of the television set he was working on. From this observation, he got the idea that the high-voltage current produced by certain television parts could be used to assist in lifting latent footwear impressions from a surface. After further research, a static electricity machine that could produce 14,000 volts was combined with an electrode plate and a black vinyl sheet to form the first electrostatic lifting device.[1] This initial machine was somewhat cumbersome and had to be plugged into a main current source in order to operate.

In 1981, England's Metropolitan Police Laboratory directed research that ultimately led to a portable high-voltage electrostatic lifting device that could operate on rechargeable batteries. The Metropolitan Police Laboratory has been successfully using this device since November 1983 (Davis R, 1985).

Today, there are two commercially available high-voltage electrostatic lifting devices, which have proven very effective in the electrostatic lifting of dry residue footwear impressions. The Dustmark Electrostatic Lifting Kit, pictured in Figure 4.1, was developed and commercially produced in late 1983 by Foster & Freeman, Ltd.[2] In 1986, a second commercial lifter, the Electrostatic Dust Print Lifter, pictured in Figure 4.2, was produced by the Kinderprint Company, Inc.[3] Both companies currently produce and sell these devices to law enforcement personnel.

Figures 4.3 and 4.4 depict some of the basic components of the electrostatic lifting apparatus. It consists of (1) a main unit housing a rechargeable battery–operated, high-voltage source of approximately 10,000 to 15,000 volts, (2) a ground plate and a cable that connects the ground plate to the main unit, (3) a metal hand-held probe, and (4) special lifting film. The lifting film can be either a black vinyl or polyester film coated on one side with a conductive metal laminate. The parts are housed in a briefcase, making them convenient to transport and use.

When the high-voltage source is turned on, it creates a static charge on the lifting film and causes some of the dust or residue particles

---

[1] "An Electrostatic Method for Lifting Footprints," *International Criminal Police Review*, 272: 287–292, National Police Agency, 1973.

[2] Dustmark Electrostatic Lifting Kit, Foster & Freeman, 25 Swan Lane, Worcester, England

[3] Electrostatic Dust Print Lifter, Kinderprint Company, Inc., P.O. Box 16, Martinez, CA 94553

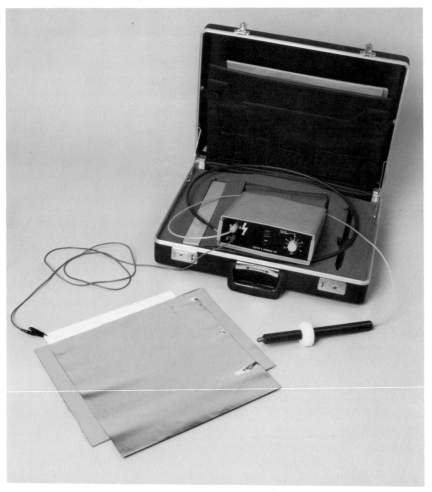

**4.1**   The Dustmark electrostatic lifting kit made by Foster and Freeman, Ltd.

composing the footwear impression to transfer to the underside or black layer of the lifting film. Since the film is in direct contact with the impression, the transferred footwear impression on the film will be the same size as the impression.

## Applications of the Electrostatic Lifting Device

With the electrostatic lifting device, footwear impressions can be lifted from virtually any surface, both porous and nonporous. The device works best on *dry dust or dry residue footwear impressions on surfaces that are relatively clean.* For impressions in that category, the device is

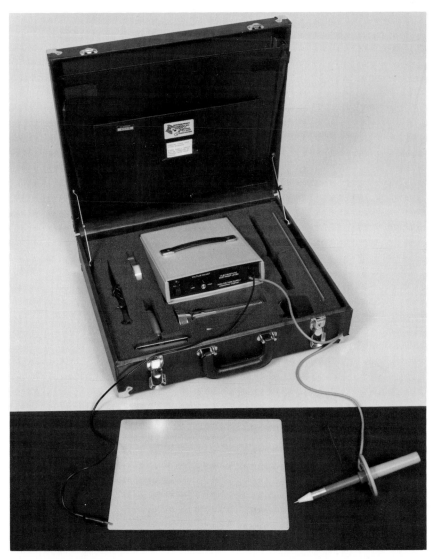

**4.2**  The electrostatic lifting kit made by the Kinderprint Company.

excellent at lifting footwear impressions. If the impressions were wet when they were made or if they become wet or damp prior to lifting, the electrostatic lifting device will work poorly or not at all. It is important to understand that the electrostatic lifting device is useful for dry impressions and *not impressions of wet origins*. It is also important to remember that impressions that do not lift are not destroyed. Therefore, in cases where it is not known if an impression is of wet or dry

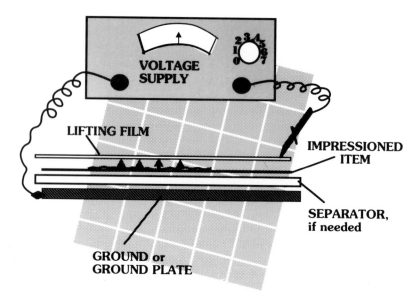

**4.3** Some of the basic parts of the electrostatic lifting devices.

**4.4** Lifting an impression from a piece of paper with an electrostatic lifting device.

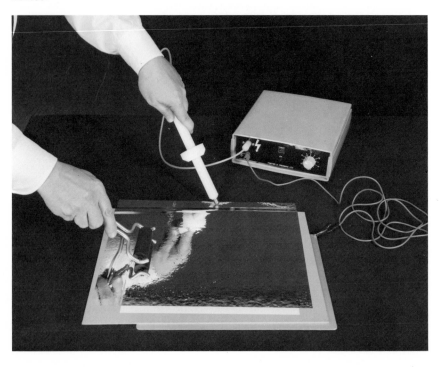

origin, the use of the electrostatic lifting device will not risk loss of or damage to the impression.

Not all dry impressions can be successfully lifted. Attempts to lift residue footwear impressions on a dirty surface that itself contains loose residue will result in both the impression and the background residue being lifted together. The lifting film will be covered with residue and the footwear impression will be lost in it. However, if the shoes of the suspect are damp or sticky and walk through a dirty surface, it may be possible to detect negative impressions where the residue on the surface adhered to the shoe and was removed, and the negative image of the shoe outsole remains.

It has always been difficult to successfully photograph and retrieve certain types of dust and residue footwear impressions, particularly if the contrast was poor or the impressions were either latent or barely visible. The electrostatic lifting device now makes it possible to locate and retrieve footwear impressions of this type that would previously have been overlooked, ignored, or lost in unsuccessful attempts to retrieve them. In fact, it may be used to lift totally latent impressions from surfaces where it is suspected footwear impressions may be present. It is therefore an excellent crime scene device with which to make a "blind search" of areas where it is likely that the suspect walked and that therefore could potentially contain latent but liftable dry residue impressions.

The best way to familiarize oneself with the usage, applications, and limitations of the electrostatic lifting device is to try different lifting procedures on a variety of both dry- and wet-origin impressions and on a variety of surfaces. Equipped with this experience, the use of the electrostatic lifting device at crime scenes and in laboratory casework becomes an easy routine.

## Procedure for Using Electrostatic Lifting Devices

To lift an impression with the electrostatic lifting device, the following procedures should be used:

*Position the grounding device.* The ground wire of the electrostatic lifting device must be attached to the ground plate or other grounding material. Some metal ground plates have a coated or covered side and an exposed metal side. Other ground plates are simply a bare metal plate. Any flat aluminum tray or plate can also be used as a ground plate. The position of the ground plate can vary depending on the type and location of the impression as set forth in the following four examples:

(1) If at all possible, position the ground plate beneath the impressioned item with the metal side facing the impression. This would be the best choice in the case of impressions on paper, loose carpeting, and

other movable items. Since the lifting film may be larger than the impressioned item, a piece of clear chartboard or similar nonconductive material must be used as a separator and should be placed between the impressioned item and the ground plate to keep the lifting film separated from the ground plate. If the metalized layer of the lifting film is in contact with the ground plate, arcing will occur, and the device will not work. The arrangement for this lifting situation is illustrated in Figures 4.3 and 4.4.

(2) Very often the impression will be on a surface such as a tile floor where the ground plate cannot be placed beneath the impression. In those instances, position the ground plate at least 2 inches away from the lifting film with the metal side of the ground plate facing down (Figure 4.5).

(3) If the impressioned item is on a surface such as a door, chair seat, etc., place the ground plate so the metal side makes maximum contact with the adjacent surface. In the case of a door, the ground plate can be taped to the rear side of the door, with the metal side facing the impression (Figure 4.6). In the case of the chair, it can be taped alongside the impression on the chair or beneath the seat. To be most effective, the metal side of the ground plate should be in maximum contact with the adjacent surface whenever possible.

(4) Occasionally, the footwear impression will be on a metal object such as a car hood or metal cabinet. In those cases, the ground plate can be used or the ground lead can be attached directly to the car frame or

**4.5**  The ground plate can be placed next to the lifting film in situations where it cannot be placed beneath the impression.

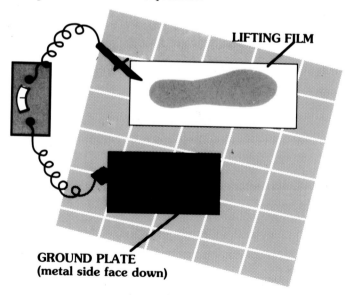

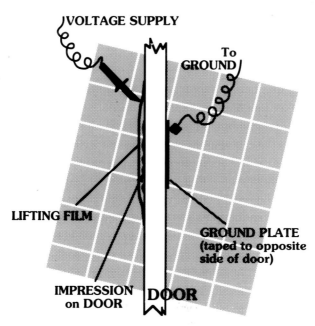

VOLTAGE SUPPLY

To GROUND

LIFTING FILM

GROUND PLATE
(taped to opposite
side of door)

IMPRESSION
on DOOR

DOOR

**4.6** The ground plate can be fastened to the opposite side of large object, such as a door.

metal cabinet. An alternate procedure should be used for the placement of the lifting film (see below).

After positioning the ground plate, attach one end of the ground wire to it or, in the case of a metal cabinet or other metal object, connect the ground lead to that object. Plug the other end of the ground lead into the voltage source.

*Prepare and position the lifting film over the impression.* Position a piece of lifting film over the impression with the black side against the impression. The black side will face down and the metalized side will face up, as shown in Figure 4.4. The placement of the lifting film should be done carefully so as not to disturb or smear the impression. *Never* slide the lifting material over the surface. The lifting film should not touch any part of the ground plate. It may be necessary to place a piece of clean chartboard between the impressioned item and the ground plate, as shown in Figure 4.4, or to make other adjustments so that the film and ground plate are not in contact with one another.

In cases where the impressioned surface is metal, carefully place a piece of clear, very thin (1 or 2 mil) Mylar or polyester over the impression. Then place a slightly smaller piece of lifting film, black side down, over the Mylar. The Mylar should be bigger than the lifting film to ensure that none of the lifting film is touching the metal surface. Continue with the lifting procedure as outlined; however, remember

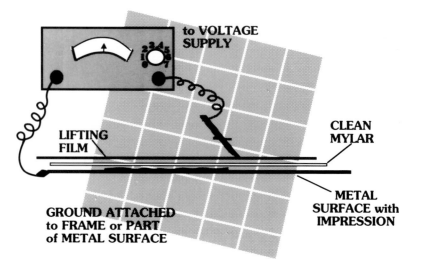

**4.7**   When lifting an impression from a metal surface, a piece of clear Mylar can be placed over the impression and then covered with a smaller piece of lifting film. The Mylar will provide a separation between the metal surface and the metalized lifting film.

that the lifted impression will now be on the Mylar. The Mylar and the black lifting film can be lifted and kept together to provide the necessary contrast. This lifting arrangement is illustrated in Figure 4.7.

The electrostatic lifting of some impressions, particularly those that are latent or may not be readily detectable after lifting, can leave the crime scene technician with a lifted impression that can no longer be oriented as to its direction in the crime scene. One examiner (Hamm ED, personal communication) has suggested marking the lifting film and the impressioned surface to later facilitate the orientation of the lifted impression. The need for this step should be considered prior to making any lifts.

*Place the probe on the lifting film.* As shown in Figure 4.4, the tip of the hand-held probe should be in contact with an edge of the metalized backing of the lifting film. There is no need to move the probe around during the charging of the film. It should remain in contact with the film during the entire procedure. The voltage can now be turned on. It is usually only necessary to turn the voltage on a low setting, although in cases where the current must travel through thicker materials, a higher setting will be required. The application of sufficient voltage will cause the lifting film to be pulled down tightly against the impression.

In some instances, air bubbles will be trapped beneath the film. These will often disappear in a few seconds. If any air bubbles remain trapped beneath the film, they may be rolled out with a clean fingerprint roller or brayer. This should be done very gently by lightly passing the roller over the film. The weight of the roller is all the pressure that should be used, because excessive pressure may damage the impression. If arcing occurs between the film and the ground, either the power is too high or part of the lifting film is touching or too close to the ground plate.

After the power is turned off, allow the probe to remain in contact with the film for approximately 5 seconds to discharge the film. As the charge leaves it, the film can be seen to relax. *Failure to discharge the film with the probe will result in a static electricity shock to the person who lifts the film off the impression!*

*Remove the lifting film.* The film can now be removed from the impressioned area by carefully peeling it off from one end to the other. Once the film is removed, lay it on a clean flat surface with the black side facing up or properly store it. In a totally dark room examine the film carefully with oblique light to see if an impression has been transferred to it. If this is not possible at the crime scene, then all lifts should be saved until they can be examined in *total darkness*. Film should never be discarded without first carefully examining the film in a darkened room with the aid of a *strong, oblique light*. Many times, film viewed in ambient lighting or without a strong, oblique light source will initially appear to contain no impressions. Further examination of that film in total darkness with a strong, oblique light often reveals the presence of valuable impressions.

Figures 1.5 and 4.8 show high-contrast photographs of impressions prior to lifting and electrostatic lifts of the same impressions. Figure 4.8C depicts an unusual lift of both a positive and a negative impression from the same shoe at the same crime scene. The subject had first tracked over the area, depositing a residue impression, then stepped in some sticky material, and later tracked across the same area, removing the dust in that area and leaving a negative impression.

Many residue impressions are so heavy that the first lifting process results in a lifted impression with too much residue. In those cases, a second lift of the same impression should be made, because it sometimes results in an impression that appears clearer and much better for examination.

*Note of caution.* Whenever using the electrostatic lifting device, it is possible to receive electrical shocks from the lifting film, the ground plate, and the metal probe. These shocks can be avoided by not touching those parts when the current is on and by allowing the probe to remain on the metalized portion of the lifting film for at least 5 seconds after the unit is turned off, thus allowing any remaining charge to dissipate.

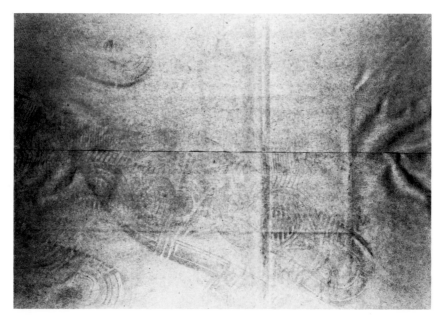

**A**

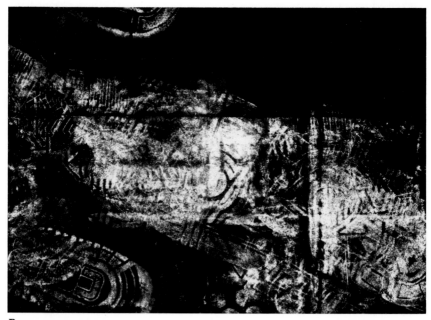

**B**

**4.8** A dry residue impression after high-contrast photography (**A**) and after lifting with the electrostatic lifting device (**B**). **C** depicts a positive and a negative impression on the same lift.

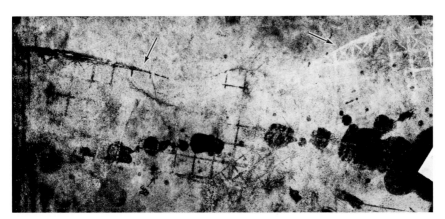

C

## Storage of the Film After Lifting

Lifted impressions are fragile and can easily be damaged if the film is not stored properly. The film often contains a residual charge that can attract dust and debris or cause the film to cling to another surface. For that reason, the lifting film should be protected immediately after being removed from the impression.

Items that contain a dry residue footwear impression *should never be wrapped in plastic or stored in a plastic bag.* If they are, a partial transfer of the impression to the plastic will take place. An example of the transfer from a piece of lifting film to a zip-lock bag is shown in Figure 4.9. To properly preserve and store the impressioned item or lifting film containing an impression, it should be stored securely in a folder or in a shallow box, as shown in Figure 4.10. If a folder is used, the film should be placed in the folder and secured with a piece of tape. If the film should slide around in the folder or be pulled out of the folder while it is closed, the delicate lift will be damaged. Whenever the lift must be removed, the folder should be opened first, followed by removal of the lift. When a shallow box is used, the impressioned item or lift can be taped securely into the bottom of the box.

Evidence can be obscured or contaminated if care is not used in preserving electrostatic lifts from crime scenes. One example of this involved the reuse of a folder that had been previously used for the preservation and transportation of other electrostatic lifts. Part of a previously lifted impression had been transferred to and retained by the side of the folder. When the folder was reused, a portion of the first impression was transferred to the lifting film that had most recently been placed in the folder. This resulted in an impression from one crime

**A**

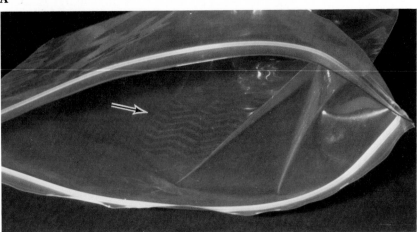

**B**

**4.9** Lifts or materials containing impressions should *never* be stored inside a plastic bag **(A)** or covered with plastic. The impression will transfer to the plastic **(B)**.

scene being transferred to a lift from a second crime scene. To prevent such occurrences, reusing folders for the storage of lifts should be avoided.

Loss of evidence can also occur if the folder, cardboard, or other material used to cover or store the lifts contains dust or dirt. In one case,

**4.10** Lifts and original items containing impressions should be stored (1) by taping them to the inside of a clean folder, thus preventing any movement inside the folder, or (2) by taping them inside a shallow box.

a lift was taped between two pieces of cardboard to preserve an impression on its way to the laboratory. Unknown to the investigator, the cardboard was filled with dust. Some types of cardboard are simply inherently dusty. By the time the lifts reached the laboratory, both sides of the electrostatic lift were covered with the cardboard dust, which had completely and permanently obliterated the footwear impression. There was no way to separate the footwear impression on the lift from the dust.

## Photographing the Impressions on the Lifting Film

The lifted impressions on the black lifting film can be photographed with an ASA 400 black-and-white film such as Kodak T-Max 400. The lighting should be directed from a very low, oblique angle. Because of the black film, a longer exposure, with the lens opened two or three f-stops more than a light meter would indicate, is usually required. The photographic prints can be reversed for direct comparison with test impressions.

## Gelatin and Adhesive Lifting

Gelatin and adhesive lifting materials permit the lifting of some footwear impressions when the electrostatic lifting device either is unavailable or, due to the nature of the impression, is unsuccessful. Gelatin lifters are relatively thick and come with a cloth or canvas backing and a clear polyester cover sheet. Some adhesive lifters are also thick, with a canvas backing and polyester cover, and closely resemble gelatin lifters.

Most commercial adhesive footwear lifting materials are thinner and have a plastic or paper backing and no accompanying protective cover.

Although gelatin and adhesive lifters are sometimes similar in appearance and are applied with the same technique, it is important to understand that they are not the same. Gelatin lifters can be used on both porous and nonporous surfaces for lifting both original residue impressions and impressions that have been dusted with powder. The gelatin lifter is therefore more versatile and, in the majority of instances, is superior to adhesive lifters. Although some of the better quality, thick adhesive lifters can be used to lift original residue impressions from nonporous surfaces and are successful in lifting powdered impressions, gelatin lifters can be used to lift impressions from all surfaces. For that reason, it would seem logical to recommend the use of gelatin lifters only. Since commercial gelatin footwear lifters have become available only recently and because some adhesive materials are acceptable in certain situations, both will be discussed.

Gelatin or adhesive lifting materials should normally be used only (1) if the impressioned item cannot be removed from the scene and taken to the laboratory, and (2) after electrostatic lifting has been tried (or if electrostatic lifting is not available).

## Application of Gelatin and Adhesive Lifting Materials

The method used to apply the gelatin lifter over the impression is outlined in Figure 4.11. Some technicians prefer to use a fingerprint roller to gently roll the gelatin material over the impression (Figure 4.11A), while others prefer to bend the lifter in the middle, setting that portion of the lifter on the impression first and allowing the ends to follow (Figure 4.11B). If the surface is rigid, either method is satisfactory. If the surface is nonrigid, like a piece of paper, only the second method should be used. With either method, it is important to *avoid any forceful rolling or spreading of the lifter*. Once the lifting material has been laid over the impression, apply only the force necessary to ensure that the lifter is firmly contacting the entire surface. This can be accomplished by gently rolling a fingerprint roller or rubbing your fingers over the back of the lifting material.

## Gelatin Lifters

Gelatin lifters consist of a gelatin material laid on a pliable backing. The gelatin layer can be colorless or can have added to it ingredients that give it a white or black opaque color. A few gelatin lifting materials are featured in Figure 4.12.

For years, the only gelatin lifting film available was the gelatin surface found on photographic films or on homemade gelatin lifters. The

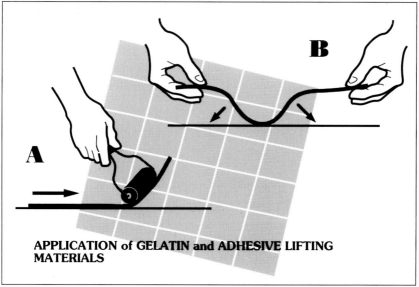

**APPLICATION of GELATIN and ADHESIVE LIFTING MATERIALS**

**4.11**   Gelatin and adhesive lifts may be applied either (a) with a roller or (b) by touching the center of the lifting material to the center of the impressioned area and allowing the sides to roll across the impression. With either choice, try to avoid air pockets, and avoid using excessive pressure, which might distort the impression.

**4.12**   Some choices of gelatin lifting materials. On the right are commercially made, transparent, black, and white gelatin lifting materials. The sheets on the left are photographic film that has been exposed (black) and unexposed (white). The commercial gelatin lifters and homemade lifters made in the same fashion are superior to the makeshift photographic film lifters.

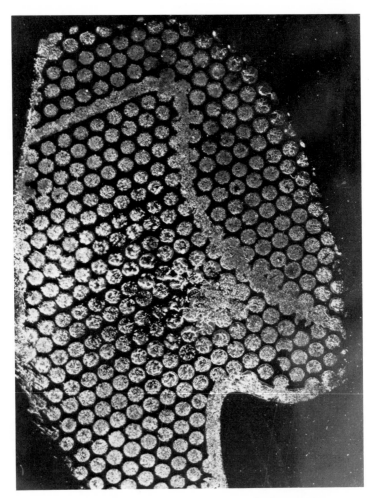

**4.13**  A lift of a wet residue impression from paper using black gelatin lifting material. This impression, because of its wet origin, would not lift with the electrostatic lifting device.

use of photographic film that has had its gelatin surface softened is referenced in much of the older literature (Hamilton D, 1949; O'Hara C and Ostenburg J, 1949).

Homemade recipes for preparing gelatin lifting films have also been advocated (Abbott J, 1941; Davis R, 1988). Currently, gelatin lifters are available from ODV (South Paris, Maine) and Lightning Powder Company (Salem, Oregon), from their source in Holland,[4] and reportedly from other sources in Europe.

---

[4] BVDA International, Willemsparkweg 58, P.O. Box 5064, AB Amsterdam, Holland

Because of the thin coating of gelatin on photographic film, as well as the fuss and the time spent in preparing it, the commercial gelatin lifters available today are the better choice. Homemade gelatin lifters made in the same fashion as the commercial gelatin lifters are also suitable, but if they are made properly, they are probably not cost effective. A lift of a residue impression of wet origin using black commercial gelatin lifting materials is pictured in Figure 4.13.

### Adhesive Lifters

Adhesive lifters include a variety of adhesive-coated materials, ranging from tapes to adhesive-coated paper and rubber. They are somewhat successful in lifting footwear impressions from nonporous surfaces, but they should be used primarily to lift footwear impressions that have been dusted with fingerprint powder, and only when gelatin lifters are not on hand.

Most of the adhesive impression lifting materials that have been used to lift footwear impressions are adhesive-coated materials that were intended for other uses (Figure 4.14). They include all forms of fingerprint lifting tape, cellophane tape, contact paper, and shelf paper, as

**4.14** Some adhesive lifting materials. On the left are black and white adhesive papers, in the center are black, white, and transparent adhesive footprint lifters, and on the right are fingerprint lifting tape and adhesive tape.

well as some commercial lifters like the rubber fingerprint or footprint lifters and the transparent footprint lifters.

### Adhesive Lifting Tape and Fingerprint Lifting Tape

When materials like fingerprint lifting tape and cellophane tape are employed, several overlapping strips must be used to cover a footwear impression. Although these materials are successfully used on fingerprints, the larger size of footwear impressions makes the use of these tapes less desirable. The awkwardness and the procedure involved in attempting lifts with strips of tape often results in poor quality lifts and loss of parts of the impression. Figure 4.15 depicts a portion of an impression that was dusted with fingerprint powder and lifted with 1-inch tape. There are several areas where the powder fails to stick well to the tape, as well as several creases, resulting in the loss of the impression in those areas. In addition, the areas of tape that overlap each other reduce or prevent visibility of the impression beneath those areas.

### Contact Paper or Shelf Paper

The quality of contact paper or shelf paper is poor, and it usually has an uneven or otherwise inferior coating of adhesive. These products often

**4.15**   An adhesive lift that involved the use of three pieces of clear tape to lift a footwear impression that was developed with fingerprint powder. Notice the creases and overlapping areas that obliterate the detail. Also notice the poor contrast.

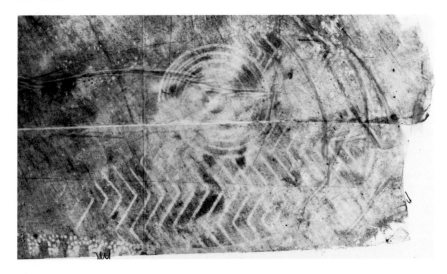

stretch, distort, and tear during the attempt to remove them from an impression. They should *not* be used to lift footwear impressions.

## Transparent Adhesive Footprint Lifters

Colorless lifters, including commercial transparent footwear impression lifters, are *not* desirable for lifting footwear impressions. *The use of transparent footprint lifters to lift original residue impressions usually results in partial or total loss of the evidence!* White and black lifting materials provide much better contrast, so colorless lifting materials are not preferred for lifting footwear impressions. Any time a transparent lifter is used, it should always be marked to prevent confusion or misunderstanding about which side of the lifter is holding the impression.

## Black and White Adhesive Lifting Materials

Black and white adhesive lifting materials of better quality that are sold specifically for footwear impression lifting are usually in the form of a rubber lifter with a clear cover sheet. They can be used to lift footwear impressions that have been successfully enhanced with fingerprint powders of contrasting colors. With fingerprint powder lifts, the protective cover that accompanies the lifter can be carefully reapplied to protect the lifted powdered impression.

In addition, the better quality black rubber adhesive lifting materials can be used to lift light-colored original residue impressions from nonporous surfaces. Problems may be encountered, however. Depending on the composition of the residue and on the adhesive, the residue may be consumed or obscured by the adhesive if the clear protective cover is reapplied to the lift. To avoid this potential loss of a successfully lifted impression, I recommend that the adhesive lifts of original residue impressions be protected by taping them, adhesive side up, in a shallow box, rather than by re-covering them with the protective cover. An adhesive lift of a residue impression is pictured in Figure 4.16. The left half of the lift was re-covered with the protective cover, while the other half was not covered. After 1 week, there was partial loss of the covered half of the impression, while the portion that remained uncovered still contained the full impression.

## Other Lifting Materials

### Carbon Paper

Carbon paper has been occasionally used to lift residue impressions. Although I have seen this done successfully, it has been my experience

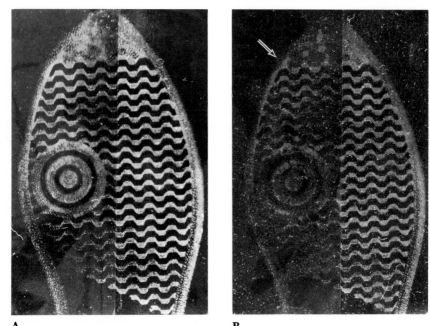

**A**                                              **B**
**4.16**   An adhesive lift (**A**) that was made of a residue impression and was
re-covered with just half of the polyester cover. After 1 week (**B**), there is
deterioration of the left side, which was re-covered.

that it works well *only* occasionally, when the residue is not tightly
bound to the surface. The electrostatic lifter and the gelatin lifting
materials are far superior.

### Silicone

Liquid silicone, if not too viscous, can be carefully poured over a residue
impression, allowed to cure overnight, and then removed. It can only be
used on nonporous surfaces that it will not bond to. The procedures
involved in adding a catalyst and mixing the silicone at a crime scene,
the expense of silicone, and the inconvenience of having to leave it
overnight before being able to remove it from the scene do not support
its routine use as a lifting material. Commercial gelatin lifting materials are more suitable and efficient for lifting residue impressions. In
some cases, however, where the residue impression may be exceptionally thick and might therefore be damaged by the application of a
gelatin lifter, or in cases where the object containing the impression is
very uneven, such as a window sill, silicone may be a good choice. If
silicone is used, it should be of a color that will provide sufficient
contrast with the impression being lifted. Figure 4.17 depicts a silicone
lift of a residue impression.

**4.17** A silicone lift of a residue impression.

## Impressions that Usually Cannot Be Lifted

*Marks in Grease or Oil*

Footwear impressions of an oily or greasy nature will not adhere well to lifting materials. Gelatin lifters, if allowed to remain on the impression for 10 to 20 minutes, can have some success in lifting impressions of a greasy material. It is more likely that chemical enhancement of such impressions followed by additional examination quality photographs of them would be more successful.

*Impressions in Blood*

Impressions in blood can be detected on a broad variety of surfaces. They are most frequently encountered on flooring materials such as tile, wood, and carpeting. They occur as a result of a suspect stepping in a pool of blood or on a blood-stained surface and then tracking the blood through the scene. Because blood is initially a relatively nonviscous liquid that quickly becomes more viscous as it coagulates and dries, footwear impressions in blood vary considerably. Depending on the viscosity as well as the quantity of blood on or beneath the shoe, some impressions are of excellent quality, while in other impressions the blood may actually obscure or fill in detail of the impression. Very often the blood impressions containing the best detail are those that have been made after excess blood has been tracked off the shoe. These impressions may be so light that they will require chemical enhancement to fully observe all of the features in the impression, but they can contain excellent detail. Regardless of the type or apparent features in a blood impression, *all* should be retrieved for comparison purposes.

Lifting blood impressions meets with very limited success. Therefore, other procedures should be carried out: Take examination quality photographs, and make every attempt to retrieve the item with the blood impression, even if it means cutting out the carpet or the flooring. Cases involving impressions in blood are usually serious enough to warrant this action.

When the item absolutely *cannot* be removed from the scene, if the impression is very faint, then chemically enhance and rephotograph it. If the impression is heavier and visibility of it is not a problem, consider dusting with a magna brush and fingerprint powder. Try a small corner of the impression first to see if this works. If successful, powder the entire impression, and lift it with gelatin lifter of contrasting color. If powdering is unsuccessful, lift the original blood impression with a white gelatin lifter. Allow the gelatin lifting material to remain on the blood impression for 20 minutes or longer before removing.

## Deformable Impressions

### Impressions on Carpets and Cushions

Temporarily deformable materials, such as carpet, cushions, grass, pillows, and other similar items, because of their resiliency, will not permanently retain the three-dimensional characteristics of a footwear impression. Impressions on those surfaces can be detected, however, in the following situations:

1. When there is some deformation of the surface still visible, such as depressed carpeting. This type of impression can be retrieved only through photography but is usually of little value beyond indicating general size and shape features and where the suspect walked.
2. When opaque materials, such as blood, grease, or visible residue, are part of the impression and contrast sufficiently with the surface to permit them to be seen. Photograph these impressions, then retain, lift, or enhance accordingly.
3. When the deformed impression also includes a latent dry residue impression that can be developed with an electrostatic lifter during the crime scene processing.

### Impressions on Skin

Impressions made by footwear on skin are frequently encountered, particularly in homicide cases. The impressions usually result from the

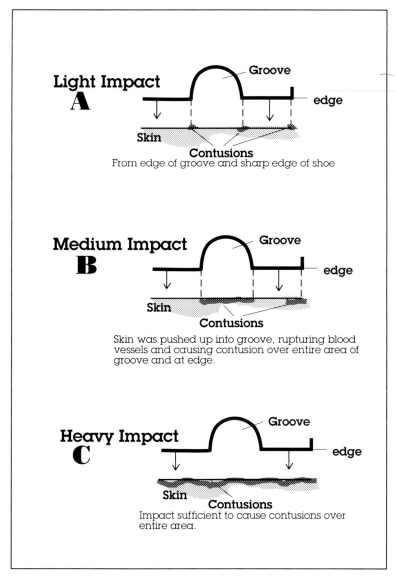

**Light Impact**
**A**

Groove

edge

Skin

Contusions
From edge of groove and sharp edge of shoe

**Medium Impact**
**B**

Groove

edge

Skin

Contusions

Skin was pushed up into groove, rupturing blood
vessels and causing contusion over entire area of
groove and at edge.

**Heavy Impact**
**C**

Groove

edge

Skin

Contusions
Impact sufficient to cause contusions over
entire area.

**4.18** Contusions vary with the degree of impact and the design of the shoe.

subject kicking or stamping on the victim. The impressions can be
found on both the skin and the clothing covering the skin. The deformation of the skin by the footwear will be a very temporary deformation;
however, footwear impressions can still be found on skin in the form of
contusions that have resulted from the impact of the footwear and that
may reflect the characteristics of the footwear that made them. Exami-

nation quality photographs of these impressions should be taken in color and with a scale held on the same plane as the impression.

If the clothing and the body has *not* been wet with water, blood, or body fluids, dry residue impressions may be found. Dry residue impressions on the skin, although probably latent, can be electrostatically lifted. Dry residue impressions may also appear on clothing that covered the area of the footwear impression when it was made.

I have observed that the combined factors of the shoe design, the degree of impact, the angle of the shoe relative to the skin, the presence of either soft tissue or bony structure beneath the skin, and the interference of clothing between the shoe and the skin all contribute to the resulting footwear impression. Contusion patterns vary primarily because of two factors: the amount of pressure applied to the skin by the impact of the shoe, and the shoe design. Figure 4.18 shows how a shoe containing a groove in its design can result in variations in the contusions simply by varying the impact. The light impact impression (Figure 4.18A) results in two slight contusion areas along the edges of the groove. If this groove were narrower or if the impact were greater, those

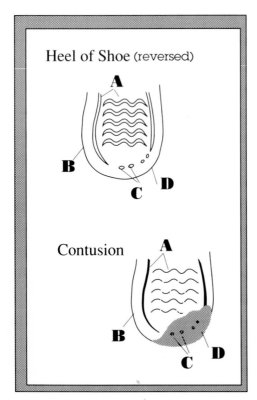

**4.19**  A contusion pattern possible from a deck shoe.

contusions would run together and appear as one, and the complete area of the groove would result in a contusion (Figure 4.18B). In these two situations, the skin is being forced around the sharp edge of the groove and, with additional impact, is forced up into the groove, causing the rupture of blood vessels beneath the skin in those areas. If a tremendous amount of impact is made, it is possible that the entire surface beneath all areas of the shoe could be sufficiently damaged to result in a contusion over the whole surface (Figure 4.18C).

A shoe design could therefore be represented well in a contusion impression if the impact, design, and other factors supported it. In Figure 4.19, a simulated example is provided of how the heel design of a

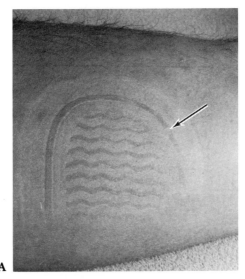

**4.20** Picture of simulated contusion pattern on skin (**A**) and deck shoe (**B**) similar to the drawing in Figure 4.19. Note the pattern of the stitching.

**A**

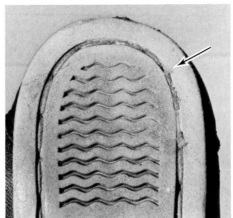

**B**

deck shoe could be reproduced in a contusion resulting from a medium-impact impression. The grooves are represented by contusions (A) as are the edges of the unworn heel (B). The stitch holes that have remained in the worn area of the heel also show up as contusions (C). In the worn area of the heel where the design has worn off (except for the stitches), the broader surface dissipates the impact and will either leave no impression or a broad, undefined contusion in that area (D). The effect of this on skin is depicted in Figure 4.20. Note how clearly one of the remaining stitches appears (arrow).

# Techniques to Enhance Footwear Impressions

# 5

Not all footwear impressions located at crime scenes are clearly visible and distinct. Many footwear impressions are latent, partially latent, or so indistinct that very little detail in them can be observed. There are a number of enhancement procedures that can render some footwear impressions more visible or distinct than they originally were. The enhancement helps the examiner use the maximum amount of information available in the impression, which in turn will enable a more thorough examination.

The many ways of enhancing two-dimensional impressions can be divided into photographic enhancement, physical enhancement, and chemical enhancement methods. Numerous factors affect the choice of what technique to use, as well as the success a given technique may have. Those factors include (1) the composition of the surface the impression is on (paper, cloth, tile, wood, carpet, etc.), (2) the texture and porosity of the surface, (3) the condition of the surface (dry, wet, damp, clean, dirty), (4) the color of the surface, (5) the composition of any contaminant on the surface (dirt, grease, etc.), (6) the composition of the impression itself, (7) whether the impression is of wet or dry origin, and (8) the humidity.

Forensic photographic enhancement methods are usually tried first, since they are nondestructive. Often, forensic photography is the only method necessary to enhance an impression so that sufficient detail is visualized to permit positive identification. If additional enhancement is necessary, the next step would be to attempt to electrostatically lift the impression. If the electrostatic lifting is unsuccessful, the attempt will not damage the impression. If it is successful, it will lift only part of the impression, allowing for possible subsequent enhancement of the remaining portions, if necessary. Additional enhancement using both physical and chemical techniques should then be considered. Original impressions that are removed from the scene should *never* be covered with tape as this will prevent the subsequent enhancement of that impression.

## Photographic Methods of Enhancement

Since enhancement through forensic photographic techniques is a non-destructive method, it should always be attempted first. Photography not only affords the opportunity for nondestructive enhancement of the impression, but also provides an examination quality recording of the impression prior to any subsequent enhancement attempts. Although some forensic photographic techniques will be mentioned in this chapter, other techniques exist, as well as improvisations and combinations of those mentioned. Some require expensive equipment or more specialized knowledge than the average photographer may possess. The methods mentioned here are discussed only briefly; however, they are some of the more often successful techniques for enhancement of footwear impression evidence. Those who wish to enhance footwear impressions using forensic photography should consult other sources for more in-depth information concerning these and other techniques.

### High-Contrast Photography

Figure 5.1 shows two photographs of an impression on paper. One has been taken with regular photography while the other has been photographed to obtain a greater amount of contrast between the light and dark areas. This kind of photography is accomplished by using a high-contrast film, such as Kodak Tech Pan, along with an appropriate developing process.

### The Use of Filters

Filters placed over the lens of a camera can be used with both black-and-white and color films. With black-and-white films, the filters can be used to vary the contrast between objects of different colors, thereby accenting certain items. For instance, a residue footwear impression on a red tile floor can be better revealed if a red filter is used. This will lighten the red floor and make the footwear impression appear darker, providing greater contrast between the floor and the impression. With color film, filters can change the color balance of the film, allowing certain colors to be accentuated or diminished. Filters are also used for infrared and ultraviolet photography.

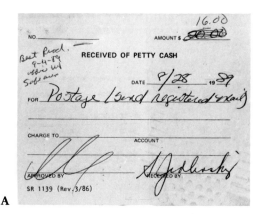

A

**5.1** A dry residue impression on paper photographed with regular film and processing (**A**), and then photographed with Kodak Tech Pan film and D-11 processing (**B**). The impression was then electrostatically lifted. The lift was photographed using oblique light and the photograph was reverse printed (**C**).

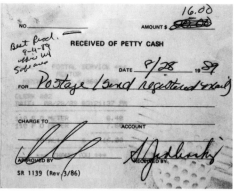

B

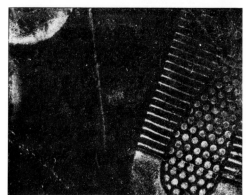

C

## Oblique Light

The use of oblique light for both two- and three-dimensional impressions has been discussed previously. It is frequently used in combination with high-contrast photography or filters to enhance footwear impressions on all surfaces. For example, if the aforementioned footwear impression on the red tile floor could also be enhanced with oblique light, the photographer could simultaneously photograph the impression with high-contrast photography, oblique light, and a red filter.

## Cross-Polarized Light

Some impressions will not show up well or at all when they are viewed from directly above, due to the amount of light being reflected from the background. The use of two polarizing filters will sometimes enable these impressions to be seen and photographed with the film plane parallel to the impression. One filter is held in front of the light source, while the other is held in front of the camera lens. One or both filters should be rotated until maximum visibility of the impression is obtained. The filters can vary the amount of light reflected from the background, possibly allowing the impression to reflect a different amount of light into the camera than does the background.

## Ultraviolet Light

Ultraviolet light (UV) ranges from 10 to 400 nm on the light spectrum, which is not in the visible portion of the spectrum. Although it is not visible to the naked eye, most films are sensitive to UV light. When a filter is used that absorbs all visible light but allows UV light to pass through it, evidence can be photographed using just the UV portion of the spectrum. An impression can be enhanced when it reflects UV light (reflected UV) or when either the impression or its background emits a fluorescence under UV light (UV fluorescence).

To photograph an impression with reflected long-wave UV light, a UV light source should be used to provide illumination of the impression. An 18A filter should be placed over the camera lens. It will filter out all of the visible light but not the light in the UV range. Either black-and-white or color film can be used. Figure 5.2 is an impression that has been photographed without and with reflected UV light. The impression was first treated with 8-hydroxyquinoline.

Reflective UV photography can also be used to successfully photograph and enhance contusion impressions, bitemarks, and other pattern injuries to the skin (Krauss T and Warden S, 1985). During the healing process, special cells called melanocytes collect the pigment melanin, which is released during injury to the skin. The melanocytes appear to migrate to the edges of the wound, providing the opportunity to photograph the injury pattern (Hempling SM, 1983). Since UV light is absorbed by melanin, reflective UV photography is able to detail and record injury patterns that otherwise might not be visible to the naked eye. In the case of contusions due to the blunt force injury of a shoe against the skin, UV photography can be used to provide increased detail and visibility. The UV photography would be most beneficial several days or even weeks after the contusion occurred, when the healing process had begun, rather than immediately after the injury. In cases where the victim was deceased, there would be no healing process and the UV photography would not work.

To photograph an impression that fluoresces under UV light (or one on a background that fluoresces), the impressioned area should be illuminated with UV light and the camera lens covered with an orange filter, which will filter out the excess UV light and blue light. A black-and-white or color film having an ISO of 400 should be used, because less light passes through the orange filter.

There are several other filters that can be used for UV photography, depending on whether the UV light is in the short- or long-wave portion of the UV light spectrum and whether the UV light is reflected or fluorescent.

## Infrared Light

In the area of the light spectrum above the visible light range is infrared (IR) light. Although IR light is not visible to the naked eye, certain films are sensitive to IR light in the 700- to 900-nm range. This film is also sensitive to the visible portion of the spectrum, so it is necessary to place an appropriate filter over the camera lens.

For photographing reflected IR light, an IR-sensitive film should be used with a tungsten light source. An 87 filter should be placed over the camera lens so that all portions of visible light will be blocked out. This technique can be used on most impression evidence, with the exception of blood impressions and surfaces having a reddish color.

For photographing IR luminescence, an IR-sensitive film should be used with an IR-free light source. This is achieved by placing the object in total darkness and then illuminating the impression with the IR-free light source. A filter such as a 29, 89B, 87, 87C, or a 113 filter should be placed over the camera lens.

## Physical Methods of Enhancement

Physical methods of enhancement include (1) methods of physically transferring the impression from one surface to another, such as electrostatic lifting, gelatin lifting, and adhesive lifting; (2) powdering an impression with fingerprint powders; and (3) detecting physical indentations with the Electrostatic Detection Apparatus.

## Electrostatic Lifting

The electrostatic lifting device, discussed in Chapter 4, is extremely useful in enhancing dry dust and residue impressions, simply through

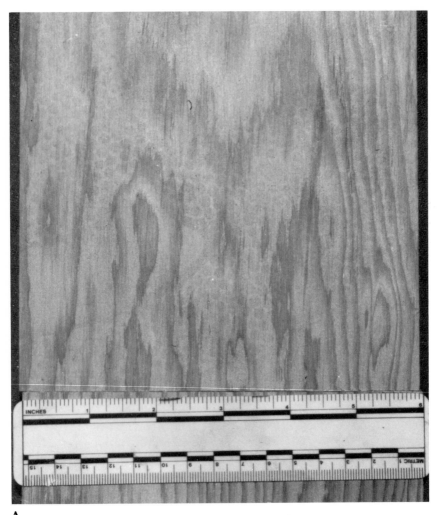

**A**
**5.2** An impression on a rough, porous wood surface (**A**) that was sprayed with 8-hydroxyquinoline and photographed with reflected ultraviolet light (**B**).

the transfer of those impressions to a surface of greater contrast. Electrostatic lifting will usually be the second method of enhancement used, after forensic photography. If the electrostatic lifting procedure is used and is not successful, the impression will not be destroyed and subsequent enhancement methods will not be affected. If the electrostatic lift is successful and a considerable amount of residue is lifted, the remaining impression may reveal sharper detail than it originally did when it contained excess residue. Rephotographing the impression

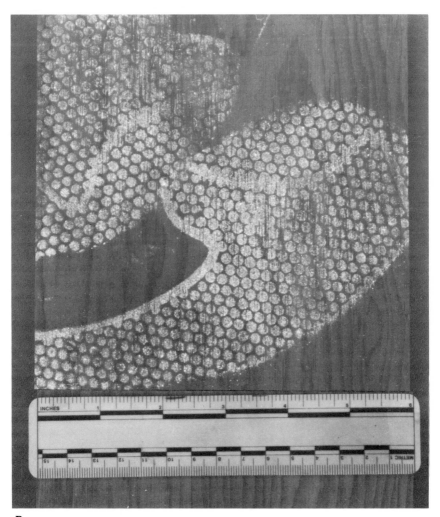

**B**

or taking a second electrostatic lift may actually reveal further detail. Figure 5.1C depicts an electrostatically lifted impression alongside the high-contrast photograph of that impression taken before being lifted.

If sufficient information can be retrieved from the impression at this point to permit an identification, it may not be necessary to perform additional enhancement procedures. Likewise, if by virtue of its composition, the impression is not a candidate for other enhancement methods, no further attempts should be made. If it is possible that more information is contained in the impression and other methods may be more successful, then additional enhancement methods can be tried. The portion of the impression that remains on the surface can still be chemically enhanced.

## Electrostatic Detection Apparatus

The Electrostatic Detection Apparatus (ESDA)[1] is an instrument used primarily for the development of indented writing on paper. It has proven to have some limited success in the development of indentations of footwear impressions on paper and thin card stock. When footwear impressions are present on such items, ESDA treatment should be attempted after photography and electrostatic lifting but prior to any other enhancement efforts. Figure 5.3 shows a piece of newspaper that contains a residue footwear impression of dry origin after ESDA treatment. The footwear impression was first successfully lifted with the electrostatic lifting device. It was then treated with the ESDA to develop indentations caused by the footwear. After treatment with the ESDA, the paper still contained the residue impression, and additional successful electrostatic lifts could be made. General procedures for the use of the ESDA are outlined with the literature accompanying the apparatus. Brennan first recommended specific procedures to be used in connection with the development of footwear impressions with the ESDA in 1981 (Brennan JS, personal communication, 1981).

## Powdering

Fingerprint powders can be used to enhance footwear impressions that have resulted from a damp or wet shoe tracking across waxed or polished surfaces, plastic or painted surfaces, and other clean, nonporous surfaces. This technique was discussed in Chapter 4 (see also Figure 1.6) in conjunction with lifting impressions. The fingerprint powders used should be very fine and are best applied with a fine brush or feather brush. The color of the powder should contrast with the color of the surface. Often, latent footwear impressions are discovered during the processing of surfaces for fingerprint impressions, in which case they are already powdered when discovered. Whenever the footwear impression is detected prior to powdering, an attempt should be made first to electrostatically lift the impression. If unsuccessful, then a very small portion of the impression should be powdered first, to determine if the

---

[1] Foster and Freeman, Ltd., Evesham, Worcester, England.

**5.3**   A piece of newspaper with a latent dry residue footwear impression. The impression was first electrostatically lifted successfully. Then the paper was treated on the ESDA to develop indentations of the footwear impression. The impression depicted here is visualized as a result of the toner being attracted to the indentations caused by the footwear impression.

technique will be successful. If it is, the remainder of the impression can be powdered. The powdered impression can be photographed and lifted with gelatin lifting materials.

Powdering should usually not be attempted on porous or textured surfaces that will attract and hold the powder, nor is it likely to be successful on dirty surfaces. If there is any doubt about whether the surface an impression is on will retain the powder and interfere with the development or enhancement of an impression, an area of the same surface away from the footwear impression can be powdered to determine the affinity the surface has for the powder.

## Gel and Adhesive Lifting

Although the use of gelatin lifting materials can effectively enhance the visibility of an impression by transferring it to a background of improved contrast, the contact of the gelatin against the impressioned surface can interfere with the use of subsequent chemical enhancement methods and powdering of the impression. For this reason, a careful evaluation of the impression should be made after photography and electrostatic lifting to determine whether chemical enhancement, powdering, or gelatin lifting should be attempted.

## Chemical Enhancement of Residue Impressions

Whether a footwear impression is of dry or wet origin, the mud, grease, oil, and other materials that are picked up by a shoe outsole are redeposited in the impression. Those materials can contain trace elements, minerals, compounds, and moisture. Often the materials that constitute the impression will not provide sufficient contrast against the surface the impression is on. During enhancement attempts, however, they could either absorb or react with certain chemicals and become more visible.

Several formulations exist for the chemical enhancement of residue impressions. Some enhancement methods using chemicals actually involve a physical attraction of the chemical to the impression, while others involve a chemical reaction with the impression. Most chemical enhancements work best on paper, fabric, untreated wood, and other hard-to-treat surfaces where physical enhancement techniques such as powdering, lifting, or photography may not work. Whenever using any chemical enhancement method involving the mixing of chemicals, the chemical reagent being used should be tested and determined to be working properly. In addition, once the reagent is known to be working, it may be desirable to test a small corner of the impression and/or the substrate it is on to see if that particular method will be likely to succeed.

Enhancements employing chemistry, like other enhancement methods, are used to increase the contrast and visibility between the impression and the surface the impression is on. Some of the chemicals and techniques are the same or similar to those used to develop latent fingerprints, to stain blood proteins, and to detect trace materials and metal ions. All of these procedures should be conducted under a ventilated hood in the laboratory or with other appropriate precautions to avoid inhalation of vapors.

### 8-Hydroxyquinoline

*Reaction.* 8-Hydroxyquinoline reacts with calcium, magnesium, iron, aluminum, and other metal ions that may be present in small amounts in the residue of footwear impressions. The reaction causes fluorescence, which is detectable under ultraviolet light. If the impression does not contain those ions, but the surface the impression is on fluoresces and the impression prevents fluorescing where it lies, a dark impression on a fluorescing background will be produced. Thus, if *either* the surface *or* the impression contain these ions, the procedure may enhance the impression. However, if *both* have a chemical composition that fluoresces, both will fluoresce and may interfere with any enhancement results. This procedure works well for the enhancement of footwear impressions made by either wet or dry residue, providing the residue contains metal ions.

One account (Fischer JE and Green E, 1980) reported success in a case involving a footwear impression on a piece of particle board, where the texture of the board interfered with photographic enhancement methods, but treatment with 8-hydroxyquinoline produced excellent results. Figure 5.2A depicts an oblique light photograph of a residue impression of wet origin on a piece of porous wood. Neither photography nor electrostatic lifting was successful in revealing much detail. Figure 5.2B shows the results after a light spraying of 8-hydroxyquinoline.

*Formulation.* Prepare a 0.5% solution of 8-hydroxyquinoline by dissolving 0.5 g of 8-hydroxyquinoline in 100 mL of a solution consisting of 90 mL of acetone and 10 mL of distilled water.

*Procedure.* First test the impression by lightly spraying a very localized area of it or by touching a small part of the impression with a cotton-tipped stick containing 8-hydroxyquinoline. If the area touched fluoresces under ultraviolet light, continue the procedure. Lightly mist the footwear impression with the 8-hydroxyquinoline solution. Then view the impression under both short-wave and long-wave ultraviolet light. The fluorescing impression can be photographed with color or black-and-white film using an ultraviolet light source, an appropriate filter, and a long exposure.

## Iodine and 7,8-Benzoflavone

*Reaction.* Iodine vapor is absorbed by many fatty, oily, and other organic materials. If those materials are present in a footwear impression, iodine vapor will be absorbed and will enhance its visibility. Where iodine is absorbed by these materials, the impression will appear yellow to brown. This method is best suited for all impressions of wet origin, as well as grease impressions and impressions of wet origin on plastics. In the case of some materials, especially fabrics, a strong background reaction may occur; therefore, it may be desirable to test a small portion of the background material prior to fuming. Dust or dry residue impressions and muddy impressions are *not* successfully enhanced using this method.

If iodine enhancement is successful, consideration should be given to following it with a 7,8-benzoflavone spray, which will produce a blue impression. Neither iodine nor 7,8-benzoflavone enhancements are permanent and both will weaken with time; therefore, photography should closely follow the treatment.

*Formulation.* The materials needed are iodine in a fuming chamber, 7,8-benzoflavone, chloroform, and petroleum ether. To prepare the 7,8-benzoflavone, dissolve 0.2 g of 7,8-benzoflavone in 2 to 3 mL of chloroform. Add 60 to 80 mL of petroleum ether to make 100 mL.

*Procedure.* Fume the impressioned item with iodine by placing it in an iodine chamber. If an iodine chamber must be made, an enclosed glass tank can be used, provided it can be equipped with a tight-fitting lid. The impressioned item should be suspended in the chamber. A saucer or small tray of boiled water that is still steaming can be placed in the chamber, and a smaller saucer or tray containing iodine crystals can be floated in the steaming water. This will provide the high humidity and heat needed to cause the iodine crystals to fume. If there is going to be a reaction, it should occur in a couple of minutes. An iodine fuming pipe can also be used; however, the relatively small quantities of iodine delivered do not produce as good results. The fuming pipe is good for crime scene applications and for screening materials to see if there will be an absorption of iodine by the impression.

Follow the iodine procedure by immediately photographing any iodine-enhanced impressions. If the iodine has developed or enhanced the impressions, then consider spraying the impression with 7,8-benzoflavone or dipping it in the 7,8-benzoflavone solution for 10 seconds. Rephotograph the enhanced impressions.

*Comments.* Iodine has long been used to develop fingerprints by reacting with the grease or fat content of the prints. Footwear impressions can also contain materials that react with iodine or iodine and 7,8-benzoflavone applications. Small amounts of wax or oily substances are often accumulated on shoe soles after walking over surfaces containing those substances. Iodine is also very successful in enhancing footwear impressions of wet origin on most surfaces.

For grease impressions that may not be retrievable from the crime scene, an iodine fuming pipe will produce some enhancement. If a positive reaction with the impression occurs, physically removing the impression (i.e., cutting a section of floor out, etc.) from the scene should be considered, so that further chemical enhancement in the laboratory can be carried out.

Figure 5.4A depicts a heel impression of wet origin on a piece of paper

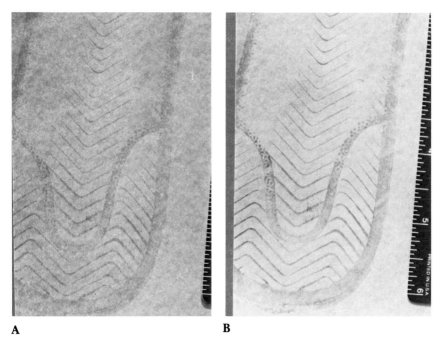

**A** **B**

**5.4** A piece of paper with a nearly latent heel impression of wet origin was first successfully enhanced with iodine (**A**), giving the impression a brownish color. It was then treated with 7,8-benzoflavone (**B**), which further enhanced it and resulted in a bluish impression.

that was treated with iodine. The impression was hardly visible before treatment. The paper was then treated with 7,8-benzoflavone (Figure 5.4B).

## Potassium and Ammonium Thiocyanates

*Reaction.* Iron will react with thiocyanate ions in an acid solution. If iron is present in the residue of footwear impressions, a positive reaction will result in a reddish-brown color. Iron is found in many residues in various concentrations, particularly in soil or mud. The procedure works well for wet residue impressions and muddy impressions on all surfaces.

*Formulation for potassium thiocyanate.* To 120 mL of acetone and 15 mL of water add 15 g of potassium thiocyanate. Then add 8.5 mL of dilute sulfuric acid. Make sure that you *add* the sulfuric acid to the acetone/water mixture. *Do not* add the acetone/water mixture to the acid or it may explode! A milky mixture will result, which, on standing, will separate into two layers. When the layers have separated, remove the top layer, which is clear. This is the solution to be sprayed on the impressions. The reagent can be stored for months.

*Formulation for ammonium thiocyanate.* There is an alternate formulation (Davis R, 1988) that uses ammonium thiocyanate: Dissolve 2 g of ammonium thiocyanate in 90 mL of acetone. *Add* 10 mL of nitric acid (2N) to the ammonium thiocyanate. No precipitation will result; thus no separation is required, as with the potassium thiocyanate method. The entire mixture can be sprayed onto the impression.

*Procedure.* The potassium thiocyanate or ammonium thiocyanate reagent is sprayed over the impression. The amount of spraying should be controlled to get the maximum reaction without causing the impression to run or bleed. The impression should then be photographed. A 58 or 61 green filter combined with high-contrast black-and-white film may help to further enhance the impression.

*Comments.* It has been reported (Davis RJ, 1988) that for faint impressions on paper or cloth a ferrous sulfate ($FeSO_4$) prewash should be considered. The prewash consists of a 0.2% solution of $FeSO_4$ in water. The impressioned item can be immersed in the prewash for 1 minute, followed by two immersions in distilled water. The item can then be placed on blotter paper and allowed to dry. Figure 5.5A shows a muddy impression on cardboard. Figure 5.5B depicts that impression after treatment with potassium thiocyanate.

## Physical Developer

*Reaction.* Physical developer, originated by the Atomic Weapons Research Establishment in England (Hardwick SA, 1981), contains silver ions that are preferentially deposited on fingerprints and footwear impressions containing certain components. Those components, although not specifically identified, are believed to be waxy, oily, or fatty materials, since they are not removed from the item in an aqueous solution. When a rubber or synthetic composition heel or sole of a shoe makes an impression on paper, plasticizers and other compounds, which are part of the chemical composition of the shoe, and oil and grease that has accumulated on the shoe, can transfer to the surface and leave an impression that may develop with physical developer.

Some advantages of physical developer are that it works well after the impressioned item has been wet or has been subjected to high humidity. Impressions may be developed on items that have been outside during heavy rains. It also works well on aged impressions. Another

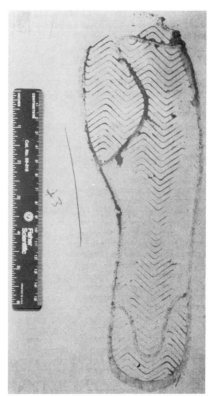

**A**                                        **B**
**5.5**  An impression made by wet, muddy footwear on cardboard (**A**) and the same impression after treatment with potassium thiocyanate (**B**). The residue or soil in the impression contained trace quantities of iron, which turned a reddish color when treated.

advantage is that physical developer is not affected by prior treatment with iodine, ninhydrin, or potassium thiocyanate, allowing it to be used after those methods.

Some disadvantages of physical developer are that it involves the meticulous mixing of several chemicals, it must be mixed fresh, and it requires a large quantity of distilled or deionized water. In addition, the glassware used for mixing and holding the physical developer must be exceptionally clean and should be dedicated for use in this process only. Any slight contamination of the glassware or the chemicals could ruin the reagent or interfere with the reaction.

*Formulation.*  Four solutions are needed in the developing process. To prepare the maleic acid prewash, make a 2.5% solution (25 g/L) of maleic acid in distilled water.

The physical developer comprises the remaining three solutions: a stock detergent solution, a silver nitrate solution, and a redox solution. To make 100 mL of the *stock detergent solution,* mix 0.27 g of *N*-dodecylamine acetate (ICN Biomedical, Plainview, NJ) with 100 mL of distilled water. Stir thoroughly in solution. Add 0.4 g of liquid Synperonic-N (Lightning Powder Company, Salem, OR) and stir thoroughly.

To prepare the *silver nitrate solution,* mix 10 g of silver nitrate in a clean beaker containing 50 mL of distilled water. Stir for 1 minute with a clean magnetic stirrer. If any solid material remains, continue stirring until it dissolves.

The *redox solution* is made by dissolving 15 g of ferric nitrate, 40 g of ammonium ferrous sulfate, and 10 g of citric acid, one at a time in the order given, in a clean beaker containing 480 mL of distilled water. After all have been dissolved, mix for another 5 minutes.

*Procedure.* Prior to processing the documents or items for impression evidence, they should first be photographed. In particular, impressions that have been developed with ninhydrin, iodine, or other chemicals should be photographed, since those impressions will most likely be washed away and lost in the physical developer processing.

Add 20 mL of stock detergent solution to the beaker containing the 480 mL of redox solution, and stir for 2 minutes. Add 25 mL of silver nitrate solution to the above mixture, and stir for 2 minutes. Let stand 5 minutes before use.

It is necessary to make up the physical developer solution fresh on the day it is to be used. It is possible to keep the solution for a few days; however, its sensitivity may suffer. Used solution should be thrown away and never reused. If the new solution should turn dark, it is contaminated and should be discarded.

Arrange a series of glass trays as pictured in Figure 5.6. These glass trays must be exceptionally clean. After washing, they should be rinsed well with tap water followed by three rinses with distilled water.

In tray 1, place the maleic acid prewash solution. In the tray or trays marked 2, place the physical developer solution. Only one item at a time should be placed in the physical developer solution, since the development of the impressions must be monitored and the item removed when optimal development is reached. More than one tray of developer solution can be used if there are many items to be processed. Tray 3 should be used for circulating distilled water. If circulating distilled water is not available in your laboratory, substitute three trays (3–5) for the circulating distilled water tray. Trays 3 and 4 contain distilled water and tray 5 can have running tap water. Deionized water can be substituted for distilled water.

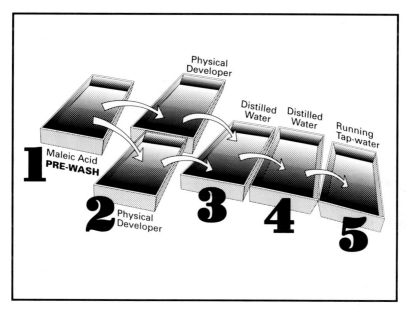

**5.6** A possible tray arrangement for the solutions used in the physical developer enhancement procedure.

Touching an item that is going to be processed with metal forceps, a finger, or rubber gloves will result in a deposition of silver in those areas when that item is processed. Therefore, items that are to be treated should be handled with cotton gloves or plastic forceps that do not have a serrated edge.

Place the item to be processed in the maleic acid prewash solution in tray 1 for 5 minutes. More than one item can be placed in the prewash at one time. Then transfer one item at a time to the physical developer solution in tray 2. Gently agitate or rock the tray occasionally. Impressions will develop slowly, appearing as dark gray images. After a while, the background will also begin to turn gray. It is important to closely monitor the development of each item so that it can be removed from the physical developer solution when it reaches the maximum contrast with the background.

All of the solutions will have to be changed occasionally, particularly if they become cloudy. If running distilled water is not available, the distilled water trays will also have to be changed frequently.

*Comments.* As more departments are beginning to use this method, its value for the development of both footwear impressions and fingerprints, particularly in a sequential treatment with other chemical enhancement methods, is being recognized. It has also been suggested

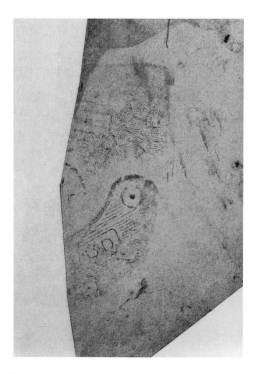

**5.7** Latent footwear impressions made by clean shoes on paper that were developed with physical developer.

that the contrast of a footwear impression developed with physical developer can be enhanced further if the item is thoroughly dried and then fumed with iodine (Beecroft W, 1989).

Figure 5.7 shows a heel impression on a piece of paper that was still wet when recovered. It was treated on one half with physical developer and not treated at all on the other half.

## Small Particle Reagent

*Reaction.* Small particle reagent (SPR) is a suspension of very fine molybdenum disulfide particles held in a detergent solution. The reagent adheres to fatty materials found in latent fingerprints and can also enhance some footwear impressions such as wet marks on *smooth,* nonporous surfaces, glass, painted surfaces, and plastic, as well as wet marks on paper. Surfaces having a textured or rough surface should not be treated with SPR. SPR can be purchased in reagent form and is applied by submersion or spray.

*Procedure.* Shake the container of SPR and place some of the SPR in a spray container. If the item being sprayed is movable, place it so that the impressioned surface will be on its edge. Spray the surface from the top

**5.8** A piece of blue plastic that contained a wet footwear impression and was treated with small particle reagent. The impression has a brownish color.

and work downward. If an impression appears, respray to further develop it. If the sprayed surface contains excess powder, use a different spray unit to spray water above the impression, allowing it to flow down and over that area. Allow the surface to dry. Photograph or lift the impression.

Figure 5.8 depicts a wet heel impression on a smooth plastic surface that has been developed with SPR.

## Antimony Trichloride

Antimony trichloride has been suggested (Davis RJ, 1988) as a possible means of enhancing footwear impressions on raw metal surfaces that have a wet origin.

*Procedure.* A few grams of antimony trichloride is placed in a small dish in a fuming cabinet. The metal containing the impression is placed in the fuming cabinet along with the antimony trichloride. A negative impression will develop as the corrosive action of the antimony trichloride on the metal etches into the nonimpressioned areas. Development can take from several hours to a day and should be monitored.

## Chemical Enhancement of Footwear Impressions in Blood

Because of the unpredictability of powdering or lifting techniques on footwear impressions in blood, it is strongly recommended that every attempt be made to retrieve the original items bearing the bloody impression so that they can be treated in the laboratory. This effort may include cutting out sections of carpeting, tile floors, or other items that frequently contain bloody impressions but are not mobile. Routinely received in the laboratory for examination are small items containing blood impressions ranging from paper and sections of carpet to larger items such as sections of stairs, doors, sections of asphalt road, bricks, and other bulky items. In most if not all of those cases, the examination was far more productive than it would have been with only photographs taken at the scene.

Chemical enhancement can be performed on bloody footwear impressions on both porous and nonporous surfaces and can both enhance and develop the impressions. The impression should be photographed first, followed by enhancement, followed by photography of the enhanced impression.

There are a number of methods and materials that can be used to develop and/or enhance bloody footwear impressions. Some of these involve serologic stains that react with the protein present in the blood, and others involve catalytic test reagents. The selection of a particular method depends on the nature of the blood impression, the background color(s) of the surface the impression is on, and the stability of the blood impression on that surface.

Most of the stains or chemicals used for enhancement are extremely sensitive to small traces of blood. Therefore, in areas where the blood impressions are very thin and faint or where the subject has tracked through blood and left a series of blood impressions, enhancement methods can develop a latent or nearly invisible blood impression into a highly valuable impression. In fact, the faint impressions, once enhanced, are normally more valuable and detailed than those containing larger quantities of blood.

In cases where a bloody impression on cloth or paper might run when it is sprayed, it has been suggested (Hamm ED, 1982) that the item first be saturated with ethanol and then permitted to dry before being treated. This procedure binds the protein matter to the paper or cloth so it will not run.

More recent research (Hussain JI and Pounds CA, 1988) has suggested that treatment with 5-sulfosalicylic acid is a more effective, more convenient, and safer way to fix bloody impressions. To fix the impression with 5-sulfosalicylic acid, the impressioned item should be immersed in a 2% weight/volume aqueous solution of 5-sulfosalicylic acid for 10 minutes, then immersed in distilled water for 5 minutes, and then allowed to dry.

It has been my experience that blood impressions usually bond well to almost any surface and therefore the pretreatment to fix those impressions has not been necessary.

## Ninhydrin

*Reaction.* Ninhydrin reacts with the amino acids found in fingerprints. A positive reaction produces a dark color called Ruhemann's purple. Ninhydrin can also be used to enhance footwear impressions in blood. Ninhydrin is commercially available in aerosol spray units.

*Procedure.* The impressioned item is sprayed with ninhydrin. Allow the ninhydrin to evaporate and spray a second time if necessary. Heat and steam can then be applied with a steam iron to speed the development of the reaction. Because ninhydrin spray is flammable, the heat should not be applied until the ninhydrin has thoroughly dried.

## Amido Black

*Reaction.* Amido black (amido 10B or naphthalene black) produces a dark blue-black stain in areas where blood is present. It is sensitive enough to provide development of blood impressions that could not previously be seen due to the extremely small amounts of blood present. Figure 5.9A depicts a piece of tile with a faint blood impression. Figure 5.9B shows the same impression after being stained with amido black.

*Formulation.* To make the staining solution, dissolve 0.2 g of amido black in a solution consisting of 10 mL of glacial acetic acid and 90 mL of methanol. The rinsing solution is a mixture of 90 mL of methanol and 10 mL of glacial acetic acid.

*Procedure.* First, consider stabilization of the impression with 5-sulfosalicylic acid. Then, treat the impression by saturating it with staining solution. This can be done by immersing the item in a tray filled with the solution or by passing the solution over the impressioned

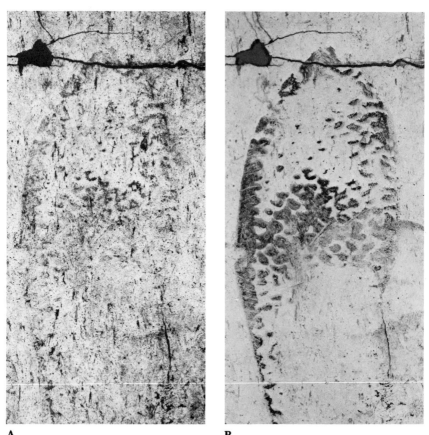

**A**                                    **B**
5.9   A piece of tile that contained a very faint footwear impression in blood
(A) and was treated with an amido black stain (B).

item. The development time depends on the surface and the impression. Staining usually occurs within 3 minutes. Rinse the impression with the rinsing solution. This helps to remove the stain from the nonimpressioned background areas. Repeat the rinsing with distilled water. Allow the impression to air dry.

An alternate amido black staining procedure using a 0.2% weight/volume solution in a 0.1 mol/L citric acid solution followed by destaining with water has been recommended as a less hazardous technique (Hussain JI and Pounds CA, personal communication, 1988). The use of the water-based amido black solution with water as a destaining solution permits the use of this procedure at a crime scene.

### Crowle's Staining Solution

*Reaction.*  Crowle's staining solution (Norkus P and Noppinger K, 1986) produces a red stain in areas where blood is present.

*Formulation.* To make Crowle's staining solution, dissolve 2.5 g of Crocein scarlet 7B and 150 mg of Coomassie brilliant blue R250 into 50 mL of glacial acetic acid and 30 mL of trichloroacetic acid. Dilute to 1 L with deionized water. The destaining solution is made by mixing 3 mL of glacial acetic acid in 1 L of deionized water.

*Procedure.* Consider stabilization of the impression with sulfosalicylic acid. Treat the impression by saturating it with staining solution. This can be done by immersing the item in a tray filled with the solution or by passing the solution over the impressioned item. The development time depends on the surface and the impression. Maximum staining usually occurs within 3 minutes. Rinse the impression with the destaining solution. This helps to remove the stain from the background areas. Repeat the rinsing with distilled water. Allow the impression to air dry.

## Luminol

*Reaction.* The luminol reaction occurs because the hemoglobin derivatives in blood contribute to the chemiluminescence of luminol when oxidized in alkaline solution (Gaensslen R, 1983). In other words, when certain luminol mixtures are sprayed onto bloodstains, luminescence will result that can be observed and photographed. Luminol is of sufficient sensitivity to luminesce in the presence of blood concentrations that are far more dilute than could be visually detected. Furthermore, luminol luminesces as well or even better after aging than it does when fresh. As a result, luminol is increasingly being used at crime scenes to allow for better and more thorough detection of blood splatter and footwear impressions. The blood can be detected months and even years later and can be reserved for treatment long after the routine crime scene processing. It is noted that luminol will cause some metals, some strong oxidizing agents such as bleaches, and even some vegetable matter to luminesce slightly. If any serologic tests are to be performed, they should take place prior to treatment with luminol.

Because of the need to apply sufficient amounts of luminol, which may cause the impression to run; because of its short-lived reaction; and because it must be photographed in total darkness, luminol should only be used to enhance footwear impressions when staining or other methods will not work. The main advantage of luminol is that it is photographed in total darkness, so background color and interferences become insignificant. Thus, in situations where faint blood impressions on red or multicolor carpeting or dark-colored objects do not allow sufficient contrast between the surface and the blood to distinguish the detail in the impression and where enhancement or staining with other materials would not be successful, luminol can be used.

*Formulation.* Luminol is sold by chemical supply houses by the names 5-amino-2,3-dihydro-1,4-phthalaziadione *and* 3-aminophthal hydrazide. Mix in a glass beaker until dissolved 0.1 g of luminol with 5 g of sodium carbonate in 100 mL of water. Just prior to using the mixture, add 0.7 g of sodium perborate and mix thoroughly.

*Procedure.* In order to ensure that the luminol formulation is working properly, first spray it on a test blood impression. In addition, since the reaction is short-lived and can only be seen in total darkness, a special method of photography should be employed to record the reaction. Most impressions that require this procedure are those with limited quantities of blood, and they will only react once with the luminol before being consumed or adversely affected. Therefore, if impressions located at the crime scene are saturated with luminol, it will not be likely that they will react a second time for photographic recording. Any impression that can be located visually before treatment should be removed and preserved first. When using luminol to examine general crime scene areas, spraying to locate footwear impressions should be as light as possible and should be discontinued when the impressions are detected. The area or areas containing footwear impressions should be marked. Any further treatment should be accompanied by photography. Night vision goggles are of great assistance at general crime scene treatments with luminol because they allow optimal detection and viewing of the luminol reaction with minimal spraying. Footwear impressions in blood that can be detected at crime scenes before treatment with luminol should be removed and photographed in the laboratory during the luminol treatment.

*Photographic procedure.* It is recommended that this procedure be tried first to gain experience before working on actual evidence. In addition, a fresh luminol mixture should always be tested on a sample blood impression, to ensure that it is working. To photograph in total darkness a footwear impression being enhanced with luminol, the following procedure should be used:

Identify the specific area where the impression is located. Be aware of the fact that the impression may occupy a larger area than the visible portion. In other words, if only the heel area is visible, consider the possibility that there may be an entire impression of the shoe that will luminesce when treated.

Place a scale next to the impression. Do not place the scale over an area that may contain a latent impression. If the impression is to be photographed in total darkness, prepare a scale by taping two pennies on a piece of cardboard with their edges exactly 6 inches apart. The copper in the pennies will luminesce when treated with luminol. A scale that fluoresces in the dark may also be used.

Select the camera and film. A larger format camera such as a 4 × 5-inch camera with a f/5.6 lens is preferable; however, a 35-mm camera with a macro lens will also work. The camera must have the capability to keep the lens in the open position for long exposures. The camera should be equipped with a shutter cable release that can be locked to hold the shutter open. Load the camera with black-and-white film having an ASA of 400 or greater. If the impression is very faint or has been previously treated, ASA 3200 film can be used.

Position the camera on a stable tripod over the impressioned area. Adjust the height of the camera so that the impressioned area and the scale fill the frame. The camera should be placed as close as possible to the impression, since the amount of light being emitted is very small. Remember, for each time the camera distance from the impression is doubled, four times the amount of light will be required to give the same exposure.

Seal off all ambient light in the room so that the photograph can be made in total darkness. Open the shutter of the camera. Spray the impressioned area lightly but enough to get a strong luminescence. Repeat spraying as necessary if the impression's luminescence begins to weaken before the exposure is over. Avoid overspraying the impression if it is luminescing well. Experience will dictate the proper amount of spraying. Close the shutter before turning the lights on.

*Photographing with attenuated light.* Impressions treated with luminol can also be photographed with attenuated light. This involves photographing the luminol-treated impression in total darkness as described above with the exception that a small amount of light is included to permit minimal recording of the impressioned item in addition to the luminescing impression.

To photograph a luminol-treated impression in this manner, have an assistant discharge an electronic flash in the corner of the room sometime during the timed exposure. The flash should be aimed away from the impression at a corner of the room or the ceiling. This will provide sufficient attenuated light to allow a minimal exposure of the impressioned object and the scale without interfering with the luminescence.

Figure 5.10A depicts a regular photograph of a blood stain on a piece of brown carpet. Figure 5.10B is a photograph of the same impression treated with luminol and photographed in total darkness. Two pennies were taped with their edges 6 inches apart for use as a scale, since copper also luminesces when sprayed with luminol. Figure 5.10C is a photograph of the same impression taken in total darkness but with the addition of attenuated light.

**A**

**B**

**C**

**5.10** An impression prior to enhancement with luminol (**A**). A photograph of a luminol-treated impression without attenuated light (**B**) requires the use of a scale that either glows in the dark or a makeshift scale that reacts to the luminol spray, like the copper pennies. The same impression after enhancement with luminol (**C**) taken with attenuated light, which also reveals the ruler and carpet.

## Tetramethylbenzidine

*Reaction.* Tetramethylbenzidine (TMB) will react with blood, generating a bluish green color where blood is present (Lee H, 1984; Olsen RD, 1986). It is very sensitive and will reveal faint and otherwise invisible traces of blood. It works particularly well on light-colored surfaces, where the bluish green color will offer sufficient contrast.

*Formulation.* First, an *acetate buffer* must be made. Dissolve 5 g of sodium acetate in 43 mL of glacial acetic acid. Add 50 mL of distilled water. Store at room temperature.

Next, 0.4 g of TMB (3,3',5,5'-tetramethylbenzidine) is dissolved in 20 mL of the acetate buffer. Mix thoroughly for 5 minutes, and filter to remove any undissolved particles. The TMB-acetate buffer *solution* should be stored in brown bottles in a refrigerator and can be kept up to 6 months.

Then, a *collodion-ethanol-ether solution* is made: Mix 30 mL of collodion with 15 mL of ethanol. Let the mixture stand for 5 minutes. Add 120 mL of ethyl ether to the collodion-ethanol solution while stirring.

Finally, the *TMB spray reagent* is prepared: Add 0.5 g of sodium perborate to 6 mL of *TMB-acetate buffer solution* and stir well. Add this to 120 mL of the *collodion-ethanol-ether solution* and stir well.

*Procedure.* TMB spray reagent should always be freshly made. Spray or mist the reagent carefully on the surface. The bloody impression should turn green or blue. Rephotograph the enhanced impression immediately after the reaction, since the color will begin to fade shortly after treatment. Parts A and B of Figure 5.11 show a faint blood impression on concrete before and after TMB treatment. Figure 5.11C depicts a faint blood impression half of which was treated with TMB, illustrating the potential enhancing a faint blood impression with this chemical has.

## Sequencing of Enhancement Techniques

Figure 5.12 is intended to provide guidance in the choice or sequence of enhancement methods for two-dimensional footwear impressions. When selecting enhancement techniques, consideration should always be given to factors such as the composition of the impression, the surface texture, whether the impression is of wet or dry origin, and other factors that have been previously discussed. The sequence chart begins by emphasizing the need to first take examination quality photographs at the scene and to then remove the impressioned item, if at all possible, so that it can be enhanced and/or examined in the laboratory. Although the laboratory is the best place to attempt enhancement, it is

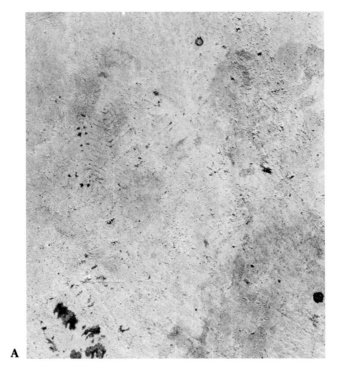

A

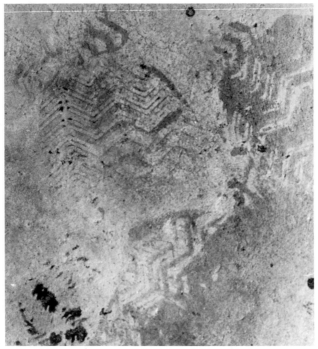

B

C

**5.11** A photograph of a faint blood impression on a concrete floor (**A**). The same impression after enhancement with TMB (**B**). An impression that was half-covered and sprayed with TMB demonstrates the ability of TMB to develop and enhance faint blood impressions (**C**).

realized that some impressions cannot be removed, and therefore some enhancement methods may have to be attempted at the scene. The first enhancement method to be considered should be forensic photography. The second method, if the impression warrants it, should be electro-static lifting. If the impression is a suitable candidate for the detection

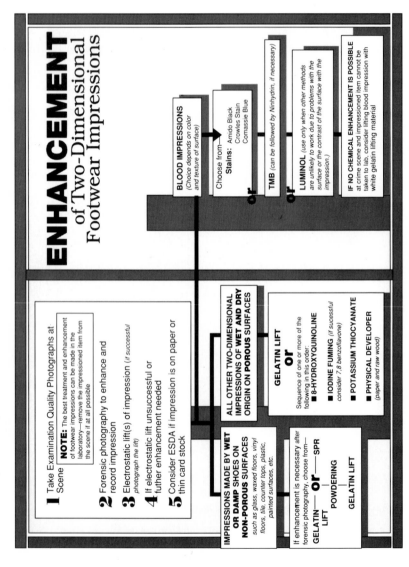

# ENHANCEMENT
## of Two-Dimensional Footwear Impressions

**1** Take Examination Quality Photographs at Scene **NOTE:** The best treatment and enhancement of footwear impressions can be made in the laboratory—remove the impressioned item from the scene if at all possible

**2** Forensic photography to enhance and record impression

**3** Electrostatic lift(s) of impression *(if successful photograph the lift)*

**4** If electrostatic lift unsuccessful or futher enhancement needed

**5** Consider ESDA if impression is on paper or thin card stock

**IMPRESSIONS MADE BY WET OR DAMP SHOES ON NON-POROUS SURFACES** *such as glass, waxed floors, vinyl floors, tile, counter tops, plastic, painted surfaces, etc.*

If enhancement is necessary after forensic photography, choose from—

GELATIN LIFT —**or**— SPR

POWDERING

GELATIN LIFT

**ALL OTHER TWO-DIMENSIONAL IMPRESSIONS OF WET AND DRY ORIGIN ON POROUS SURFACES**

GELATIN LIFT
**or**

Sequence of one or more of the following in this order:

■ **8-HYDROXYQUINOLINE**

■ **IODINE FUMING** *(if sucessful consider 7,8 benzoflavone)*

■ **POTASSIUM THIOCYANATE**

■ **PHYSICAL DEVELOPER** *(paper and raw wood)*

**BLOOD IMPRESSIONS** *(Choice depends on color and texture of surface)*

Choose from—
**Stains:** Amido Black
Crowles Stain
Comassie Blue

**TMB** *(can be followed by Ninhydrin, if necessary)*

**LUMINOL** *(use only when other methods are unlikely to work due to problems with the surface or the contrast of the surface with the impression.)*

**IF NO CHEMICAL ENHANCEMENT IS POSSIBLE** at crime scene and impressioned item cannot be taken to lab, consider lifting blood impression with white gelatin lifting material

**5.12** A chart listing some general guidelines for the enhancement of two-dimensional footwear impressions.

of indentations on the ESDA, that also should be considered at this time.

After these preliminary considerations, the impressions can be divided into those that are blood impressions and those that are not. If the impression is in blood, several choices exist. The selection should take into consideration the contrast of the impression against its background and the type of surface the impression is on. For instance, a faint blood impression on a light-colored tile floor could be enhanced with almost any stain. On the other hand, a blood impression on a very dark floor might not be a candidate for a dark stain, but might be enhanced with luminol.

Impressions that are not blood impressions can be divided into two general categories: those of wet origin on nonporous surfaces and all other impressions. Impressions that might have been made by damp or wet shoes on nonporous surfaces could potentially be enhanced with powdering or SPR, after which they could be photographed and/or lifted. If the surface was dirty before the impression was made and powdering or SPR are not likely to work, a gelatin lift of the impression might be the best choice. Other two-dimensional impressions, particularly those on paper, cardboard, and similar porous items, can possibly be chemically enhanced using one of or the sequence of 8-hydroxyquinoline, iodine, potassium thiocyanate, and finally physical developer. If the impression is on a porous surface that is not a candidate for the chemical sequence, a gelatin lift of the impression should be considered.

The enhancement of two-dimensional impressions, because of the almost unlimited variety in their composition and because of the wide variety of surfaces and conditions in which they are found, cannot be summarized as simply as the diagram in Figure 5.12. However, the diagram, along with the experience gained by trying all of the enhancement methods in this chapter, will hopefully provide a general understanding of the approach that must be taken when enhancing an impression and the potential success of each method on any particular impression.

## Enhancement of Three-Dimensional Impressions

Photographing three-dimensional impressions with oblique light, making casts of those impressions, and spraying snow impressions to highlight the characteristics are all methods that can enhance the amount of detail seen under normal conditions. These methods were previously discussed in Chapters 2 and 3. For three-dimensional impressions, the enhancement techniques are incorporated in the procedures for retrieving the impression.

## Computer Enhancement

Computers can assist the footwear impression examiner in a couple of ways. Through manipulation of the gray tones in a black-and-white photographic image of a footwear impression, whether it be a negative or a print, computer enhancement may provide greater contrast. It does this by recalculating the gray level of each picture point on the computer screen.

The computer can also assist the footwear impression examiner by correcting the perspective in photographs in which the film plane was not parallel to the footwear impression. Occasionally, through erroneous photographic methods, but also sometimes intentionally in cases where the impression can only be seen from an angle, a footwear impression will be photographed at an angle. When this happens, the perspective problem in the photograph can severely limit any subsequent examination.

In order for the computer to be able to correct the perspective, a square or rectangular ruler completely surrounding the impression will

---

**5.13**  A footwear impression that was photographed at an angle on a square tile floor **(A)**. A computer program was used to correct the perspective problem **(B)** and then to provide a greater amount of contrast **(C)**.

**A**

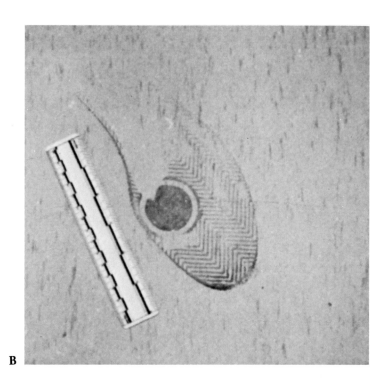

B

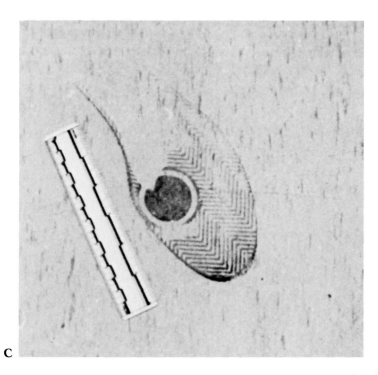

C

be needed in the photograph. In some cases, it is possible to use existing right angles in the photograph, such as the right angles of the four corners of a piece of tile along with the known dimensions of the tile. The computer program can stretch or shrink the image of the impression to correct the perspective and provide a normal image.

Correction of out-of-perspective photographs has traditionally been done on rectifying photographic enlargers. In most cases, this is still the best method. Occasionally, where *extreme* perspective problems exist, such as in pictures taken at a very low angle, the photographic enlarger would have to be tilted to the point where it would be difficult or impossible to get the entire photographic print in focus.

Figure 5.13A is an improperly taken photograph of a light footwear impression on a tile floor. Figure 5.13B shows a computer perspective-corrected photograph made from the photograph in Figure 5.13A. Figure 5.13C shows the same impression after the computer has enhanced the contrast in the impression.

Computer enhancement procedures work differently from case to case and do not always provide the desired results. The use of computers and special rectifying photographic enlargers to correct mistakes is usually a last resort technique. The proper procedures for taking examination quality photographs, as set forth in this book, should always be followed.

# Footwear Sizing

# 6

## Shoe Sizing Systems

*Origin of Shoe Sizing*

Footwear, or foot coverings, in the crudest sense, have probably existed as long as humans have walked. Early humans, from the time of the cave dwellers, to the later, more developed civilizations, used a variety of materials to help tolerate rough terrain, hot desert sands, and colder climates. These materials included papyrus, braided grass, cloth, wood, and animal skins.

Until the later part of the nineteenth century, most footwear was not mass produced, but was custom made to fit a particular foot. The materials were either wrapped and bound around the foot or the foot was placed on the materials, which were then cut to fit. Naturally, there was no need for shoe sizing systems as long as shoes were made in this fashion.

The first recorded shoe sizing system was introduced in 1688 in England by Randle Holme and was based on a $\frac{1}{4}$-inch system.[1] It was not until 1856 that the next recorded description of a shoe sizing system was published by Robert Gardiner, also in England.[1] This system used a scale in which each larger size was $\frac{1}{3}$ inch longer.

In 1839, the vulcanization process of curing rubber was developed by Charles Goodyear, and in 1846, Elias Howe invented the sewing machine (Cheskin MP, 1987). The specific adaptation of these two discoveries as well as others in the nineteenth century, contributed significantly to the mass production of footwear. With mass production came the need for a more detailed and broadly used shoe sizing system.

---

[1] The True Story of Shoe Sizes, Sterling Last Corporation, NY (undated).

**6.1**  Comparative chart of shoe sizing systems.

The first detailed shoe sizing system was introduced in 1880 by an American named Edwin B. Simpson.[1] Simpson's system was adopted by the American and British footwear industries around 1888.[1] Simpson also introduced a system of shoe widths.

## Current Shoe Sizing Systems

There are several shoe sizing systems in use in the world today. The chart in Figure 6.1 shows the American system (for both men and women), the English system, the Continental or French system, and the centimeter system.[2]

The English system measures sizes in increments of $\frac{1}{3}$ inch in length, with half-sizes of $\frac{1}{6}$ inch. Sizes begin at 4 inches with size 0. After size 13, which measures $8\frac{1}{3}$ inches, the sizing begins again at the next $\frac{1}{3}$-inch increment with size 1.

The American system also uses size increments of $\frac{1}{3}$ inch and half-sizes of $\frac{1}{6}$ inch. The difference from the English system is that the American system begins at $3\frac{11}{12}$ inches instead of 4 inches (Figure 6.1). The sizing repeats after size 13 and begins again with size 1. In addition, the American sizing system is different for women's shoes than for men's. Both are divided into $\frac{1}{3}$- and $\frac{1}{6}$-inch increments, but the women's system begins at a point between youth size $12\frac{1}{2}$ and size 13 instead of $\frac{1}{3}$ inch above size 13. Thus, a woman's size, for the same foot length, will always be slightly more than one size number greater than a man's size.

Today, some American-made shoes are made in as many as 15 different widths (AAAAAA to EEEEEE). In other parts of the world, most shoes are made in only one or two widths. In the more common widths,

---

[2] Professional Shoe Fitting, National Shoe Retailers Association, 1984.

| MADE IN THAILAND | | | |
|---|---|---|---|
| USA | EURO | UK | CM |
| 7 | 40 | 6 | 25$\underline{0}$ |

**6.2** It is becoming more common to see shoe sizes from more than one shoe sizing system printed on shoe boxes and shoe size labels.

American shoes are made on approximately 300 different size and width combinations. The majority of shoes sold in the common adult sizes fall into about 50 size-width combinations.[2]

The Continental, or French, system is divided into Paris Points, beginning with 0 cm and continuing without repetition. Each size is $\frac{2}{3}$ cm longer than the previous size. Shoes measured in this system usually are not further divided into half-sizes.

The centimeter system, used in some European countries, uses a size increment of 1 cm for each size, with $\frac{1}{2}$ cm representing a half-size. The centimeter size scale begins at 0.

The Mondopoint system, not included in Figure 6.1, is the most recent shoe size system. It was developed as a universal shoe sizing system; however, as of yet, it has not gained wide acceptance, and the Mondopoint system is rarely used. It has size increments of 5 mm or $7\frac{1}{2}$ mm for length, as well as a size interval for width. An example of a size for a man's shoe in the Mondopoint system would be 260/94. This would fit a foot 260 millimeters long and 94 millimeters wide.

As you can see in Figure 6.1, a size 8 in an American-made adult men's shoe would be a size 41 in a shoe sized by the French system and a size $7\frac{1}{2}$ in the English system. Because of the worldwide distribution of footwear by many companies and the need to list sizes for people accustomed to different sizing systems, shoe size labels and shoe boxes now often have more than one size printed on them (Figure 6.2).

## Shoe Fitting Devices

There are two predominantly used devices in this country for measuring feet to determine shoe size. They are the Brannock device[3] and the size stick (Figure 6.3). Many other foot-measuring devices or gauges exist as well. Instructions accompanying some of these devices recom-

---

[3] Brannock Device Company, Syracuse, NY.

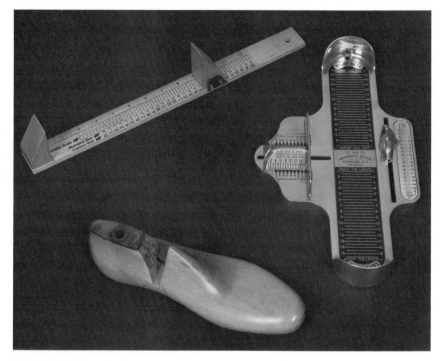

**6.3**   The Brannock device, top right, and size stick, top left, are two common foot-measuring devices. The wooden last, in the foreground, is a foot form around which a shoe is built. Lasts are shaped and sized for each different style and each different shoe size.

mend that the person be seated when the measurement is being made. Studies that show how the size of the foot can change slightly between sitting and standing have resulted in some devices being marked for either weight-bearing or non-weight-bearing measurements. Many shoe fitters now measure the foot in both the sitting and standing positions.

The Brannock device can measure overall foot length (toe-to-heel length), ball-to-heel length (arch length), and ball width. The device is reversible, so that the left and right feet can be separately measured. When the foot is properly positioned in the device, the three measurements can be made simultaneously. The size stick primarily measures heel-to-toe length but can also be used to measure width.

These measuring devices can help in the proper fitting of a shoe; however, there is no such thing as a perfect fit. In order to obtain a perfect fit, each shoe would have to fit the respective foot with regard to many measurements. The fit would take into consideration not only heel-to-toe length, heel-to-ball length, and ball width, but additional factors such as toe room, heel width and fit, and instep and arch fit. In addition, since a person's left foot and right foot are of slightly different dimensions, a pair of shoes will usually fit one foot better than the other.

## Lasts

A last is a wooden, plastic, or metal foot-shaped form around which the shoe is constructed. A wooden last is pictured in the foreground of Figure 6.3. During manufacturing, the upper materials of the shoe are pulled tightly over the last. The materials remain on the last until the outsole has been attached to it and the shoe construction is complete. The final shape, appearance and fit of the shoe will relate to the specific size and shape of the last. Consequently, different lasts are constructed for each different design, size, and type of footwear.

Lasts often contain over two dozen measurements, a few of which are shown in Figure 6.4. Model lasts are made by skilled craftspersons and can then be commercially copied in a full range of sizes.

Lasts can be straight or can have a degree of curve or flair to them. Figure 6.4 depicts a sketch of a straight and a curved last. The straight last is fairly symmetrical and is divided by a line that extends from the center of the heel to the toes. This type of last would be used for shoes that would best fit a straight foot. The curved last will have a curve to accommodate a foot that is curved in the same manner.

**6.4** Lasts.

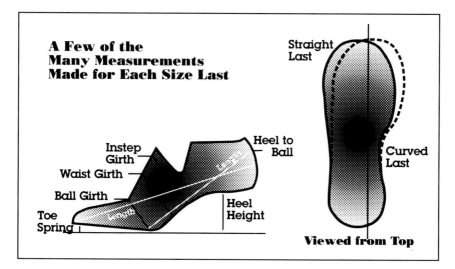

## Variables Involved in a Single Shoe Size

With all of the shoe sizes and widths, and with shoes being made on specifically designed lasts, one would expect that the sizing of shoes would be rather exact and would be consistent, not only for a particular manufacturer, but also from one manufacturer to the next. And one would expect that a particular shoe size would always represent the same dimensions. This is not the case at all. The specific dimensions of a shoe will vary with style and pattern. Materials that shoes are made of will also have some effect on size, since some materials stretch more than others. Different types of shoes, whether work boots or casual, athletic, or dress shoes, will be provided with different size allowances to account for their specific materials, construction, and usage. Thus, the internal and external dimensions of different styles of shoes of a single size made by the same manufacturer will vary.

## Variables Among Individuals

Aside from the manufacturer's shoe sizes, there are still other factors to consider when trying to assign a particular shoe size to an individual. A person's feet are not exactly matched and therefore have slightly different dimensions. In addition, a person's foot dimensions vary slightly from morning to evening, from winter to summer, when standing versus sitting, when standing versus running, and when in a heeled shoe versus a flat shoe. The particular usage of a shoe should also be considered. Some shoes are intended to fit more tightly, while others are intended to be loose fitting. Personal choice is a big factor. Some individuals simply prefer a loose-fitting shoe, while others prefer a tight-fitting shoe. Socioeconomic factors may also influence the selection of size. Some individuals might not have the choice of the exact size they would prefer because their shoes may be handed down, donated, or traded or because a particular pair of shoes they were able to buy at a good price was a size only close to theirs.

## Forensic Considerations

Investigators often ask questions concerning footwear impressions from crime scenes. Those questions quite commonly include "What size shoe made the impression?" and "Can you tell anything about the physical make-up of the person who made those impressions?"

Some studies have shown a correlation among the size of footwear impressions, the size of shoes, and the height of the person who wears them. Information of this type, at best, is useful for limited investigative assistance and is not a method of positive determination. For example, in a particular case involving a footwear impression of a certain dimension, it may help to know that that dimension is usually associated with shoes between the sizes of 7 and 8. This fact may contribute toward the elimination of a potential subject having a shoe size of 12 or 13. It should not, however, be used to eliminate a suspect having the closer shoe size of 9.

## *Shoe Size and Outsole Size and Shape*

There is a correlation between the size of a shoe and the size of its outsole; however, that correlation is not particularly high for many reasons.

Different shoes of the same shoe size, by virtue of their design, construction, purpose, and different origins, will vary in the physical shape and size of their outsole. Although this range of variance will be limited in a general sense, it nevertheless will be larger than might be expected.

Figure 6.5 illustrates the type, size, length, and widest dimension of the outsoles of several shoes that one person currently owns and uses. The chart shows that the shoe size for that person ranges from size 8 to

**6.5** Survey of shoes currently owned and used by one person.

## Survey of Shoes Currently Owned and Used by One Person

| Type of shoe | Size | Length (mm) | Widest part (mm |
|---|---|---|---|
| Black Overboots | medium | 308 | 112 |
| Nike Tennis Shoes | 8 1/2 | 279 | 90 |
| Nike Tennis Shoes | 8 1/2 | 285 | 94 |
| Nike Jogging Shoes | 8 1/2 | 290 | 111 |
| New Balance Jogging Shoes | 8 1/2 | 295 | 108 |
| TretornTennisShoes | 9 | 295 | 97 |
| Bostonian Loafers | 8 1/2D | 285 | 98 |
| Bostonian Tassel Loafers | 8 1/2D | 295 | 109 |
| Hush Puppies (leather) | 8 1/2M | 280 | 99 |
| Bass Duck Boots | 9 | 280 | 103 |
| Sperry Top-siders (deck shoe) | 8 1/2M | 286 | 103 |
| Nike Deck Shoe | 8 1/2D | 284 | 100 |
| Bass Sandals | 10  M | 282 | 90 |
| Snow Boots | 8 | 295 | 111 |

### Average Length Measurements and Standard Deviations of Five Major Brands of Sneakers

| | ADIDAS | | CONVERSE ALL STAR | | CONVERSE STD. PATTERN | | NIKE | | PUMA | |
|------|------|----------|------|----------|------|----------|------|----------|------|----------|
| Size | mm. | std. dev. | mm. | std. dev. | mm. | std. dev. | mm. | std. dev. | mm. | std. dev. |
| 6 | -- | -- | 273..5 | 1.08 | 267 | -- | -- | -- | 271.5 | 0.58 |
| 6 1/2 | 272 | 0 | 277.5 | 0.93 | 271 | -- | 267.6 | 1.82 | 274.8 | 0.96 |
| 7 | 277.8 | 0.79 | 282.2 | 1.48 | 275 | -- | 271.9 | 2.33 | 278.9 | 1.36 |
| 7 1/2 | 281.4 | 1.35 | 286.0 | 1.15 | 279 | -- | 275.2 | 0.75 | 283.2 | 1.99 |
| 8 | 284.9 | 0.99 | 290.1 | 0.88 | 283 | -- | 283.3 | 1.03 | 289.5 | 0.71 |
| 8 1/2 | 289.6 | 1.51 | 294.7 | 1.16 | 287 | -- | 285.4 | 1.06 | 293.2 | 0.92 |
| 9 | 293.9 | 1.10 | 298.6 | 0.84 | 291 | -- | 288.3 | 1.37 | 297.3 | 1.06 |
| 9 1/2 | 297.9 | 1.25 | 301.8 | 1.40 | 295 | -- | 290.2 | 0.44 | 302.1 | 0.57 |
| 10 | 303.3 | 0.89 | 306.1 | 1.29 | 300 | -- | 294.8 | 2.66 | 305.5 | 0.53 |
| 10 1/2 | 308 | 0 | 310.6 | 1.51 | 304 | -- | 300.9 | 2.18 | 310.2 | 0.79 |
| 11 | 310 | 1.10 | 315.0 | 0.82 | 308 | -- | 302.5 | 1.29 | 313.8 | 1.17 |
| 11 1/2 | -- | -- | 318.6 | 1.17 | 313 | -- | -- | -- | 320.5 | 2.38 |
| 12 | 320.8 | 0.71 | 322.8 | 0.96 | 317 | -- | 311.7 | 1.64 | 322.4 | 0.84 |

**6.6** Average length measurements and standard deviations of five major brands of sneakers (courtesy of Harvey Van Hoven).

size 10, the length of the outsoles ranges from 279 to 308 mm, and their width ranges from 90 to 112 mm.

Shoes of the same general type whose labels are marked with the same shoe size, but that originate from different manufacturers, also vary in outsole dimensions. In a study of 450 court shoes, length measurements of the outsoles of five brands were taken of shoes from four different manufacturers (Van Hoven H, 1985). These length measurements, some of which are presented in Figure 6.6, show variations between the five different brands. For instance, in the study reflected in Figure 6.6, for the shoe size 10½, the physical length of the outsole for Adidas was 308 mm, for Converse Chuck Taylor All-Star was 310.6 mm, for Converse standard pattern was 304 mm, for Nike was 300.9 mm, and for Puma was 310.2 mm.

There are reasons why this occurs. Every manufacturer has design specifications for each size and each dimension of the shoes they make. Slight differences in the materials, styling, and manufacturing methods for a particular shoe can cause changes in the overall dimensions. This is clearly shown in the comparison of length measurements between the Converse Chuck Taylor All-Star pattern and the Converse standard pattern. The Converse All-Star pattern has an extra layer of rubber on the toe, known as a toe guard or bumper guard; a rubber label on the heel; and a layer of rubber, known as a foxing strip, that wraps around the perimeter of the outsole. These added areas are included in the overall outsole dimensions and are, in fact, part of the outsole that would leave an impression. The result is an additional 5 to 6 mm of length in the Converse Chuck Taylor All-Star over that of the Converse standard pattern.

## Shoe Size, Stature, and Foot Size

In a recent study I conducted, which involved the acquisition of the bare footprints of 399 males and 101 females, I also collected the contributors' shoe sizes and their heights. The data display some correlations between the actual maximum length of people's feet and the manufacturer's shoe size they believe they should wear.

At the same time, it also shows that a person's height, although somewhat related to manufacturer's shoe size, can in no way be used to accurately predict either one. Referring to the men's shoe size 10½ in the American system in Figure 6.7, the following will apply: Based on the data in the survey, the height of a person wearing a size 10½ shoe could range from 68 to 76 inches, with the majority of persons in the survey being from 70 to 73 inches in height. This kind of information may have some limited investigative value, so long as its limitations are fully understood.

In a separate and independent study conducted by Michael J. Cassidy of the Royal Canadian Mounted Police (Cassidy MJ, 1980), it was reported that for a size 10½ athletic shoe size, the wearer's height can range from 70 to 74 inches, with 80% accuracy. Some of the figures from that study are reprinted in Figure 6.8 and provide very similar information to that obtained in the survey reported in Figure 6.7.

Also reprinted from Cassidy's study, and provided in Figure 6.8, is a shoe size calculation chart that gives the measurement of the actual impression made by running shoes and flat-bottomed casual shoes of different sizes. This same type of information, obtained directly from the shoe dimensions, can be extracted from Figure 6.6.

The statistics provided in Figures 6.5 through 6.8 clearly show that there is a correlation between the length of the foot, shoe size, height, and outsole dimensions, but also show the limitations of those correlations. Because shoe outsole sizes vary from manufacturer to manufacturer, both within a single style and between different styles, and because of the other reasons for variations previously discussed, additional statistics will not provide much more specific information. Once again, although this information can be of value in some investigations, there is a limit to its accuracy, which must be understood by the investigator.

## Survey of 399 Males Shoe Size

| Height in Inches | 6 | 6 1/2 | 7 | 7 1/2 | 8 | 8 1/2 | 9 | 9 1/2 | 10 | 10 1/2 | 11 | 11 1/2 | 12 | 12 1/2 | 13 | 14 |
|---|---|---|---|---|---|---|---|---|---|---|---|---|---|---|---|---|
| 63 |  |  |  | 1 |  |  |  |  |  |  |  |  |  |  |  |  |
| 64 |  |  |  |  |  |  |  |  |  |  |  |  |  |  |  |  |
| 65 | 1 | 1 |  | 4 | 1 |  | 1 |  |  |  |  |  |  |  |  |  |
| 66 |  | 1 |  | 2 | 1 |  |  | 2 |  |  |  |  |  |  |  |  |
| 67 |  |  | 2 | 2 |  | 3 |  |  | 2 |  |  |  |  |  |  |  |
| 68 |  | 1 | 1 | 4 | 9 | 7 | 7 |  |  | 1 | 1 |  |  |  |  |  |
| 69 |  |  | 1 | 3 | 8 | 14 | 10 | 8 | 3 | 2 |  |  |  |  |  |  |
| 70 |  | 1 |  | 3 | 4 | 13 | 15 | 15 | 18 | 3 | 1 |  |  |  |  |  |
| 71 |  | 1 |  | 3 | 3 | 7 | 5 | 14 | 9 | 7 |  | 2 |  |  |  |  |
| 72 |  |  |  |  |  | 7 | 11 | 11 | 21 | 11 | 4 | 3 |  |  |  |  |
| 73 |  |  |  |  | 2 | 1 | 2 | 4 | 11 | 8 | 1 | 7 |  |  | 1 |  |
| 74 |  |  |  |  |  | 1 | 1 | 7 | 8 | 5 | 3 | 4 |  |  | 1 | 1 |
| 75 |  |  |  |  |  |  |  | 1 | 2 | 3 | 2 | 5 | 1 | 2 |  |  |
| 76 |  |  |  |  |  |  | 1 | 1 | 1 | 1 | 3 |  |  | 1 | 1 |  |
| 77 |  |  |  |  |  |  |  |  |  |  |  | 4 |  | 3 |  |  |
| 78 |  |  |  |  |  |  |  |  |  |  |  |  |  |  |  |  |
| 79 |  |  |  |  |  |  |  |  |  |  |  |  |  |  |  | 1 |
| 80 |  |  |  |  |  |  |  |  |  |  |  |  | 1 |  |  |  |
| 81 |  |  |  |  |  |  |  |  |  |  |  |  |  |  |  |  |
| 82 |  |  |  |  |  |  |  |  |  |  |  |  |  |  | 1 |  |
| Totals | 1 | 3 | 3 | 8 | 18 | 27 | 54 | 54 | 63 | 74 | 40 | 12 | 28 | 1 | 10 | 3 |

## Survey of 101 Females Shoe Size

| Height in Inches | 4 1/2 | 5 | 5 1/2 | 6 | 6 1/2 | 7 | 7 1/2 | 8 | 8 1/2 | 9 | 9 1/2 | 10 | 10 1/2 | 11 |
|---|---|---|---|---|---|---|---|---|---|---|---|---|---|---|
| 56 |  |  |  |  |  |  |  |  |  | 1 |  |  |  |  |
| 60 | 1 |  | 2 | 3 | 2 |  |  |  |  |  |  |  |  |  |
| 61 |  | 1 | 1 | 3 | 2 | 2 | 1 |  |  |  |  |  |  |  |
| 62 |  | 2 |  | 1 | 2 |  |  |  |  | 1 |  |  |  |  |
| 63 |  | 1 |  | 1 | 1 |  | 1 | 2 |  |  |  |  |  |  |
| 64 |  |  |  |  |  | 6 | 2 | 1 | 1 |  |  |  |  |  |
| 65 |  |  |  |  |  |  | 1 | 2 | 3 | 3 | 1 |  |  |  |
| 66 |  |  |  |  | 1 | 1 | 4 | 3 | 2 | 1 | 1 |  |  |  |
| 67 |  |  |  |  | 1 | 1 | 2 | 2 | 2 |  |  |  |  | 1 |
| 68 |  |  |  |  |  |  | 3 | 4 | 2 |  |  | 2 |  |  |
| 69 |  |  |  |  |  |  | 1 | 2 | 1 | 1 |  |  |  |  |
| 70 |  |  |  |  |  |  |  | 1 | 1 | 2 |  |  |  |  |
| 71 |  |  |  |  |  |  | 1 | 2 |  |  |  |  |  |  |
| 72 |  |  |  |  |  |  |  |  |  |  |  |  |  |  |
| 73 |  |  |  |  |  |  |  |  |  |  | 1 |  |  |  |
| 74 |  |  |  |  |  |  |  |  |  |  |  |  |  |  |
| Totals | 1 | 4 | 3 | 8 | 9 | 11 | 12 | 15 | 17 | 11 | 6 | 6 | 0 | 1 |

6.7   Survey of 399 men's shoe sizes (**A**) and 101 women's shoe sizes (**B**).

A more accurate way of determining shoe size, based on outsole dimensions and characteristics, is to associate an impression with a particular shoe of the same design from that shoe's manufacturer. The best method would be to ascertain that the impression was made by a shoe from a particular mold. Information concerning mold characteristics is covered in the chapter on footwear manufacturing.

## Height Calculation Chart

| | | | | | | | | | | | | | | | |
|---|---|---|---|---|---|---|---|---|---|---|---|---|---|---|---|
| Approximate HEIGHT | 5'2 to 5'6 | 5'3 to 5'7 | 5'4 to 5'8 | 5'5 to 5'9 | 5'6 to 5'10 | 5'6 to 5'10 | 5'7 to 5'11 | 5'8 to 6' | 5'9 to 6'1 | 5'10 to 6'2 | 5'10 to 6'2 | 5'11 to 6'2 | 6' to 6'4 | 6'1 to 6'5 | 6'1 to 6'5 |
| SHOE SIZE | 6 | 6 1/2 | 7 | 7 1/2 | 8 | 8 1/2 | 9 | 9 1/2 | 10 | 10 1/2 | 11 | 11 1/2 | 12 | 12 1/2 | 13 |
| % of ADULT MALES | 1% | 1% | 3% | 3% | 11% | 11% | 15% | 15% | 14% | 11% | 7% | 2% | 3% | 1% | 1% |

## Running Shoes & Flat Bottom Casuals—shoe size

| | | | | | | | | | | | | | | | | | | | | | | |
|---|---|---|---|---|---|---|---|---|---|---|---|---|---|---|---|---|---|---|---|---|---|---|
| RANGE of SHOE SIZE | 6<br>4 1/2 | 6 1/2<br>5 | 6 1/2<br>5 | 7<br>5 1/2 | 7 1/2<br>6 | 8<br>6 1/2 | 8<br>6 1/2 | 8 1/2<br>7 | 9<br>7 1/2 | 9<br>7 1/2 | 9 1/2<br>8 | 10<br>8 1/2 | 10 1/2<br>9 | 10 1/2<br>9 | 11<br>9 1/2 | 11<br>9 1/2 | 11 1/2<br>10 | 12<br>10 1/2 | 12 1/2<br>11 | 13<br>11 1/2 | 13<br>11 1/2 | 13 1/2<br>12 |
| IMPRESSION—length in inches | 9 7/8 | 10 | 10 1/8 | 10 1/4 | 10 3/8 | 10 1/2 | 10 5/8 | 10 3/4 | 10 7/8 | 11 | 11 1/8 | 11 1/4 | 11 3/8 | 11 1/2 | 11 5/8 | 11 3/4 | 11 7/8 | 12 | 12 1/8 | 12 1/4 | 12 3/8 | 12 1/2 |
| IMPRESSION—length in millimeters | 251 | 254 | 257 | 260 | 263 | 266 | 269 | 272 | 276 | 279 | 282 | 285 | 288 | 291 | 294 | 298 | 301 | 304 | 307 | 310 | 313 | 317 |

**6.8** Height calculation chart and shoe size calculation chart (courtesy of Michael Cassidy).

## Shoe Size Survey

Often the question is asked, "What percentage of the population wears a certain size of shoe?" Footwear Market Insights[4] conducts a yearly survey, part of which includes statistics on what percentage of the population wears each size of shoe. Figure 6.9 is a summary of part of that survey, which included 226,007,000 pairs of men's shoes in 1986. Of those, 99,847,000 were athletic shoes. Figure 6.9 includes the size breakdown for the total number of men's shoes in all categories, as well as the size breakdown for men's athletic shoes.

## Shoe Size Codings and Markings

In some footwear examinations, it is necessary to determine what size a particular shoe or pair of shoes is. If the label or markings in the shoe or on the bottom of the outsole are still present, this poses no problem. Size markings on the inside areas of the shoe or on labels are frequently still visible. These markings sometimes consist simply of the size, such as "8½" or "9M." In other cases, there may be a longer number, for example, "07-14832-04--3." This particular number was found on a pair of shoes being sold in a national chain shoe store. The numbers "07" represent the department number, "14832" represents the style number, and the "04-3" represents administrative numbers necessary for a computerized cash register and inventory system. None of the numbers represent the size. In other cases, a number, such as "7 324586" may represent a size 7 shoe, style 3245, made in 1986. There is no universal coding system concerning these numbers, what they represent, and where they are placed on the shoe. Only the manufacturer or distributor will be able to provide their exact meaning and significance.

Often a shoe will not contain any surviving markings of the shoe size. Approximate sizing of the shoes can be made from a measurement of the outsole dimensions and the information printed in Figures 6.6 and 6.8. This will provide a general idea of the size of the shoe.

Some of the individual shoe components are separately size coded and offer a more accurate way, if necessary, of determining the manufacturer's shoe size. Figure 6.10 depicts a photograph of the top side of a compression-molded shoe outsole. The size and mold number is often contained on the upper portion of the mold, which then records this information on the top side of the molded outsole. This is usually accessible only in certain types of shoe construction, such as basketball and tennis shoes having molded unit outsoles. The mold number and

---

[4] Footwear Market Insights, Nashville, TN.

Based on United States sales figures for 1986, of 226,007,000 pairs of mens' shoes which had a length measurement, the following gives a breakdown of the numbers sold / percentage sold for each half size.

| | | | | | |
|---|---|---|---|---|---|
| 6 | 4,848,000 / | 2.2% | 11 | 22.495 ,000 / | 10% |
| 6 1/2 | 3,403,000 / | 1.5% | 11 1/2 | 4,714,000 / | 2.1% |
| 7 | 6,763,000 / | 3.0% | 12 | 17,127,000 / | 7.6% |
| 7 1/2 | 8,230,000 / | 3.6% | 12 1/2 | 777,000 / | .3% |
| 8 | 14,457,000 / | 6.4% | 13 | 6,517,000 / | 2.9% |
| 8 1/2 | 19,596,000 / | 8.7% | 13 1/2 | 106,000 / | .1% |
| 9 | 25,942,000 / | 11.5% | 14 | 871,000 / | .4% |
| 9 1/2 | 30,516,000 / | 13.5% | 15 | 316,000 / | .1% |
| 10 | 31,301,000 / | 13.9% | 15 1/2 | 38,000 / | --- |
| 10 1/2 | 27,897,000 / | 12.3% | 16 | 48,000 / | --- |

The fraction of the 226,007,000 which constitute mens' athletic shoes, of which there were 99,847,000, are broken down by the number sold / percentage sold for each half size.

| | | | | | |
|---|---|---|---|---|---|
| 6 | 3,733,000 / | 3.7% | 11 | 9,902,000 / | 9.9% |
| 6 1/2 | 2,528,000 / | 2.5% | 11 1/2 | 2,261,000 / | 2.3% |
| 7 | 3,818,000 / | 3.8% | 12 | 7,412,000 / | 7.4% |
| 7 1/2 | 4,121,000 / | 4.1% | 12 1/2 | 296,000 / | .3% |
| 8 | 6,564,000 / | 6.6% | 13 | 3,035,000 / | 3.0% |
| 8 1/2 | 8,130.000 / | 8.1% | 13 1/2 | 76,000 / | .1% |
| 9 | 10,880,000/ | 10.9% | 14 | 282,000 / | .3% |
| 9 1/2 | 12,392,000/ | 12.4% | 15 | 125,000 / | .1% |
| 10 | 12,943,000/ | 13.0% | 15 1/2 | 38,000 / | ----- |
| 10 1/2 | 11,264,000/ | 11.3% | 16 | 21,000 / | ----- |
| | | | 17 & over | 28,000 / | ----- |

**6.9** Footwear size figures from 1986 (courtesy of Footwear Market Insights).

**6.10**   Photograph of the back of a molded outsole, showing its size.

size number can be accessed by removing the insole. In shoes made in other ways, this number usually does not exist or has been permanently cemented over.

Other components of the shoes often contain notches, which are size codings used to assist in the proper assembly of the many shoe components during manufacture. Figure 6.11 depicts part of the material of a shoe upper that contains two V-shaped notches. Figure 6.12 is an example of a shoe size coding chart used by one manufacturer to translate what size is meant by the notches. If the chart in Figure 6.12 was valid for the shoe component in Figure 6.11, it would indicate that the component was a size 10. The coded sizes for shoe upper components do not necessarily correspond to the shoe size. For instance, the upper component in Figure 6.11, coded for a size 10, may be used on a size 8 shoe. Further, the shoe size codings that a manufacturer uses are often

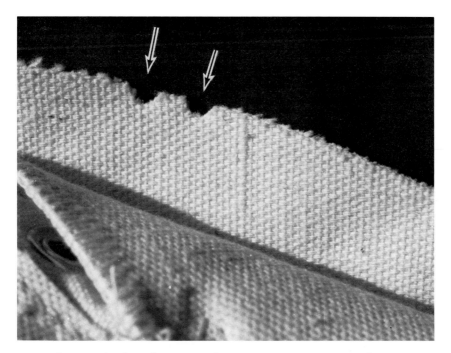

**6.11** Photograph of notches cut in shoe upper components to reflect size.

**6.12** Photograph of shoe size coding card.

| SIZE CODE SCHEDULE | | | | | |
|---|---|---|---|---|---|
| 1 | U | 5 1/2 V | v | 10 | V V |
| 1 1/2 U | v | 6 V U | | 10 1/2 V V | v |
| 2 U U | | 6 1/2 V U | v | 11 V V U | |
| 2 1/2 U U | v | 7 V U U | | 11 1/2 V V U | v |
| 3 ⊔ | | 7 1/2 V U U | v | 12 V V U U | |
| 3 1/2 ⊔ | v | 8 V ⊔ | | 12 1/2 V V U U | v |
| 4 ⊔ U | | 8 1/2 V ⊔ | v | 13 V V ⊔ | |
| 4 1/2 ⊔ U | v | 9 V ⊔ U | | 13 1/2 V V ⊔ | v |
| 5 V | | 9 1/2 V ⊔ U | v | | |

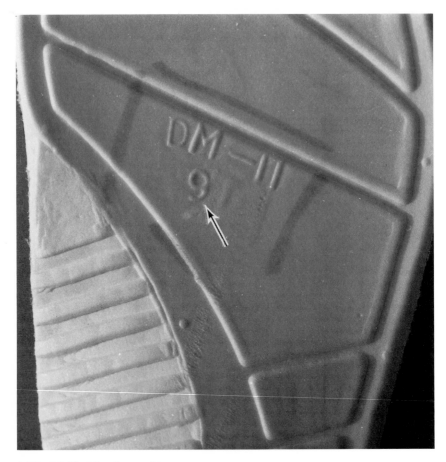

**6.13**   Molded insole markings.

their own and do not necessarily correspond to another manufacturer's codings. As shown in Figure 6.13, the insole often contains size codings. The codings on the back of the insole in Figure 6.13 read "DM-11 9." For this particular manufacturer, "D" represents the identification of the factory at which the insole was made, "M-11" represents mold number 11, and "9" represents the shoe size.

Date coding information is frequently placed on the back side of molded heels, which are then nailed or glued to the outsole or heel base of the shoe. By separating the heel from the shoe, these codings can be revealed and may not only provide information about the shoe size but may provide information as to the manufacturer, the date the heel was made, and the mold it was formed in.

The use of size markings on outsoles, insoles, and other components of the shoe can best be used to determine the size of a shoe with the cooperation and assistance of the manufacturer. Sometimes this is not possible, as in cases when the shoe cannot be tracked to a manufacturer or when the manufacturer is known but is in another part of the world. This obstacle can sometimes be overcome if another shoe, identical in style and manufacturing source, can be located in a local shoe store. The codings in the new shoes, whose size is known, could then be used as a reference for determining the size of the questioned shoes. For instance, consider the hypothetical case of a shoe whose size and manufacturer is unknown and that contains the code "74321-B4." If a shoe of the same style, containing the same number in the same format and in the same area within the shoe can be located at a local shoe store, it can provide a means of identifying both the manufacturer and the size of the shoe.

## Shoe Terminology

There are literally hundreds of words specific to the footwear industry, including those used to describe the components of the shoe, lasts, anatomy of the feet, outsole compounds, and numerous other items relating to footwear technology.

Figure 6.14 depicts some basic parts of a running shoe. Shoes of other designs or shoes made with different methods, such as boots, basketball shoes, high-heeled shoes, and men's welted dress shoes, will have some different components, and therefore the terminology varies slightly with each.

Of most importance to the footwear examiner, a few basic words and definitions that apply to most shoes are offered as follows:

*Direct attach:* a process wherein the lasted upper of a shoe is lowered into the mold cavity, where the midsole or outsole is molded directly onto that upper.

*Dual density:* a term used for a midsole-outsole combination in which the outsole and midsole are composed of materials having different densities.

*Foxing strip:* a shoe component, usually a strip of unvulcanized material, wrapped around the lower part of the shoe, covering and adding strength to the joint between the outsole and the shoe upper.

*Heel:* a separate component attached to the rear portion of the outsole or, in a continuous outsole, a raised area in the rear portion of the outsole. In a flat shoe, the heel area.

*Heel area:* in a flat shoe, the rear portion of the outsole; the area occupied by a separate heel component in a heeled shoe.

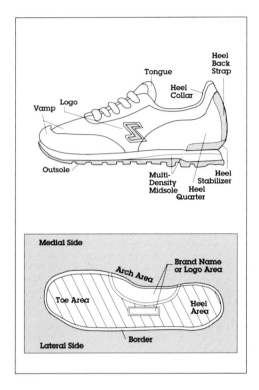

**6.14**  Simple nomenclature of a running shoe.

*Heel backstrap:* a piece of material centered at the rearmost portion of some shoes and extending from the heel collar down to the upper portion of the midsole or outsole.

*Heel collar:* the highest portion of the shoe upper in the rear of the shoe that surrounds the ankle when the shoe is worn.

*Lasted:* a shoe upper that is on a last and is ready for the bottom to be cemented or molded onto it.

*Logo:* a name, design, or pattern that often appears on the sides or outsole of athletic shoes and that is a trademark of the manufacturer.

*Midsole:* the component, found on some shoes, that is placed between the outsole and the shoe upper.

*Multidensity midsole:* a midsole composed of materials of two or more densities.

*Outsole:* the extreme bottom layer of the shoe that makes contact with the ground.

*Shoe upper:* the components of the shoe excluding the outsole and midsole.

*Toe bumper guard:* a thick strip of rubber placed around the front perimeter of the shoe, surrounding the toe area.

*Toe cap:* a piece of rubber or material placed across the top of the toe area or vamp of a shoe to increase the durability and strength of the shoe in that area.

*Tongue:* a strip of material that covers the instep of the foot and lies beneath the shoe laces.

*Unit soles:* a molded heel-sole unit of a predetermined size.

Although a more extensive vocabulary is not needed for the footwear examiner, a much more comprehensive list and an explanation of shoe fitting and shoe terminology can be found in the following sources:

The Dictionary of Shoe Industry Terminology
Edited by Ruth J. Schachter
Footwear Industries of America
1420 K Street NW, Suite 600
Washington, DC 20005

Professional Shoe Fitting
National Shoe Retailers Association
200 Madison Avenue
New York, NY 10016

The Complete Handbook of Athletic Footwear
By Melvin P. Cheskin
Fairchild Publications
7 East 12th Street
New York, NY 10003

# Basic Manufacturing Processes of Athletic Shoe Outsoles

7

Traditionally, footwear impression comparisons have concerned themselves with four areas of examination: (1) the physical size and shape of the outsole, (2) the outsole design, (3) wear characteristics, and (4) identifying characteristics.

In addition to the traditional four areas of examination, knowledge of the way a shoe is manufactured can also be of great importance in footwear examinations. Many of the characteristics in the outsoles of footwear are class characteristics shared by *all* other footwear from that manufacturer in that size and design. But most outsoles reflect at least one and often numerous variations or random characteristics acquired during the various steps of the manufacturing processes. In some processes, the amount of the randomness in a particular manufacturing step may be limited, that is, it can and will recur, but only a percentage of the time. In other processes, the randomness of certain features can be so great that the shoes are unique before ever being worn. Manufacturing techniques and characteristics should, therefore, always be considered during a footwear examination. They can assist the examiner in both identification and elimination of shoes.

The footwear industry of today is highly competitive on a worldwide basis. This, along with current footwear trends, is causing the production of a larger quantity and assortment of styles and designs of shoes. There are many thousands of shoe outsole designs available on the world market, each made in many sizes. Many of those designs are short-lived and, for marketing reasons, are rapidly replaced with newer designs just months later. This is particularly true with regard to athletic shoes and other nonleather footwear.

This chapter will introduce the reader to some basic manufacturing methods used for athletic and other nonleather shoes. Examples are provided showing how this knowledge could contribute to footwear examinations. This information will demonstrate the importance to the examiner of having some basic knowledge of the manufacturing methods used to produce shoes. The following information is by no means a complete representation of all the methods and variations that can occur during the manufacturing of footwear. *It should be regarded only as an introduction to manufacturing and as an encouragement to the reader to seek additional information concerning the way a shoe is made if that information is significant and obtainable in a particular case.*

## How the Footwear Industry Has Changed

In the early 1900s, athletic shoes were largely of the "sneaker" variety. Originally called pumps, they consisted of a canvas upper and a gum rubber outsole material. The manufacturers of these shoes at that time included, among others, Converse, Goodrich, Spalding, and U.S. Rubber. During the 1940s and 1950s, the canvas vulcanized sneaker, in both high- and low-top versions, became increasingly popular. In the 1950s and 1960s, shoe manufacturers such as Adidas, Puma, and Tiger played leading roles in the beginning development of more specialized footwear for specific sports such as soccer and track. Then, in the 1970s, with the running boom and the new emphasis on exercise in the United States, the sales of athletic shoes skyrocketed. Competition from foreign manufacturers and the number of imports increased. Nike, Pony, Converse, Hyde, Adidas, New Balance, Brooks, Etonic, Tiger, Saucony, and other companies brought innovative ideas to the construction of specialized athletic footwear. Many even conducted their own research concerning the biomechanics of the foot in order to better understand how to develop their footwear. In the last decade, additional technology, including computer-aided design–computer-aided manufacture (CAD-CAM), dual-density combination soles, air-filled midsoles, molded insoles, and even shoes with a built-in computer, has reflected the continuous changes and competitiveness in the athletic shoe industry.

Today, the percentage of imports of nonleather footwear in the United States exceeds 80%. The number of surviving footwear factories in this country has been reduced considerably. In efforts to produce footwear in this country as well as in other countries where labor costs are high and still be competitive with the imports, the footwear industry has resorted to some new technology and methods in footwear manufacture. At the same time, footwear is still being made with the older methods, especially in parts of the world where labor costs are low. As a result, there is an abundance of shoes in the United States and in the world marketplace being made by each of these methods.

There are many methods of manufacturing athletic shoe outsoles. Some methods use cutting processes in which the outsoles are cut from previously molded or milled outsole materials, while others use molding processes in which the final outsole units are formed in a mold. For that reason, I have divided the way in which outsoles are manufactured into (1) those that are cut or trimmed in some way before reaching their final size and shape and (2) those that are molded into their *final* size and shape. The cut and the molded processes will be discussed separately.

## The Cut Processes

### Materials for Cut Outsoles

Cut outsoles, as distinguished from molded outsoles, are those that are literally cut or trimmed into the size and shape required for a shoe. In order to fully understand the forensic significance of the cut outsoles and the process itself, it is first necessary to understand the various types of outsole materials and their characteristics.

Materials to be cut into outsoles can be (1) calendered rubber, i.e., that milled from unvulcanized rubber, usually on location, in a calendering process; (2) premolded (and therefore vulcanized) sheets of outsole material that is available in a large variety of designs; (3) premolded but individual oversize unit outsoles, i.e., outsoles that are larger than needed and that are trimmed or cut down to a specific-size outsole; or (4) individual premolded outsole units in exact sizes, subject only to finish trimming as needed.

*Calendered rubber outsole material.* Some manufacturers mix the chemicals and raw rubber ingredients and then mill their own rubber outsole material through a calendering process. This method is labor intensive and is therefore no longer commonly found in factories in the United States. In this operation, once the raw, unvulcanized rubber compound is mixed, it is heated and then fed through a calendering machine having a series of several smooth rollers. These rollers serve to further heat and form the material into a continuous sheet of rubber having a uniform thickness. The soft sheet of rubber exits the calendering machine between the design roller and the final smooth roller, both depicted in Figure 7.1A. Often found in the design of outsole material made in this fashion is a strip of design that reads "Made in USA" or "Made in China" or similar wording (Figure 7.1B).

The cylindrical design rollers used to mill this material can be of uniform diameter or can have one end with a smaller diameter. Cylinders with a uniform diameter can have an area on one end that is void of design (which represents the area to which a heel can later be attached) or can have a design covering the full surface. Other design rollers have

188

A

B

**7.1** The engraving roller of the calendering machine that contains the design next to the final smooth roller (**A**). The soft, unvulcanized rubber exits between those two rollers. Note the strip of design that contains the words "Made in USA" (**B**).

**7.2**   Some of the many different design rollers that can be used interchangeably on the same machine. Note that one roller has a smaller diameter at one end (arrow). A thicker sheet of calendered rubber will be formed at that point and will represent the heel area.

a smaller diameter on one end, which results in the milling of a thicker area of the outsole at that point. When the outsole material is cut, the thicker area will be positioned on the heel end. Figure 7.2, which shows some of the rollers being used in a particular factory, shows one that has a smaller diameter on one end and therefore produces material with a thicker heel area. The design rollers are interchangeable, so many different designs can be made on one machine simply by changing the roller.

Once the design roller has impressed its design into the soft, unvulcanized rubber, the newly formed outsole material exits the machine on a conveyer belt, as shown in Figure 7.3. This material, because it is still unvulcanized, is very soft and pliable. Workable slabs, in lengths of about 4 feet are cut from the continuous sheet of this newly formed outsole material. As these newly milled, warm slabs of outsole material cool, they will undergo some shrinkage. The slabs are then taken to the cutting area where outsoles will be cut from them. (Figure 7.31 depicts a

**7.3** A calendering machine in operation. The sheet of calendered rubber exits below the engraving roller and travels over a conveyer belt. It will then be cut into shorter slabs.

slab of this material that had outsoles cut from it.) Figure 7.4 is a diagram that illustrates the calendering process.

Many variations occur during the calendering operation that contribute to making the outsole material, and therefore the resulting outsoles, extremely individual. Some of these variables are:

1. Variations in the chemistry of the components used to produce the rubber plus unstrained impurities in the mixed rubber before calendering.
2. Flaws or damage to the design roller that have occurred during the life of the roller and are reproduced in the calendered outsole material. Because of the random manner in which outsoles are cut, this flaw, although repeated with each turn of the calendered roller, will show up in different positions on the outsoles cut from it (Figure 7.5A).
3. Variations in the heating of the calender rollers and design rollers

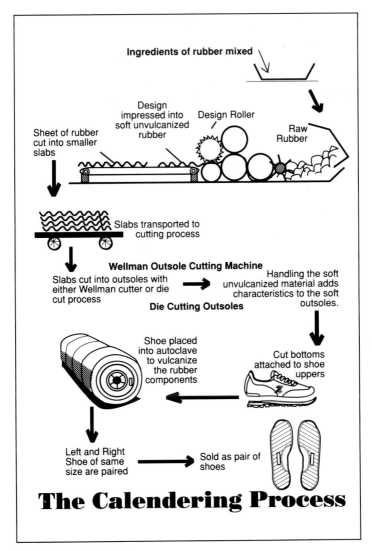

**7.4**   The calendering process.

and variations in the preheating of the raw rubber before entering the calendering machine. The amount of heat, as well as the evenness of the heating of the material before it is calendered, will affect the ability of the calender roller to impress the design into the material. In addition, the amount the material is heated when calendered will affect the amount it cools and therefore shrinks afterward.

4.  Stretching of the soft material as well as damage resulting from the

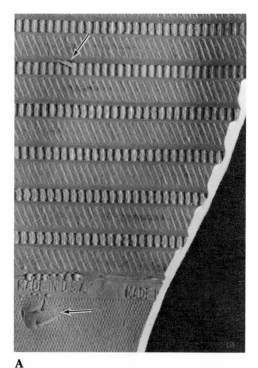

**A**

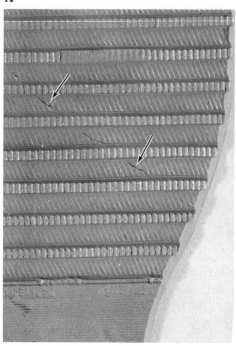

**B**

7.5 Enlarged sections of two outsoles cut from soft, calendered rubber. One has two flaws that are due to damage in the calender roller (**A**). The other outsole has acquired random damage during handling of the soft material (**B**).

**7.6**   Incomplete pressing of the rubber into the calender roller can result in numerous random void areas.

operator handling the slabs of the soft, unvulcanized outsole material before the cutting process. The calendered material is both soft and warm. When it is held, it can easily stretch under its own weight. In addition, anywhere the material is touched, it can acquire damage. If something sharp touches it, it will acquire random cut-like characteristics, as shown in Figure 7.5B. If something blunt touches it, it will be flattened in that area.

5. Incomplete pressing of the rubber into the calender roller. This results in random void areas that vary immensely in shape and depth (Figure 7.6).
6. Uneven shrinkage of the slabs of outsole material as they cool.
7. The possibility for the outsole material to acquire additional random characteristics, such as those shown in Figure 7.5B, as a result of handling during the subsequent outsole cutting operation and during the attachment of the outsole to the shoe upper. Both steps come before vulcanization, when the material is still very soft.

Calendered material, because it is soft, can be easily cut into outsoles using either a die-cutting process or the Wellman outsole cutting process. These methods are discussed later in this chapter.

**7.7**   A sheet of premolded outsole material, measuring 30 × 36 inches. Outsoles can be die cut from this sheet with dies like the one shown in Figure 7.11.

*Premolded sheets of outsole materials.* Another way for the manufacturer to obtain outsole materials for making shoes with cut outsoles is to purchase premolded sheets of outsole material. The premolded sheets of outsole material come in a large variety of designs and in different materials, such as natural and synthetic rubbers, ethyl vinyl acetate (EVA), and expanded EVA. The premolded sheets are compression molded and therefore will take on the same characteristics of each mold, sheet after sheet. Unlike the soft, unvulcanized rubber, their surface is cured and will not acquire any additional defects as a result of being handled during the manufacturing process. Figure 7.7 depicts a sheet of outsole material measuring 30 × 36 inches and having a herringbone design. Some premolded sheets of outsole designs, like the one in Figure 7.7, are directional, i.e., they must be oriented on the bottom of a shoe in a particular direction for functional reasons. Outsoles with directional designs must therefore be cut from the sheet of this material in certain directions. Others, like a textured design, can be positioned in any direction on the shoe and can therefore be cut in any direction.

**7.8** An individually molded oversize outsole that will later be combined with a midsole to form a blocker unit and then be die cut to size.

*Premolded oversize unit outsoles.* Cutting different sizes of shoe outsoles from premolded sheets can result in a large amount of waste. It also limits the content of the design itself. As a result, either individual premolded oversize unit outsoles or specific-size outsoles can be obtained instead of the sheet outsole material. The oversize unit outsoles can be cut and/or trimmed to the precise size. Figures 7.8 and 7.9 depict two types of oversize outsoles, one that has been individually molded and another that has been molded, several at one time, in a sheet. Both will have to be cut and trimmed to the final size for a particular shoe. Note the asymmetric design that these outsoles contain. This would not be possible using a sheet of *continuous design* outsole material, such as that shown in Figure 7.7.

**7.9** A series of oversize outsoles molded in a large sheet. Both oversize and specific-size outsoles can be molded this way but will have to be cut and trimmed from the sheet.

*Premolded specific-size unit outsoles.* Figure 7.10 depicts a specific-size premolded outsole that will be fitted and glued to other precut midsole pieces. Specific-size outsoles are designed and molded to fit the midsole components almost perfectly but usually still require some minor trimming or adjustments.

Although the premolded specific-size outsoles could be discussed in the molded outsole section, they are more appropriately placed here because of their blocker unit assembly and because there is almost always some cutting, trimming, or grinding to the edge of the midsole-outsole unit prior to completion of the shoe.

## Die Cutting

Die cutting employs a steel die, like that pictured in Figure 7.11. Each die has been formed for a specific size and shape of a shoe outsole. That die will conform to the size and shape of the last that the upper of the shoe is built on. Separate left and right dies exist for each half-size.

**7.10** A specific-size, premolded outsole unit. This outsole will be glued to precut and specific-size midsole components and will require only minor cutting, trimming, or grinding. Note the thicker heel area with a thin border around it. Designs like this are a clue that the outsole was not oversize.

During the die-cutting operation, the die, which has a sharpened edge, is positioned on a sheet of calendered or premolded material as shown in Figure 7.12. Using what is known in the industry as a "clicker" machine, shown in Figure 7.13, the die is stamped through the outsole material in a cookie-cutter fashion. A die can be used to cut outsoles from either soft calendered material or premolded outsole materials.

If the material being cut is a sheet of premolded outsole material, the die-cutting operator is concerned with both getting the most cuts from each sheet of outsole material and cutting the outsoles as quickly as necessary to meet production quotas. The operator is often not concerned with, and usually makes little or no effort to duplicate, the

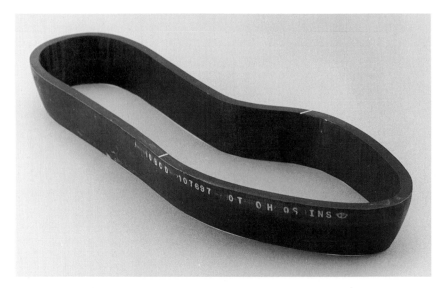

**7.11** A steel die having a sharpened edge on one side, specifically made for one size and shape of outsole. The die can be used to cut through any type of premolded outsole material as well as through the calendered outsole material.

**7.12** A steel die positioned over a sheet of calendered outsole material with the clicker machine arm to the side.

**7.13** A sheet of calendered outsole material being cut with the use of a clicker machine and the steel die.

positioning of the die over the design of the outsole. In some instances, the operator may try to orient the die in a certain way when a particular design must cross the bottom of a shoe in a preferred direction; even so, a great deal of variation occurs in successive cuttings. In some factories, when certain designs of outsole materials are used, marks are placed on the dies to help the operator line up the die with a particular point in the design of the outsole material.

The methods and procedures used in die cutting outsoles result in a series of shoe outsoles that have been cut with the edge or perimeter of the die in a slightly different position almost every time. The specific point in the design of the material along the edge of the outsole around the entire perimeter will vary considerably from one outsole to the next. Figure 7.14 represents a die of the exact same shape and size positioned in four different places on a sheet of premolded herringbone design. Note how much the design varies at the perimeter from one cut to the next. The exact position of the die cut will eventually be duplicated simply because there is a limit to the number of different positions that the die could be in. In factories where the cutting methods and materials involve this type of variation, one outsole can be distinguished from the vast majority of other outsoles cut. How distinguish-

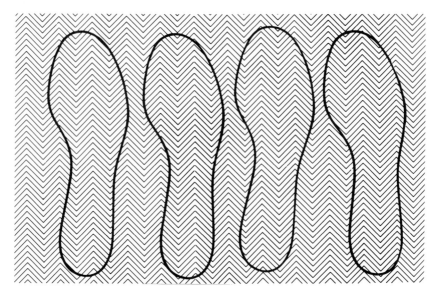

**7.14** Four identically shaped and sized dies placed over a sheet of premolded herringbone design will result in variations in the precise cut of the outside material. The variations are best seen where the design intersects the perimeter of the cut.

**7.15** An enlarged section of an outsole die cut from a sheet of premolded textured material. Note that the slightest movement of the die cut would result in an easily distinguishable difference in the pattern at the perimeter.

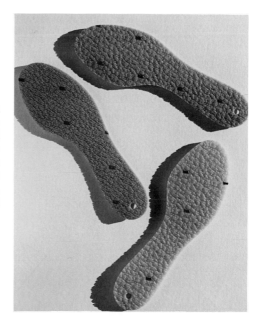

**7.16** Three outsoles cut from a sheet of textured outsole material with the same size and shape die. The outsoles are positioned as they were cut from the sheet. The textured design allows for greater flexibility, and thus greater variation, in the cutting of outsoles.

able each outsole is depends on the repetitive nature of the design of the outsole material, how many times the pattern repeats on any particular sheet of outsole material, whether the design requires that the die be lined up in a certain direction, and whether any markings on the die or efforts by the operator are used to assist in aligning the die and material. This can be elaborated on as illustrated in the examples below:

Figure 7.15 represents an outsole cut from a sheet of premolded material consisting of a finely patterned design. With a design of this type a die could be turned in any direction and would still cut out an acceptable piece of outsole material. Figure 7.16 shows the positions in which three outsoles were die cut from a sheet of premolded material. Because of the fine pattern of the design in Figure 7.15, the slightest movement or change in position of the die would cause an easily discernible change of the design at the perimeter. With a design that can be arranged in any direction, the operator will use every position of the die to get the most cuts from the sheet of outsole material. Outsole materials having designs like this allow for a very large number of possible cutting positions. In order to duplicate any outsole that is cut, the die would have to cut through the exact position on another sheet of identical premolded outside material.

Another example concerns outsole material that, by the very nature of its design, must be positioned on the shoe bottom in a certain direction. Examples are outsole materials having a thicker heel area, those with a name or logo on or across the outsole material, and those having designs, like a herringbone design, that for functional reasons

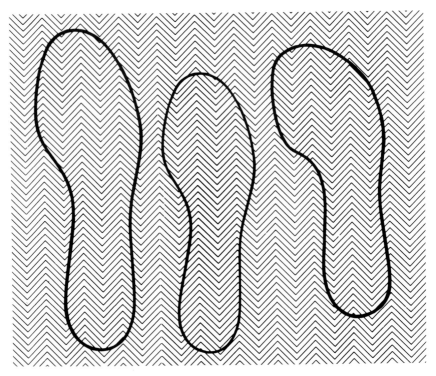

**7.17**   Three dies of different shape or size cannot result in outsoles with identical cut characteristics.

must run across the shoe in a certain direction. Although this restriction somewhat limits the possibilities, there are still an enormous number of distinguishable positions in which the die can cut through outsoles of that type.

The above discussion and examples concerned one die or several dies of the same shape and size. Any time a different shape or different size of die is used, the precise cut will have to change. There is no way in which a cut outsole of one shape or size can be an exact duplication of any other cut outsole of a different shape or size (Figure 7.17).

Outsoles that have been die cut will have a characteristic edge that is straight and contains vertical striations that the cutting die has left in the rubber. In the finishing process, the edge of the die-cut outsole is usually ground smooth or covered with a foxing strip; therefore, those characteristics are usually no longer visible or obvious. In some inexpensive shoes, like the beach thongs shown in Figure 7.18, the die-cut characteristics are still present. These beach thongs also provide an excellent example of the randomness of the cutting process. Figure 7.19

**7.18** Straight edges and striations left from the die blade are characteristic of the die-cut process. In most cases, these striations will be ground away or covered up. In the case of these inexpensive beach thongs, the characteristics still remain.

**7.19** The die cut of the design on these beach thongs as well as the relative position of the strap plugs that pass through the design illustrate the variables of this process.

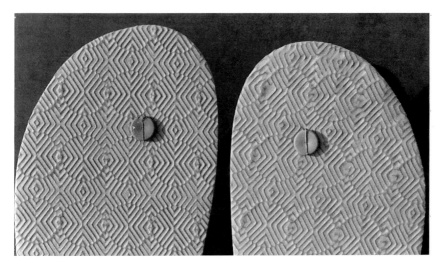

**7.20**　A cast (**A**) and two pairs of shoes (**B** and **C**), from the same subject. Both shoes are the same color, make, size, and style. Based on the size and shape of the logo, which can vary across the premolded sheet of herringbone design, as well as the variables of the die cut process, only one of these shoes (**C**) could have made the impression represented by the cast. The direction of the design on the perimeter (arrows) and the number of rows of design elements from the logo to the toe and heel of the shoe are two of several distinguishable variables of the die-cut process.

**A**

shows the bottoms of two beach thongs. Note the variation in the cut of the material, as well as in the point in the design where the strap plugs intersect the bottoms of the thongs. The chances of finding a second pair of beach thongs, where both the left and right shoes are cut in the same manner and where the strap plugs are in the same positions is possible, but very unlikely.

One case study (Birkett J.) of 78 Adidas sole units die cut from a calendered herringbone material showed that 77 of those were clearly distinguishable. Only one was close to being duplicated, but it was still not a perfect match. The differences were mainly attributable to the

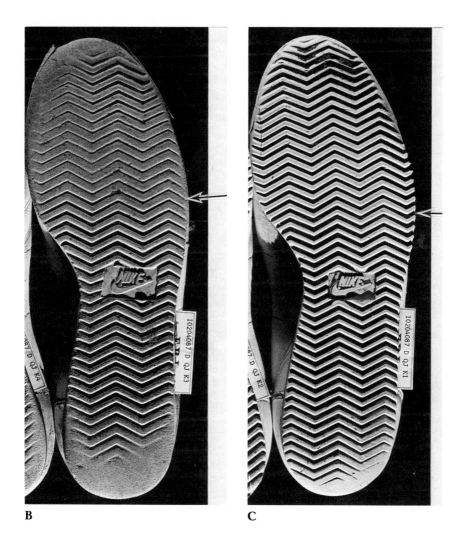

B                                        C

precise position of the cut of each unit and the resulting change in the position and direction of the design around the perimeter.

In another case, illustrated in Figure 7.20, two pairs of shoes of the same make, style, color, and size were obtained from one subject. The outsoles of these shoes were cut from a sheet of premolded material. The logo, which repeats many times across the sheet of the premolded herringbone material, would be centered beneath the die in approximately the same area when the outsole was cut with the die. In this case, the exact size and shape and positioning of the logo in relation to the herringbone design varied in each position across the sheet mold

(Figure 7.20). Each outsole was cut from a different part of a sheet from one mold, or from sheets from two different molds. The shoe outsoles have a different number of herringbone design elements ahead and behind the logo areas. In addition, the herringbone direction is different around the perimeter. These variables reflect the positioning of the die during cutting. Only one of the subject's shoes corresponded with the cast impression.

## Blocker Units

For certain types of shoes, most notably some of the wedge-soled jogging-type shoes, there will be two or more layers or components of midsole and outsole materials combined. Some of these midsole-outsole combinations are referred to as blocker units. The outsole portion of a blocker unit can use either premolded outsole material from sheets, or premolded oversize or premolded specific-size outsoles. The traditional blocker is assembled and then glued to the upper, but in the industry, one-piece, oversize molded midsole-outsole units are also referred to as blockers. In blockers having a separate midsole portion, that portion can be composed of one material or of several materials glued together. The amount of variation between one shoe and the next depends on the manner in which they were assembled and the nature of the components.

In some instances, the blocker unit is purposely made oversize. The entire blocker unit is then die cut into the rough final size and shape (Figure 7.21). Since only the outer edges of these blocker units are cut away with the die and later trimmed or ground, there is far less room for outsole variation from one blocker to the next one of the same size, in contrast to the variation possible with the regular die cutting of sheet goods. Although varying with the design and the particular manufacturing techniques, in most cases there is still enough room in a blocker unit for sufficient variation to distinguish one die-cut blocker outsole from the majority of other blocker outsoles cut with the same die. Figure 7.22 depicts the classic wedge-soled jogging shoe. The blocker unit for this shoe consisted of an oversize outsole-midsole blocker unit that was then die cut and ground to get a beveled wedge look. It was then glued to the shoe upper as evidenced by the glue still visible between the upper and midsole. The edges of outsole units cut in this way will be ground to eliminate any cutting marks left by the die and to even the edges of the midsole and outsole components. If the edges of the outsole and midsole are ground evenly and completely, it indicates that the outsole was probably oversize, cut to rough size with a die, and then ground even with the midsole.

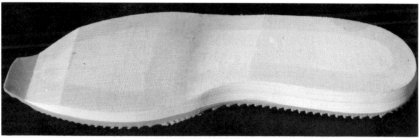

**A**

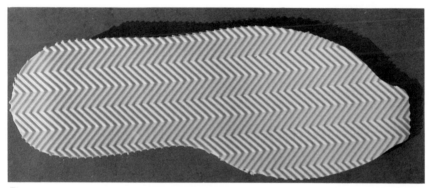

**B**

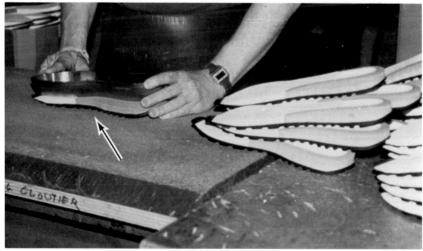

**C**

**7.21** A blocker unit consisting of midsole and outsole glued together (**A**), then die cut to specific size (**B**). A die positioned over an oversized blocker unit (**C**), which will be placed under the clicker machine and cut to final size.

**7.22**   A die-cut blocker unit that has had its edge ground to the wedge-shaped bevel typically found on jogging shoes. The midsole-outsole blocker unit is then glued to the upper.

If the edges of the outsole are not completely ground, but the ground portions are even with the ground midsole (Figure 7.23), it indicates that the outsole was a specific-size outsole that had to be ground only to even its edge where it joined the midsole and possibly to obtain the wedge shape. There will be far less variation possible in shoes of this type.

One published account (Groom PS and Lawton ME, 1987) of a homicide, where both the left and right footwear impressions were left at the scene, provides another good example of how the knowledge of the manufacturer of premolded oversize outsoles, which are later die cut to specific size, can assist in the examination. The questioned left and right impressions showed noticeable differences between them that were attributable to manufacturing variables and the random pairing of mismatched outsoles. The left sole was originally intended for one size of shoe and the right sole for another size. Inventories at the end of the day caused intentional mismatching of the outsoles. The suspect's

**7.23** An enlarged area of the edge of a blocker unit showing a specific-size outsole that was glued to the midsole to form a blocker unit and was then ground to make the joint between the two even. The black outsole was not ground completely and still has part of its original smooth edge, indicating that it was a specific-size outsole.

shoes corresponded with the mismatched size, design, and cut features of the respective left and right impressions. Although there were no identifying characteristics, contact with the manufacturer revealed it would be extremely unlikely that another mismatched pair, exactly like the shoes in question, would exist.

I have investigated numerous cases involving boots or shoes that were mismatched due either to different size blocker units or to variables in the final cutting process. Figure 7.24 depicts the toe areas of two boots in one case that left impressions reflecting those characteristics.

*Using specific-size components to make blockers.* Premolded outsole and midsole components that are carefully precut to fit together in a blocker usually need only minor trimming or grinding to reach completion. Figure 7.25A depicts a blocker unit consisting of a midsole component, an outsole component, and a stabilizing device on the heel. These components were premolded in specific sizes and were then carefully fitted and glued together. The outsole of this unit is featured in

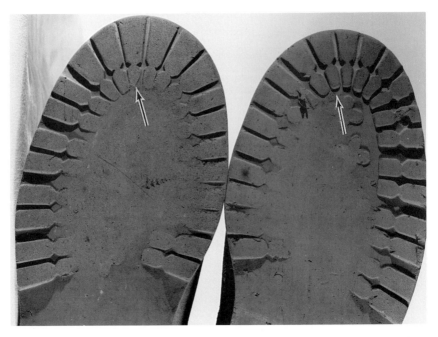

**7.24** A portion of a pair of blocker cut boots showing the mismatch in both pattern and cut. Note the larger "lugs" in the toe area of the outsole on the left.

**7.25** A blocker unit having a midsole component, an outsole component, and a heel stabilizer (**A**). These components were all specifically sized to minimize any necessary trimming, cutting, or grinding. The specific-size outsole on the boots of this unit (**B**).

**7.26**  A specific-size molded outsole glued to the specific-size midsole, which in turn is glued to the upper. The components did not receive any trimming or grinding. Note at the arrow the fine lip of flash protruding from the edge of the black outsole. Also note the smooth edges of the black outsole.

Figure 7.25B. The edges of this outsole, shown in Figure 7.26, reveal the glue between the upper and the white midsole, a small lip of flashing (see arrow) on the specific-size black outsole that was not ground, and the smooth edges of the molded outsole. The edges of a blocker unit like that in Figure 7.25 were obviously not ground like the ones in Figures 7.21, 7.22, 7.23, and 7.27. Close examination of the edges of a shoe of this type, after production, will reveal the method of assembly and the degree of trimming or grinding, if any, that was necessary.

## The Wellman Outsole Cutting Machine

A second method of cutting outsoles is achieved with the Wellman outsole cutting machine, shown in Figure 7.28. This machine uses a knife blade guided by a template to cut each outsole from calendered outsole material. The knife blade and template can be seen in Figure 7.29. The Wellman outsole cutting machine *cannot* be used to cut premolded sheet materials or premolded outsoles because those materials are already vulcanized and are too hard. It can *only* be used to cut the soft, calendered (unvulcanized) rubber.

**7.27** An enlarged photo of a section of the edge of a blocker unit like the one in Figure 7.23, which shows the amount of trimming or grinding. Note that the complete edge of the black outsole and the white midsole are ground evenly. This indicates that the outsole was possibly not a specific-size outsole and therefore may have significant variations from others of the same type and size.

The outsole cutting process uses a different template for each half-size and shape. The outsole material is passed beneath the head of the Wellman outsole cutter. With each cut, the template presses against the material as the cutting knife rapidly travels around the template and cuts the outsole from the calendered material. An experienced operator can quickly guide and move a slab of calendered outsole material through the machine, cutting six to ten outsoles in a few seconds. The knife will ride around the edge of the template at an angle, which can be adjusted. It will therefore cut the edge of the material at an angle, resulting in an outsole with a angled edge. The angled edge can slope either way, depending on whether the outsole material was cut with the design facing up or down. In addition, the knife blade will often draw the soft, calendered material into a fine, raised edge around the perimeter. Both the angle of the cut and the fine edge can be seen in Figure 7.30. The angled edge may or may not still be evident in the finished shoe.

The end result of the methods and procedures used in the outsole cutting process are similar to those that occur in the die-cutting method

**7.28** The Wellman outsole cutting machine. The sheet (or slab) of material is pulled beneath the cutting head where a template guides a knife to cut out each outsole. The operator controls the rate at which the material is pulled through and thus the speed at which the outsoles are cut. During each cut, the material must stop while the template is pressed against the material and the cutting takes place.

**7.29** A closer view of the cutting head of the Wellman outsole cutting machine shows the cutting knife (arrow) traveling around the template.

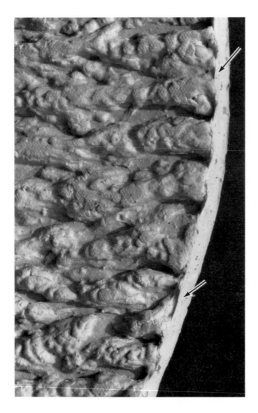

**7.30** An enlarged area of an outsole cut from soft, calendered rubber on a Wellman outsole cutting machine. Note the randomly cut angled edge and the lip of rubber that results from the knife blade spreading the soft material.

**7.31** A slab of calendered rubber that had seven outsoles cut from it. Only one has been removed. The point at which the edge of the sheet begins and the point and position of the first cut, the angle at which the slab passes beneath the cutting head, and the distance between each cut outsole are all random.

**7.32** Two successive outsoles from the sheet pictured in Figure 7.31. Note the position of the number 10 (arrows) and the variations in the cut around the perimeter.

inasmuch as the perimeter of the cut also varies considerably from one outsole to the next. In addition, since only the soft, calendered outsole material (and not premolded outsole material) is used with this process, Wellman-cut shoes will also include the variation associated with soft, unvulcanized calendered material.

Figure 7.31 depicts a slab from which seven outsoles were cut. The machine operator usually positions the slab of outsole material so that the portion comprising the heel area will be proportionally correct. This is particularly necessary when the material is thicker in the heel area or has a dividing strip that contains repeating words like "Made in USA." For that reason, variation within each size will be greater laterally (along the direction the slab is fed through the machine), than longitudinally (heel to toe). Variation will also occur due to slight changes in the position of the slab as the operator pulls it beneath the cutting head. If the slab passes beneath the cutting head at an angle, it will cause the design and any marking, like the size, that may be impressed by the template with each cut to shift in its position on each subsequent outsole.

Figure 7.32 depicts a pair of outsoles from the slab in Figure 7.31. Note the different positions of the number "10." This size number was pressed into the outsole by the template. Since the slab passed beneath the template at an angle, the position of the "10" and the entire cut shifted slightly. Also, the slabs of calendered outsole material are randomly cut from a continuous feed of outsole material from the calendering operation, so the beginning point of each slab is also random. In addition, as previously discussed, the soft, pliable nature of calendered outsole material, which has not been vulcanized, is subject to stretching (from handling) and shrinking (from cooling) and is also very prone to pick up random defects during the handling and assembly of the shoe. Figure 7.33 depicts an enlarged view of a portion of those outsoles. Note the variance in the cut, as well as the defects in the outsole's soft material. One area of this particular design is actually void of any texture and contains totally random characteristics in the form of air entrapped in the rubber compound as it was mixed.

Wellman cutting is found predominantly on boots and shoes. The outsoles of the boots in Figure 7.34 have been cut on a Wellman cutting machine from soft, calendered material that has no design in the heel area. The beveled cut is still visible on the edge of the outsole. Molded heels were then added, as was a foxing strip, a steel shank label, and a size label. In the popular "duck boot," shown in Figure 7.35A, the beveled edge is cut at a sharp angle with the design facing down, so it can be pulled around the rubber upper and stitched in that position (Figure 7.35B). The outsole is then vulcanized to the shoe upper in that position.

## Finishing Cut Shoes

In addition to cutting or molding outsoles, many additions and modifications are made during the assembly and finishing of a shoe that can leave characteristics in an impression. Some of those are:

*Positioning the outsole on the lasted upper.* Many outsoles are glued to the shoe upper. Shoes glued in this manner usually have visible glue lines or evidence of glue where the midsole meets the upper. The glue

**A**

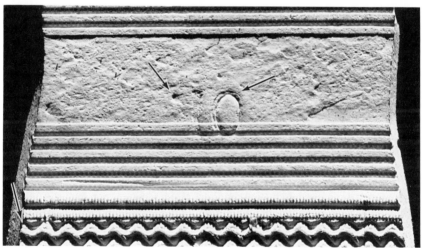

**B**

**7.33** An enlarged area of the two outsoles in Figure 7.32. Note the varied position of the number 10, the variance of the edge, the damage to the outsole from handling it, and the void spaces in the nondesigned area, which are totally random.

merely establishes that the outsole or outsole-midsole unit was made separately before being attached to the shoe. If the components of the shoe were unvulcanized, they would be attached in a different manner. The upper of the shoe would be dipped in a latex glue bath, deep enough

**A**

**7.34** These boots are typical of the type of boot made with calendered materials and the Wellman outsole cutting machine. Note the angled edge of the outsole, which is still visible in this type of boot, the added foxing strip, the size tag, and the mispositioned heels.

**B**

to cover and penetrate the lower areas of the upper that will contact the outsole and foxing strips. The outsole, foxing strips, separate heels and other items could then be pressed against the latex glue areas of the shoe upper and would be temporarily held in place. They would be permanently bonded to each other and to the upper of the shoe when vulcanized. In the case of unvulcanized outsoles, which are soft and pliable and able to stretch and adapt to the lasted upper, the precise positioning and contouring of each outsole can vary more.

*Stitching.* The term stitching refers to the use of a hand tool to press the various soft rubber components to one another. Marks left by the stitching tool resembling serrations can be seen in the boots in Figures 7.35B and 7.36. The heel in Figure 7.36A is a molded heel that is temporarily attached to the soft outsole and permanently bonded during vulcanization. Its smooth sides and edges are characteristic of a molded heel. Figure 7.36B shows a heel that has been die cut from soft, calendered material and then stitched to the upper. Note the rubber drawn over the edge of the heel as a result of the die cutting through the soft, calendered material.

*Positioning the heel.* Figures 7.34, 7.35, and 7.36 depict outsoles that were cut from material that has no heel design. The heels, either

A

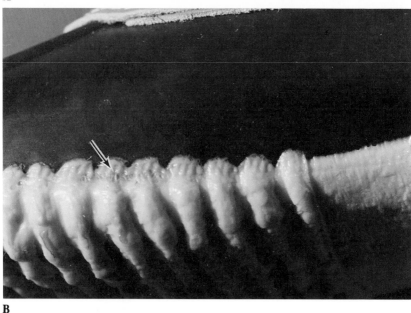

B

**7.35** These boots, sometimes called duck boots (**A**), are also cut on the Wellman machine but with the outsole design facing down. The angled edge of the outsole is then drawn around, stitched tightly to, and vulcanized to the upper (**B**).

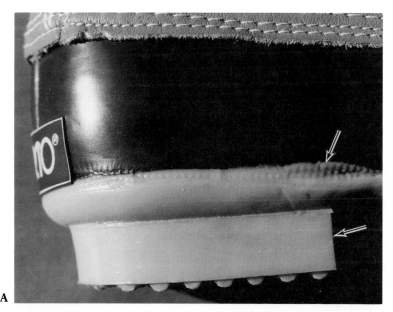

A

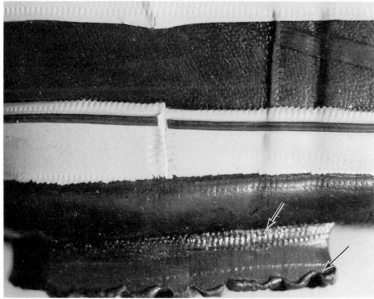

B

**7.36** Two boots that have Wellman-cut outsoles. The boot in **A** has a pre-molded heel. Notice the straight and smooth edges. The boot in **B** has a heel that has been die cut from soft, unvulcanized material, as evidenced by the soft rubber that has been pulled over the edge and by the stitching on the sides of the heel. Note in both boots the numerous stitch marks used to temporarily hold the pieces together.

**7.37**   A premolded heel with torn flashing that has been positioned on an unvulcanized outsole. The torn edge (arrows) is a random identifying characteristic.

molded or cut from unvulcanized, calendered material are then positioned temporarily until they are bonded during the vulcanization process. As a result, a number of additional variations can occur.

1. If the heels are molded, they can come from a variety of different molds, each possibly having distinguishing features. For example, if there is a choice of eight heels, each of the same general design but still distinguishable, the chance of having a pair of shoes with two heels from the same mold will be far less than if there were only one possible molded heel. In addition, some heels may have distinctive features associated with them. Figure 7.37 depicts a random edge where the flashing of a molded heel was torn. This was not an accident; the usual way of removing the flash from the heel in this particular factory was to tear it off.
2. The heels can be die cut from calendered material, adding a random cut heel pattern in combination to the already random cut outsole.
3. The heels will vary in their exact position and angle, since they are positioned by hand.
4. Another factor associated with the heel is string that occasionally protrudes from premolded heels; these pieces of string are used to temporarily tie it to the outsole until it is vulcanized.

*Foxing strips.* An item known as a foxing strip is frequently used to give added bond between the outsole and the upper and also to cover the edges of the various outsole materials. This foxing strip, made of unvulcanized rubber, is wrapped around the perimeter of the shoe. The area where it begins and ends is either a butt joint or an overlap joint. The exact location and characteristics of these joints vary immensely and provide additional random features that often show up in an impression.

*Adding toe guards.* As explained later in the description of the construction of the Converse Chuck Taylor All-Star shoe, the addition of a toe guard, particularly an unvulcanized toe guard, contributes another potential variable to the outsole area of the shoe. Toe guards are frequently added to boots and athletic shoes.

*Adding labels, logos, size tags, etc.* Small pieces of rubber containing the shoe size, brand name, and other information are placed by hand on the heel, the sides, or the bottom of the shoe. Since these labels are often hand cut or have a variety of shapes, they can add yet another variable to the bottom surface of a shoe (Figure 7.34A).

The entire assembled shoe would then be placed in a pressure chamber, like the one pictured in Figure 7.38, where the materials would be vulcanized and would be permanently bonded together.

## Word of Caution

Many of the features of the cut processes, such as the appearance of the cut material, the presence of the foxing strips, and the duck boot look, are copied, for aesthetic reasons, in the molded processes. In other words, when a mold is made, the designer of that mold will sometimes place certain features in the mold that simulate various characteristics usually associated with cut shoes. Some examples of these are shown in the section on molded shoes. It is essential, therefore, to initially distinguish between a cut shoe and a molded shoe.

## Siping Shoes

Siped outsoles have had a series of small cuts (sipes) placed in them *after* they are molded. Sipes are commonly found in deck or boat shoes. They are added to the outsole to increase the traction of the shoe on wet surfaces. Sipes that are cut into the outsole should not be confused with the similar, but larger, grooves that are actually part of the molded design in some shoes. Figure 7.39 depicts shoes that have molded grooves. The molded grooves will be the same for all shoes from a particular mold. The shoes in Figure 7.40 have true sipes that have been

**7.38**  Pressure chamber for vulcanizing shoes.

**7.39**  A molded deck shoe. The grooves in this outsole were molded, not siped.

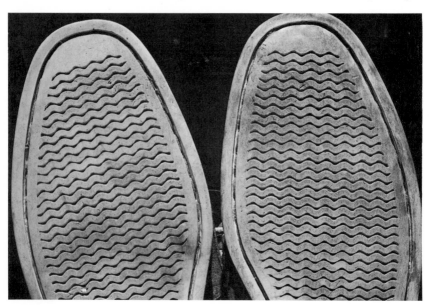

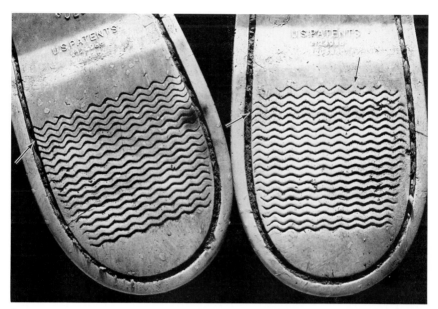

**A**

**7.40** Heels of a pair of deck shoes with true sipes (**A**). Note that the heel on the left has 19 sipes while the one on the right has 20 sipes. Note the uneven spacing of the sipes on the heel on the left. The direction of the sipe design where it intersects the perimeter also varies. Also note that portions of the first sipe on the heel on the right have disappeared after some wear, indicating they were not of an even depth. In another area (**B**), the contrast between worn and unworn sipes can be seen. The general appearance of the worn sipes appear significantly different although they once were the same as the unworn sipes.

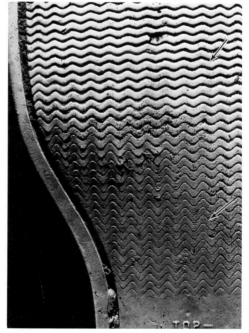

**B**

A

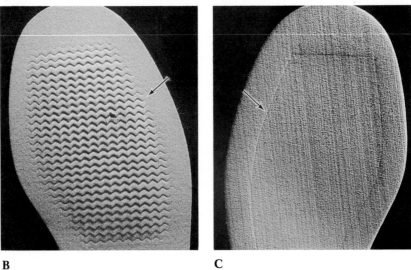

B                                        C

**7.41** A siping machine cutting one row at a time across the full outsole. The arrow points to the wavy cutting blade (**A**). Part of an outsole that has been siped in a specific area by placing a template beneath that area (**B**). The corresponding impression of the template on the opposite side of the outsole is still visible (**C**). By placing a hard template, shaped like the area depicted in **C**, beneath the outsole and running the outsole beneath a siping machine like the one shown in **A**, only the area as depicted in B will be siped.

cut into the outsole. True sipes will vary considerably from one shoe to the next. True sipes are usually tightly closed unless the shoe outsole is flexed. It is noted, however, that the tightly closed sipes can get filled with dirt, which, combined with wear, causes them to appear more open. This can be seen in the worn and unworn areas of the shoes in Figure 7.40.

True sipes can be cut into the outsole with either a single siping blade or a series of siping blades. If a single siping blade is used, each row of sipes will be cut individually while the outsole is advanced beneath the siping blade. This is shown in Figure 7.41A. If a series of siping blades is used, the entire number of sipes can be cut into the outsole at one time. Whether a single blade or a series of blades is used, the location of the sipes can be controlled by varying the surface beneath the outsole. For instance, if an outsole is placed against a hard surface, such as in Figure 7.41A, the siping blade will cut across the entire outsole. If a hard template of a particular shape is placed beneath the outsole, then the siping blade will only cut the area over top of that template, resulting in a siped area of the same shape as the template. The areas not having a hard surface beneath them will simply be pushed away by the siping blade. Parts B and C of Figure 7.41 depict the front and back of a portion of a siped outsole using a template. Note the limited area of the siping in the outsole and the impression left by the template on the corresponding back side of the outsole.

There are many variations associated with the siping of a shoe outsole. The exact position of each cut can vary immensely because of the relationship of the positions of the outsole to the blade. This is most noticeable at the point where each row of sipes ends, whether it be at the edge of the shoe or within the border of the outsole. In other operations, particularly where forms or templates are used, the position of the sipe cuts may be very close from one outsole to the next. In addition, because sipe blades become dull and because of other variables, there are frequently areas along each sipe that are not cut as deeply as adjacent areas. As the outsole is worn down, those areas will become smooth sooner. With the use of single sipe blades, the outsole may not advance evenly beneath the blade, thus causing some rows of sipes to be spaced differently (Figure 7.40).

## The Molding Processes

Molded outsoles are manufactured using different molding processes, such as compression molding, injection molding, and open-pour molding. In the case of the previously discussed cut outsoles, some of the outsole material was initially molded but was then cut, trimmed, or siped to reach its final shape, size, and design. In molded outsoles, as discussed hereafter, the entire outsole is formed in a mold, resulting in an outsole that has taken on the shape, size, and detailed design of that specific mold cavity. One or more mold pairs are usually made for each half-size of shoe.

## Mold Manufacturing

Most molds for shoe outsoles are made by a process known as hand milling. Two additional methods of mold making are being used increasingly but still represent a small percentage of the molds made. Those methods include (1) molds that are milled at the direction of a computer-assisted design–computer-assisted manufacture (CAD-CAM) machine and (2) molds that are cast from a shoe model.

*Hand-milling or hand-engraved molds.* The hand-milling technique is by far the most predominant method of mold making. It uses a pantograph to transfer the design from precut templates or patterns into a steel or aluminum alloy mold blank. Many variables are encountered throughout this operation. As a result, successive hand-milled molds being made for the molding of shoes of identical size and design will have distinguishable differences in their *gross design.* The term gross design refers to the portions of design that are milled from the mold and does not include any stippling or texture that may later be placed into the mold surface.

The variables in the hand-milling method occur for a number of reasons. The same template can be, and often is, used to rout out molds for different sizes of the same design. This results in different quantities of that design being transferred to each mold. In other words, as the size of the mold increases or decreases, there will be more or less of the design transferred from the same template to each mold blank. In addition, templates of the same general design, but with slight differences, can be used to rout out identically sized molds, that, as far as the mold maker is concerned, are the same design. For instance, a mold maker may have many templates of a general herringbone design; however, each may be slightly different. If the shoe outsole is composed of several different designs, more than one template, each having a different design, might be used. These various possibilities, combined with the fact that each of these templates, as well as the mold blanks, are readjusted or repositioned during the mold-making process, prevent different molds made in this manner from being exactly the same, even though they are being produced to make shoes of the same size and design (Figure 7.42). (The results of this can also be seen in cases cited in this book, such as in Figure 10.2.)

*CAD-CAM manufacturing of molds.* Another way in which molds are engraved is with the use of a CAD-CAM process, wherein a design is

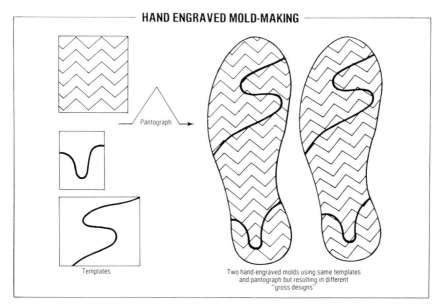

HAND ENGRAVED MOLD-MAKING

Pantograph

Templates

Two hand-engraved molds using same templates and pantograph but resulting in different "gross designs"

**7.42** A simplified illustration of how hand-engraved (hand-milled) mold-making results in differences between molds made for outsoles of the same size and design.

generated and stored in a computer. The computer then directs the engraving machine to mill that design into the mold blank. In this system, two successive molds will usually have identical or closely identical gross designs.

*Casting a shoe model to make a mold.* Another way to make a mold is by casting, which is commonly used for low-pressure molding processes such as those used in open-pour polyurethane outsoles. This involves first making a model of the shoe. The model can be of wood, metal, or a combination of materials. On this model, the shoe name, texture, and other characteristics can be added. Figure 7.43 shows a wooden model that has been covered with different design materials. The gaps at the joints or seams where the different materials meet are visible and can be seen in the outsoles made from this group of molds (Figure 7.44). The model is then mounted on a base around which a mold frame is built. The model is then sprayed with a thin metal coating. An epoxy-based fill with aluminum resin is poured around the model. When the cast is set, the model is removed. Then the top half of the mold is similarly prepared. Because of the softer alloy usually used,

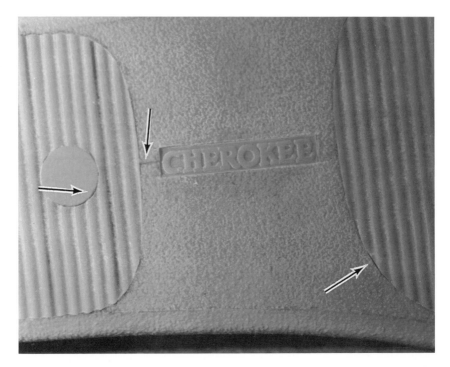

**7.43**   Wood mold model covered with materials to create a design. Note the areas where the different materials are joined together unevenly. This model will be covered with metal by a special metal spray deposition process. A mold will then be cast from it.

these molds easily acquire nicks, dents, and scratches, which will then be transferred to the outsole. Two outsoles made from the same original model are depicted in Figure 7.44; they contain numerous nicks that can be used to distinguish one from another.

*Molds with inserts placed into them.*  Some molds are made with an area void of a design or logo that can hold a premolded insert. The insert, which can be either a portion of the design in a different color or a logo, can then be placed into the mold before each outsole is molded. Figure 7.51A depicts a portion of an outsole that has a premolded insert. In this case, it was placed into the mold prior to the addition of the biscuit of rubber in a compression-molding process.

Other molds, such as the one used to mold the outsole in Figure 7.45, have a removable piece containing a logo that can be removed from the mold and replaced with either a different logo, a blank, or a piece having the same design as the rest of the outsole.

**A**

**B**

**7.44** Two outsoles from two molds made from the same model. Although the gross designs of the molds are identical, since they were cast from the same model, differences have resulted from nicks and other accidental occurrences to the molds, a few of which are pointed out.

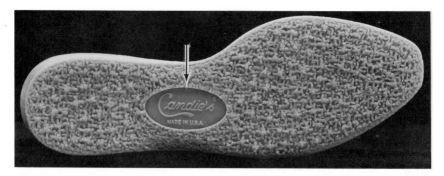

**7.45**   An outsole that originated from a mold having a removable slug containing the logo. By changing the slug, the same mold could be used to mold an outsole with another logo, with a slug having the same design as the rest of the outsole, or with no design at all.

## *Stippled or Textured Areas of the Mold Surface*

Many molds have portions of their surface stippled or textured. This stippling or texture must be added after the gross design of the mold is made. Regardless of whether a mold is hand milled or is milled with the CAD-CAM operation, the stippled areas are added to the molds by hand with the use of a steel die punch. This is accomplished by a skilled craftsperson who uses the steel die punch and a hammer and artfully punches the design into the selected areas of the mold. Figure 7.46 depicts a steel die and some of the innumerable choices of stippling. The surface of the die is small and is repositioned with each strike of the hammer. Many strikes of the die are required to stipple the entire area. Variations in the force and angle with which the punch is struck, as well as the exact relationship of the position of successive strikes of the punch to both each other and the gross design of the mold, result in a random and unique pattern of hand stippling on each mold. The combined positioning of characteristics of the stippling is so unique that it becomes a "fingerprint" of the mold. In most cases, only a small area of stippling is needed to reach this uniqueness. The significance of this method is that it enables specific items of footwear, in which the hand stippling is still present, to leave footwear impressions that can be found through comparisons not only to correspond in size and gross design but to have come from the exact same mold. This can be determined without ever seeing the mold, simply through the knowledge that this stippling is unique to only one mold.

In the case of molds made by casting a model of the shoe, it is possible that more than one mold could be made from the same model, although manufacturers say that this is not usually done. If different models were used for multiple molds of one size, any textured or stippled material that might be laminated onto the mold model would be in different positions.

Very fine texturing is also placed on some mold surfaces instead of stippling. Texture can be placed on mold surfaces in a variety of ways, such as sandblasting or chemical etching. These types of textured surfaces are also random, but usually do not leave as detailed an impression, since they are more shallow. They also wear off the outsole more rapidly.

Some molds also contain a few stippled marks, usually put on at the factory and not in the mold-making operation. These marks are used for various reasons, one of which is to identify each specific mold. (One such mark is featured in Chapter 10, Figure 10.9A.) In addition, some manufacturers will place a coded pattern of stipples or marks on the back side of the molds of both heels and soles, which is a date code that will later enable them to determine when that heel or sole was molded. An example of this is shown in Figure 7.46D. This kind of information could be used to identify the make and date of manufacture of shoes found with skeletal remains.

## The Significance of Mold Making to Casework

The understanding of how molds are made and the recognition of characteristics associated with molds can enhance footwear impression examinations. Figure 7.47 depicts a questioned impression, and the respective portion of the known impression. The stippling pattern is the same. Figure 7.48 shows a lifted impression and the corresponding area of a test impression and the known shoe. The arrows are pointing to milling marks that remained in the mold and are transferred to each outsole formed in that mold. In addition, the stippling is still evident in certain areas and also corresponds. In both of these cases, because the mold markings and stippling are unique to only one mold, it can be determined that the shoe that made the crime scene impression came from the same exact mold as the known shoe.

In Figure 7.49, an impression on a piece of board was compared with a shoe that belonged to a suspect. The shoes were found not to be identical based on mold differences. Several days later, another suspect was investigated that had shoes that were identical to the first suspect's shoes in size, brand, color, and design. The shoes of the second suspect agreed in mold characteristics and also contained identifying characteristics that resulted in a positive identification. Enlarged areas of the shoes of both suspects revealed some of the mold characteristics that enabled elimination of one suspect's shoe and contributed to the identification of the second suspect's shoe.

In another case, a pair of casts representing a left and a right basketball shoe were submitted along with the shoes of a suspect. The casts

A

B

**7.46** A steel die (**A**) is used to place a stippled design (**B**) on mold surfaces. The steel die is hand struck with a hammer (**C**). The combination of the precise placement, angle, and force of each strike will create a pattern that is unique to each mold. Similar markings are also sometimes found on the reverse sides of outsoles or heels (**D**). They are placed there to enable the manufacturer to later determine the approximate date of manufacture.

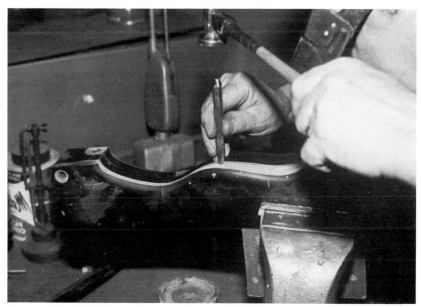

C

D

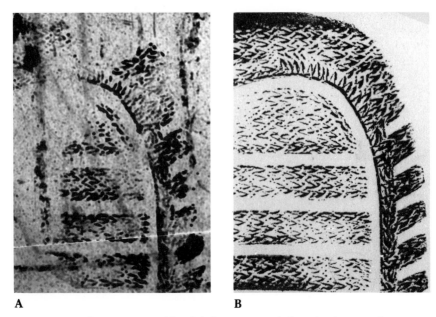

**A**                                    **B**

**7.47**   A stipple pattern in blood **(A)** corresponded with the stipple pattern evident in the test impression of the known shoe **(B)**. From that comparison, it can be determined that the shoe that made the impression and the known shoe came from the same exact mold.

were of deep impressions, made in thick, wet, claylike mud. Portions of impressions represented by the cast were somewhat distorted and reflected some twisting or movement during the impression-making process. Other areas of the cast reflected clearer detail. The overall lengths of the impressions were $\frac{1}{2}$ to $\frac{3}{4}$ inches shorter than the respective shoes. Dimensions of other parts were also slightly smaller. It was likely that the heavy soil was totally saturated with water and therefore collapsed back into the impressions the shoes had made. There were several mold characteristics evident in the cast impressions, and they agreed with the respective characteristics in the suspect's shoes. The manufacturer was contacted, and it was determined that the suspect's shoes and the shoes that made the impression could have originated from only one right mold and one left mold. Figure 7.50 depicts a small portion of one of the casts and the respective area of the suspect's shoe.

## Compression-Molded Outsoles

The compression-molding process is an "open-mold" process. Open mold means that the mold is open when the outsole material, usually rubber or ethyl vinyl acetate, is placed into the mold cavity. The mold

**7.48** A lift of a dusted impression (center), the known impression (bottom), and a reverse photograph of the known shoe (top) all show identical milling marks and stippling.

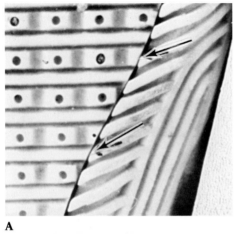

A

B

**7.49** Enlarged portions of the known shoes of the first suspect (**A**) and the known shoes of the second suspect (**B**) show the minor, but very significant, mold differences between two pairs of shoes of the same brand, design, and size. The first suspect's shoes did not make the questioned impression in this case.

closes during the molding process. Compression molds are usually two-piece molds. Some are hinged together, while others have a top half and bottom half that are opposingly mounted in the compression-molding machine. A premixed and weighed *biscuit* of rubber, ethyl vinyl acetate, or other outsole material is placed between the two halves of the mold. The mold is closed and placed under considerable heat and pressure for several minutes. This melts the outsole materials and allows them to conform to the size and shape of the mold. Excess material escapes from the side of the mold where the two halves of the mold meet and is referred to as flash. The flash is later trimmed off. The resulting molded outsoles are accurate representations of the mold, and each contains the specific class characteristics of that mold. This method may be likened to making waffles, where the batter is placed on

**7.50**   An enlarged area of a cast
**(A)** and of the suspect's shoe **(B)**
with the same mold characteristics. None of the other seven
molds in that size and none of
the molds of adjacent sizes
shared the same combined characteristics. A couple of those
characteristics are pointed out.

A

B

the bottom waffle iron, the top half of the waffle iron is closed, and the
excess batter leaks out the sides. Figure 7.51A depicts a compression
mold. In this particular operation, an insert with the manufacturer's
logo is first placed into the mold and is then covered with a large biscuit
of rubber. Figure 7.51B depicts the molded outsoles being removed. The
finished outsole was shown in Figure 7.51B.

Compression-molded outsoles can also be made with two colors
using a three- or four-piece compression mold. A four-section mold is
pictured in Figure 7.52. This four-section mold consists of (1) a section
that contains the outsole design, (2) a section that is a cover plate that
will fit over the top of the first section, (3) a section that represents the
side walls of the outsole-midsole area, and (4) a section that represents
the top part of the mold. To explain how a two-color outsole-midsole
unit can be made, an example of a two-color unit having a blue outsole
and a white midsole will be used. First, a small biscuit of blue rubber is
placed into the first section of the mold, which contains the outsole
design. The cover plate (second section) is placed on top of the first
section and the two sections are then placed into the compression-
molding machine for approximately 1 minute. The cover plate will
confine the melted blue material to a restricted area over the outsole

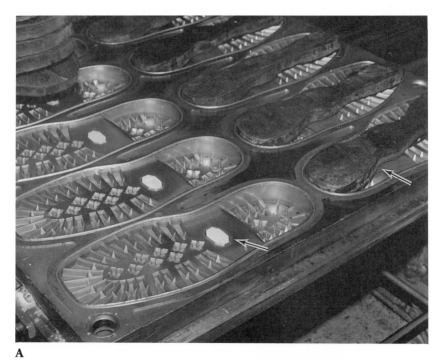

A

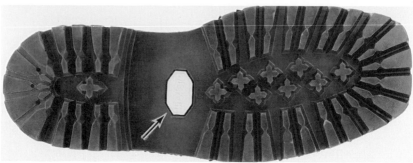

B
**7.51** A compression molding machine process. A small, premolded piece of rubber containing a brand name is placed into position on the bottom half of the mold (**A**). A biscuit of black rubber is then placed over it. The bottom half of the mold is then joined with the top half and, under heat and pressure, the black biscuit of rubber melts and conforms to the size and shape of that mold and the small rubber logo insert. The resulting outsole contains the logo in one color with the black outsole (**B**).

**7.52** A four-section mold used to prepare two-color, compression-molded outsoles (**A**). An enlarged area of a pair of outsoles made with this mold (**B**). Note the area of flash between the two colors that has been trimmed (see arrow).

A

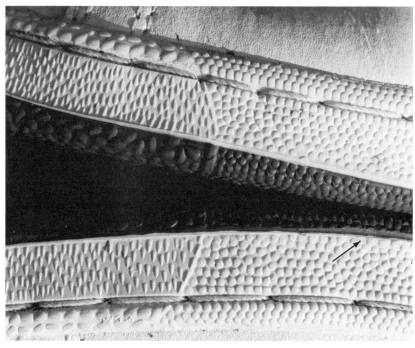

B

design, thus forming a thin blue layer of outsole. Next, the mold is removed, the cover plate is taken off, and section three is placed over section one. Section three represents the sidewalls of the mold, which contain the design of the midsole area. The white biscuit of rubber, which will be formed into the midsole, is placed on top of the already melted blue outsole. Then the fourth section is placed on top of the biscuit and section three. Sections one, three, and four, still containing the already formed blue outsole and now containing the white biscuit material, are then placed back into the compression-molding machine for the duration of the molding process. The white biscuit melts and conforms to the midsole area and also covers and adheres to the already formed blue outsole. When the mold is opened, a two-colored molded outsole can be removed.

Many of the outsoles having two, three, or even more colors are made in this manner. Instead of placing a blue biscuit of rubber to cover the entire bottom, the mold will have "dammed" sections into which different color rubber could be placed.

There will be some flash, usually at the point where the mold parts meet, that will need to be trimmed. The precise hills and valleys and beginning and ending points where the flash is manually trimmed are very individual and are occasionally reproduced in deep three-dimensional impressions or in impressions on clothing, sheets, etc., in which the material may wrap around the side of the shoe during the impression-making process. An enlarged area of a pair of two-color compression-molded outsoles that were molded in a four-piece mold like the one described above is depicted in Figure 7.52B. Note that the flash formed at the point where the two colors meet has been trimmed away.

In almost all instances, especially in the popular size ranges, a manufacturer using compression molding will have more than one mold for each size in a particular design. This is because it takes several minutes to mold each outsole using the compression-molding process. In most instances, the precise gross design in these molds, even though they may have been made by the same mold manufacturer, will vary from mold to mold because they are almost always made by the hand-milled method. As an example, in one particular design of shoe currently being sold, the manufacturer has over 30 different mold sets (left and right together) for a single common size. These molds have been produced by several different mold makers over a span of 40 years. All the molds have distinctive variations in the gross design features and can easily be distinguished from one another.

*Converse Chuck Taylor All-Star shoes.*   A good example of the compression-molding process and the way in which a shoe having a unit sole is assembled can be seen in the Converse Chuck Taylor All-Star

(CCTAS) basketball shoe (Bodziak WJ, 1986; Hamm ED, 1989). This shoe provides an example of some of the incredible number of variables that can be encountered in the manufacturing of footwear. The CCTAS shoe is one of the most popular and most widely recognized basketball shoes made. First introduced in the early 1900s, its design was like that of many other sneakers, having a canvas upper and a rubber sole. Variations of its current outsole design have been used for over 50 years.

The CCTAS outsoles are compression molded. A pair of CCTAS shoes is shown in Figure 7.53. With the exception of a few of the large sizes, the manufacturer has and uses many molds for each size of outsole. These molds have been made and accumulated over a number of years. Additional molds have occasionally been made to increase production or to replace the older ones.

During the factory production of these outsoles, several hundred molds covering the normal size distributions, will be used. The molds have all been hand milled. The gross design of each mold is distinguishable from other molds, both within the same size and between different sizes. The outsoles are compression molded in pairs of left and right outsoles of the same size; however, as they are taken from the molds, the left outsoles and the right outsoles are intentionally separated. There is no factory requirement or logical need to keep together the respective left and right outsoles that originated from a particular mold pair. Instead, as the shoes near the completion stage, a left shoe is paired with a right shoe of the same size and color.

As an example, if there were 15 different mold pairs in one size, each distinguishable from the other due to variations in the gross mold characteristics, and the left and right outsoles from each were separated during the assembly process, the chances of the same left and right outsoles being paired together for sale would be small. Figure 7.54 depicts the variable mold features found in two pairs of purchased size 9 CCTAS shoes. Close examination of these two pairs of size 9 outsoles will reveal that gross mold characteristics of the two left shoes and those of the two right shoes are different in many respects. In addition, the left and the right shoes of each pair, as well as the left and the right shoes in Figure 7.53 are not mirror images of each other.

Some of the variation that can be found between the outsoles from different molds can be seen in the three pairs of shoes represented in Figures 7.53 and 7.54; they are numbered in the impression in Figure 7.55 and include:

*Variations, in both the number and design of the transverse bars that cross the toe and heel areas.* The number of bars varies significantly throughout the population of all sizes of outsoles and also varies significantly within each size. For instance, in Figure 7.54, three outsoles have four bars in the toe, while one has five bars. Of

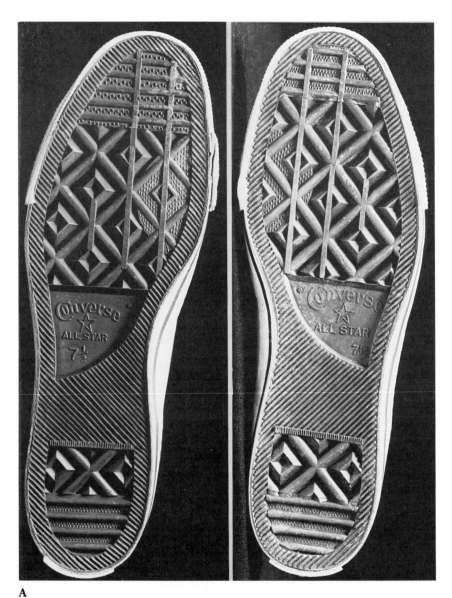

**A**

**7.53** A pair of size 7½ CCTAS outsoles (**A**) and an enlarged area showing the gap produced by the overlap of the second foxing strip (**B**). A factory worker placing the foxing strip on a CCTAS shoe (**C**). The person placing the foxing strip on the shoe will not do so exactly the same way each time.

B

C

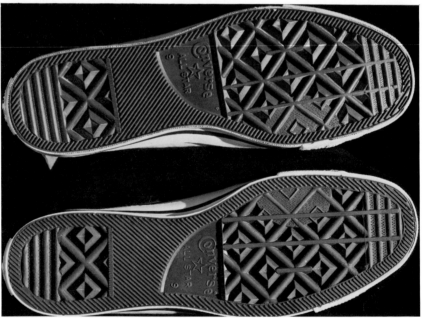

**7.54** Two pairs of size 9 CCTAS outsoles that depict the many variations found between CCTAS shoes.

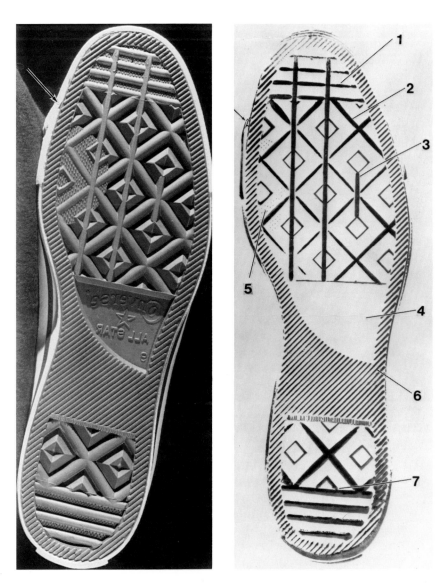

**7.55** An impression of one of the shoes in Figure 7.54 and a reverse photograph of that shoe. Numbers on the impression refer to (1) the transverse bars found in the toe and heel areas, (2) the diamond design, (3) longitudinal bars, (4) shoe brand and size area, (5) stippling, (6) diagonal lines, and (7) flash (see corresponding area of shoe).

the three shoes that have four bars, all are distinguishable from one another based on the specifics of the bar design alone. Variations also occur between the exact configurations of the heel bars as well in each of the four shoes, even though all four shoes contain four bars in the heel. Variations occur both in the toe bars and in the heel bars; however, they are usually more pronounced in the toe area.

*Variations in the features and position of the diamond designs on the outsole.* The outsole design includes numerous diamond shapes that in turn have a smaller diamond located within them. In adult sizes, these diamonds are the same size from one outsole to the next, regardless of the outsole size. The diamonds are found in both the heel area of the outsole and in an area of the sole between the transverse bars of the toe area and a transverse border that runs across the middle of the shoe. Because the size of those diamonds remains the same, the number of them will increase as the size of the outsole increases, and thus the position of those diamonds relative to the border and other design elements will change. Even on outsoles of the same size, because of variation in the way molds are made, there will be different positioning of these diamonds relative to the surrounding design. The variation in the position of these diamonds in usually most noticeable where they intersect the toe bars, the transverse border, and other design elements on the outsole. In the heel area, the general positioning of the diamond design is somewhat similar from mold to mold, however, the overall size of that area can also vary, as can be seen in one heel area in Figure 7.54B.

*Longitudinal bar designs.* Running lengthwise, intersecting the corners of the diamonds in the front half of the outsole, perpendicular to and passing through the transverse toe bars, are longitudinal bars. Their presence and intersection with other design elements helps to further distinguish outsoles from different molds. Other longitudinal bars are shorter and pass through only a small portion of the diamond design.

*Shoe brand and size area.* Just behind the transverse border in the middle of the outsole is a pie-shaped area that contains the Converse name, a star, and the shoe size. The size of this area, as well as the style, size, and position of the Converse name, the star, and the shoe size, can vary from one mold to the next.

*Variations in stippling.* Between the transverse bars of the toe and heel area, and also in a semicircular area of design positioned beneath the ball area of the foot, there are a series of stipples. These stipples have been hand struck, and therefore the specific design,

exact number, and position of these stipples is unique to each mold. In addition, there is a strip of stippled lines that runs across the heel of the shoe, just in front of the diamond design. The characteristics of these stipples are unique to each mold.

*Diagonal lines.* The spacing and thickness of the diagonal lines that run across the perimeter of the entire outsole border and across the area behind the pie-shaped logo area vary between molds. Through their intersection and relative positioning with the other design elements and characteristics on the outsole, the diagonal lines can help to distinguish outsoles. These lines run diagonally in one direction on right shoes and in the other direction on left shoes.

*Other.* There are also miscellaneous pieces of flash that occur at certain parts of some molds. These occur where some parts of the mold designs meet.

In addition to the variations between outsoles from different molds, other characteristics that are acquired during the manufacturing of these shoes and are reproduced in impressions made by the CCTAS shoe are very significant. The CCTAS shoes are assembled by several persons in an assembly line. The upper of the shoe is stitched together and is placed on a metal last. The bottom of the lasted shoe is dipped in a latex bath. This latex material acts as a temporary glue to hold on the foxing strips, toe cap, and outsole, which are about to be added. The first foxing strip is hand wrapped around the bottom of the lasted upper. Next, the outsole is attached by pressing it against the bottom of the latex-coated shoe upper.

After this step, a second foxing strip is hand wrapped around the shoe and extends to the bottom of the outsole, covering the entire edge of the outsole. Both of the foxing strips are made of soft, unvulcanized rubber that can easily stretch. The foxing strip is wrapped around the shoe slightly differently each time. The exact position at which the operator begins the second foxing strip must be within a certain area that will subsequently be covered by the toe cap. At the point where the second foxing strip overlaps itself, a small space, usually triangular, will be left (Figure 7.53B). Because of the variation that occurs from the precise wrapping of each subsequent foxing strip, the exact point of this overlap, as well as the exact size and shape of the space, will vary a great deal from shoe to shoe, as can be seen in the shoes in Figures 7.53 and 7.54 and in the impression in Figure 7.55B. In addition, the height of the foxing strips in relation to the bottom of the outsole will usually vary, with some spots being slightly higher than the outsole and some being lower. If the foxing strip is below the level of the outsole, it may temporarily prevent the edge of the outsole adjacent to that point from touching the ground until the foxing strip is worn down. This can be seen in the impression in Figure 7.55B. Where the foxing strip is included in the impression, it is touching the surface. When it is not included in the impression, the foxing strip is not touching the surface. As a low foxing strip wears down, it will sometimes become frayed, separated, or torn along those areas, adding further characteristics to the impression.

Next, a toe bumper guard is added. The toe bumper guard material is also placed by hand around the toe area of the shoe, with very little attention being given to its exact position. Thus, the beginning and ending positions of the toe guard also vary a great deal from shoe to shoe. Like the toe guard, a heel label is added to the heel area of the shoe. Its positioning is also done by hand; therefore, its exact placement will vary. The toe guard and heel label vary in their position, with some areas extending below the level of the outsole and some areas staying above or even with the outsole. The exact way in which they vary is random.

All of these characteristics can be reflected in impressions made by the shoe. They are visible in the shoes in Figures 7.53 and 7.54, and some are visible in the impression in Figure 7.55. As shoes wear down, some of these characteristics change or disappear while others become more apparent. The assembled shoe now goes into an autoclave where it is vulcanized and the various rubber components and outsole are bonded together.

The variables that occur in the assembly of CCTAS shoes are extremely significant in an examination. There is no precise way in which one could accurately predict the mathematical likelihood of a specific left or right CCTAS shoe being exactly like another left or right CCTAS shoe based on characteristics of the molded outsole, foxing strip overlap, toe guard, and heel label. Nor is there any precise way to predict mathematically the even more unlikely chance of a pair of CCTAS shoes being alike in all respects to another pair. The knowledge of the variation that exists in CCTAS shoes will significantly strengthen a footwear examination involving those shoes.

The example of the CCTAS shoe is another excellent illustration of why manufacturing information is important and significant in the examination of footwear impression evidence. Some variables and components, such as the toe guard, foxing strip, and heel label, are also found in many other brands of shoes where cut or molded outsoles are joined together and then bonded in an autoclave.

*Compression-molded oversize unit soles.* In addition to making compression-molded outsoles that are specific in their size and shape, as in the case of the CCTAS shoes, some compression-molded unit soles are molded in an oversize version and are later die cut or trimmed to a specific size. Unlike the thin, premolded outsoles used in the

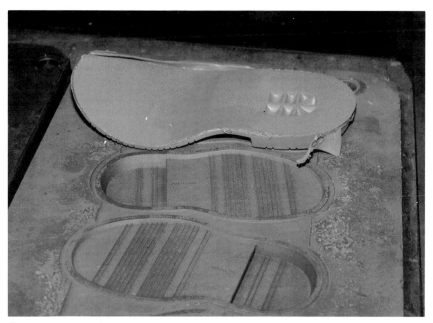

**A**

**B**

**7.56** Expanded ethyl vinyl acetate sole on mold (**A**). Note how the outsole has expanded to nearly twice the size of the mold cavity. Two outsoles taken from the same mold (**B**). The difference in expansion and the die cutting has caused variations in portions of the outsole design. For instance, note the difference in the size of each area between the arrows and the tip of the outsole.

blocker units, these outsoles are thicker and can be used on boots and casual shoes. They are, however, still referred to by some manufacturers as blockers, even though they are a single molded piece.

A good example of another variable associated with some compression-molded outsoles, in this case expanded microcellular soling material, is depicted in Figure 7.56. The microcellular material used is expanded ethyl vinyl acetate (EVA). The EVA is placed in the mold in a premeasured biscuit form, as in any other compression-molding operation. When molded in the compression-molding process, the EVA attempts to expand but cannot, because of the pressure exerted on it while it is in the mold. When the mold is opened, the microcellular EVA outsole instantly expands to a much larger size than the mold cavity. The tremendous difference in size between the mold and the outsoles can be seen in Figure 7.56A. The molds are much smaller than those for similarly sized outsoles in a material that would not expand, such as rubber. Although the amount of expansion is considerable, there is still a separate mold size for each shoe size. The oversize outsoles are then die cut into a specific size. Variations can occur, as previously discussed, in the exact positioning of the die when cutting oversize outsoles. In addition, the amount of expansion can vary from one batch of EVA to the next and will also vary during different seasons of the year. An example of two EVA outsoles from the same mold that were cut with the same die is in Figure 7.56B. One outsole expanded slightly more than the other. Even though they were both cut with the same die and are now the exact same size and shape, they are not exact duplicates.

## Injection-Molded Outsoles

Injection molding can best be described as a *closed-mold* process, i.e., the mold is first tightly closed and then the outsole material is injected into it through a small port or ports. The point of injection and the method of injection can vary with the particular machinery and the materials.

Injection molding is very versatile. Injection molding machines have molds with one, two, or three separate injection steps and injection stations. This enables the manufacture of one-, two-, or three-colored outsoles composed of one, two, or three different types of midsole and outsole materials. For example, a two-color injection-mold process could produce a high-density gray polyurethane outsole having a white midsole of a lower density polyurethane. The particular materials used in these outsoles are selected for a certain set of qualities. The outsole material may need to have excellent traction on a specific surface, while the injected midsole material may need to be a lower-density material used to reduce the weight of the shoe, to increase the flexibility of the shoe and to give the shoe more "bounce." A shoe made in this manner with a lighter density midsole combined with a heavier and more durable outsole is known as a *dual-density* shoe.

Injection molds and molding machines are, as a rule, much cleaner and quicker than the hot and dirty compression-molding operation. The mixing and injection of the outsole or midsole materials into the mold cavity in some processes can involve chemical reactions with little heat or pressure. In other cases, the process involves simply melting and injecting, under much greater pressure, the outsole materials into the mold. Injecting an outsole takes less time than compression molding an outsole. As a result, in injection-molding operations, there are on the average fewer molds per size and sometimes only one or two molds found in each size of each design.

The process itself involves, in simple terms, the injection of the outsole substance into a closed mold. Trapped air and any excess materials are bled through the seams. Some molds will also have special air-release ports. Flash is formed in the areas where the mold parts come together. Thermoplastic rubber, polyvinyl chloride, ethyl vinyl chloride, and polyurethane are the most commonly used outsole substances in the injection molding process.

There are two general categories of injection molded outsoles. The first is individual *unit* outsoles. Unit outsoles made with the injection-molding process are like compression-molded unit outsoles inasmuch as they must be cemented, stitched, or otherwise attached to the upper portion of the shoe. The second category is *direct-attached* injection-molded outsoles. These are outsoles that are injected directly around the shoe upper, resulting in a completed shoe.

*Injection-molded unit outsoles.* Injection-molded unit soles are injected into a closed mold but are not directly attached to the shoe upper. Unit soles can be made on direct-attach machinery with the use of a dummy last (Figure 7.57), or they can be manufactured on separate, unit sole injection machines. Injection-molded unit outsoles are difficult and sometimes impossible to distinguish visually from compression-molded outsoles based on observation of the outsole after the shoe has been assembled. However, from a footwear examination standpoint, the determination that it is a molded unit outsole (whether compression or unit injection), as opposed to a cut outsole or direct-attach injection molded outsole, is all that is important in most instances.

*Direct-attach injection outsoles.* Footwear made by the direct injection of the outsole onto the upper are easier to recognize. The mechanics of this process require a mold assembly (side rings and soleplate) that can open and close around the upper portion of the shoe. The points where the left and right mold side rings come together, usually in the

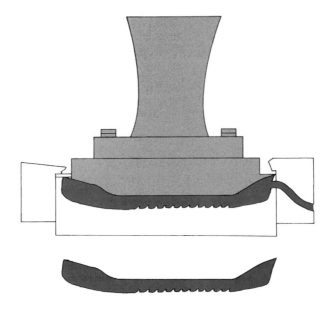

A

B

7.57 A drawing of a mold using a dummy plate to cover the top of the mold cavity and allow injection of an outsole (**A**). A multistation injection machine fitted with dummy plates (arrow) for the injection of unit outsoles (**B**).

toe and heel area, leave a visible seam. In addition, with some injection machines, there is a mark left on the toe or heel area where the injection device injected the midsole through a small port in the mold. Presence of the seams and/or injection port marks in the toe or heel areas is characteristic of the direct-attach injection molded process and is therefore proof to the examiner of the manufacturing method used. Figure 7.58 shows how this will appear on the shoe.

One-component direct-attach systems (Figure 7.59) inject the soling material into the mold assembly, which has closed itself around the shoe upper. The entire one-component sole is molded directly onto the shoe upper. Material that seeps between the mold side rings or other components is referred to as flash. The material that remains attached to the outsole at the point of injection and which is later pulled or cut off is referred to as sprue. Figure 7.59A depicts a direct-attach process where the outsole is injected from the heel. Figure 7.59B is a drawing of a process where the outsole is injected through the bottom of the heel and sole.

Other direct-attach injection-mold systems use two or three components. These components can be different colors or different materials or both. In one type of two-component process, a multiple station machine rotates like a merry-go-round, while the operator is stationary (Figure 7.60A). The outsole is first injected using a smooth dummy last in place of the shoe upper (Figure 7.60B). If the process were interrupted and the outsole from the first step pulled out of the mold, it would appear as in Figure 7.60C. After the outsole has been formed, the dummy last is rotated out of position and the shoe upper is lowered into the mold assembly and rests on top of the already formed outsole (Figure 7.60D). The side rings of the mold assembly close and then the midsole is injected through a second injection port, directly attaching itself to the previously injected outsole and the shoe upper (Figure 7.60E). The finished shoe has a visible seam in the heel and toe area, where the two halves of the mold side rings come together. Depending on the arrangement of the mold assembly, there may also be spots where the points of injection were and the sprue was cut off. There will also be flash between the first and second injection stages until it is trimmed from the shoe. The diagrams in Figure 7.61 provide a profile of the two-step direct-attach injection process depicted in Figure 7.60.

With the large variety of direct-attach injection-molding machines in the world, as well as the manufacturing variations that can be employed in the direct-attach injection molding of outsoles, it stands to reason that the significance each variation may have on footwear examinations may also vary. The recognition that an item of footwear is injection molded is in itself helpful, since many injection-molded outsoles, as previously illustrated in Figure 7.58C, have been designed for aes-

**A**

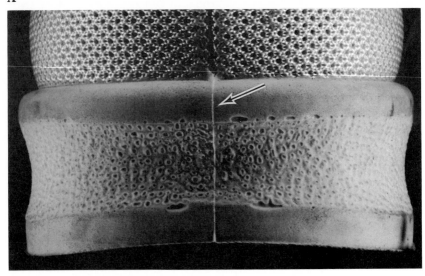

**B**
7.58 In shoes made by a direct-attach method, the midsole and/or outsole in the toe area (**A**) and in the rear of the heel (**B**), where the mold halves met, usually have flash that is visible. In some direct-attach shoes, such as this two-color, direct-attach outsole (**C**), flash from the seam where the mold halves closed, as well as a round injection port, is present on the heel area. This particular shoe is a direct-attach injection-molded simulation of the CCTAS style of shoe. It even simulates the foxing strip, toe guard, heel label, and other features characteristic of a hand-built shoe but will not have any of the variables like the CCTAS shoe.

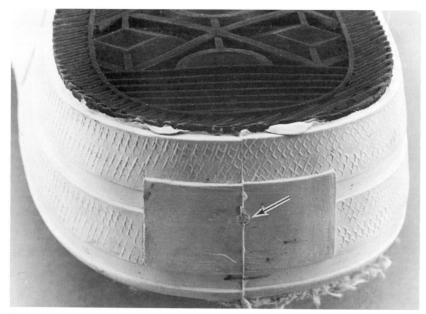

C

thetic reasons to simulate shoes made by die-cut, outsole-cut, and hand-wrapping processes. Failure to recognize shoes that have imitated those designs and that actually have injection-molded outsoles could result in erroneous evaluation of the characteristics in the impression.

*Direct-attach injection-molded outsoles using polyurethane.* Although many injection-molded outsoles are made using polyvinyl chloride, thermoplastic rubber, and other materials, the use of polyurethane (PU) for the outsole is becoming more common because of its superior qualities (Bodziak WJ, 1986). In addition, many PU outsoles contain air bubbles generated during the molding process with varying degrees of randomness (Music DK and Bodziak WJ, 1988). Although the examiner can compare void areas in a questioned impression with corresponding air bubbles in an outsole, determining the significance of those bubbles and what weight they may contribute toward an identification requires some knowledge of PU outsole processes (Keijzer J, 1990; Katterwe H, 1990).

PU solings are formed by a process called reaction molding. Two materials, a resin and an isocyanate, are metered into a mixing chamber and are then injected into the mold cavity while they are reacting to form a polyurethane. This reaction is a very quick one. The time it takes for the PU to harden after it is mixed and injected involves only a few seconds. The mixed PU must therefore rapidly enter the mold and expand across the mold surface, filling the mold cavity. The amount of

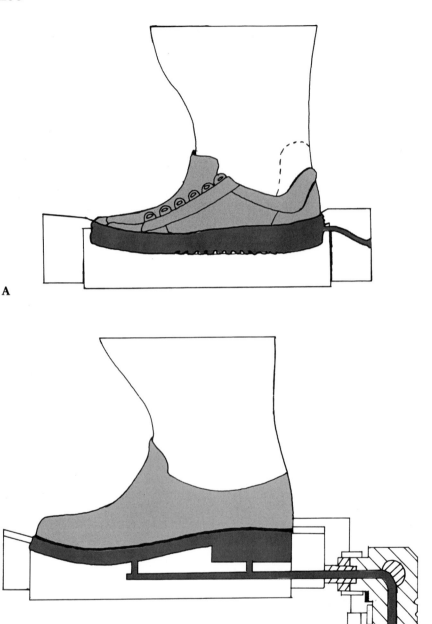

**A**

**B**

**7.59** Two examples of one-component, direct-attach injection systems. One injects the material from the heel (**A**). The heel in this type of system would look like the heels in Figure 7.58C, having both a port and seam flash. The other injects the material from the bottom (**B**). In this method, flash would still be visible where the mold halves meet, but the injection port sprue on the bottom of the shoe would wear off quickly.

PU injected into a mold cavity will not initially cover the entire bottom surface of the mold but will expand over the surface. During this expansion, air may become trapped between the PU and the mold surface, which cannot escape through the viscous and quickly hardening PU. Other air is contained in the PU mixture itself and is simply suspended in the PU mixture when it hardens. In either case, the trapped air will leave a void area that becomes permanently fixed in the outsole as it hardens (Music DK and Bodziak WJ, 1988).

Variables that influence the frequency, size, and positioning of air bubbles in PU outsoles can be attributed to (1) chemical variables— those relating to the precise chemistry of the PU; (2) mechanical variables—those relating to the mechanical mixing of the components by the mixing screw and the mechanical process of injecting the PU into the mold; and (3) physical variables—those relating to the physical properties of the mold such as the design, the stippling, the use of release agents on the mold surface, and the presence of any contaminants in the mold. The diagram in Figure 7.62 illustrates a few of the variables that influence the air in PU (Music DK and Bodziak WJ, 1988).

*Chemical.* Polyurethane outsoles are made of (1) a resin blend composed of polyol resins and other materials such as blowing agents, chain extenders, and catalysts and (2) an isocyanate. Either polyester-type or polyether-type base resins are used. Blowing agents are used to expand the PU. This can be accomplished by using the reactions of water with an isocyanate to produce carbon dioxide gas, expanding the liquid to create a foam, or it can be accomplished by the addition of low boiling point hydrocarbons, such as Freon to the mixture. Surfactants may be included to control the structure and size of the foam cells. Pigments may be added to color the PU (Music DK and Bodziak WJ, 1988).

The resin and the isocyanate are maintained at a precise temperature. At the time of mixture, they are combined in precise amounts in a mixing chamber, where they are mixed with a mixing screw. The mixture is then injected into the mold cavity. As the PU foam expands within the mold, heat is generated and an integral skin is formed where the PU touches the mold's surface. This skin is thinner in polyester-based PU and thicker in the polyether-based PU (Figure 7.63) (Music DK and Bodziak WJ, 1988).

*Mechanical.* The PU is mixed immediately prior to its injection in the mold cavity, or, in the case of open-pour processes, immediately before pouring. The PU components must be mixed rapidly, since the mixture begins expanding in a few seconds. The components are metered into the mixing chamber, where a mixing screw (Figure 7.64) turning at high speeds rapidly mixes the two components. Some of the PU will remain and harden on the mixing screw. Consequently, after a

A

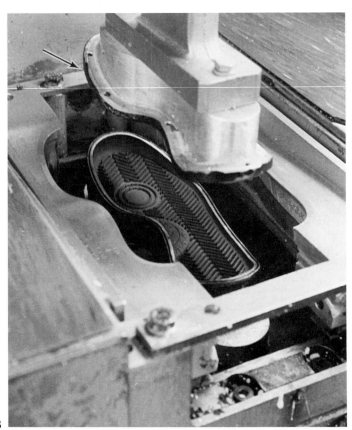

B

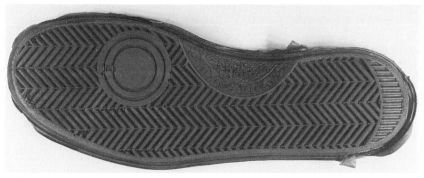

C

D                                                    E

**7.60**  A multiple-station, rotary-injection machine (**A**). The outsole is injected with a smooth dummy last over the top of the mold assembly (**B**). The thin outsole (**C**) has been injected at this point and remains in the mold cavity. The dummy last is rotated out and the lasted shoe upper is lowered into the mold assembly (**D**) over top of the already molded outsole (**C**). The side rings of the mold assembly close, and the midsole is injected, directly attaching itself to both the outsole (**C**) and the shoe upper (**E**).

period of time, the mixing screw will become dirty or clogged and will not perform as efficiently as a mixing device. This necessitates the periodic cleaning of the mixing screw to assure a rapid and complete mix. The mixing screw on the bottom in Figure 7.64 is clean, while a similar screw on the top is full of hardened PU. In Figure 7.65, the PU sample on the right has been taken from the mixing chamber just after a clean mixing screw was inserted. The PU sample on the left was taken just before a dirty mixing screw was removed from the mixing chamber.

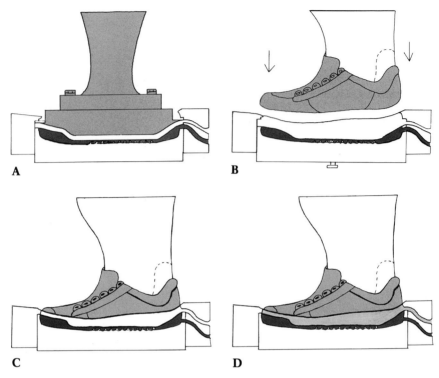

**7.61** Diagrams shown of the two-step, direct-attach injection molding process as shown in Figure 7.60.

**7.62** Some of the variables that can influence the air bubbles in PU soiling.

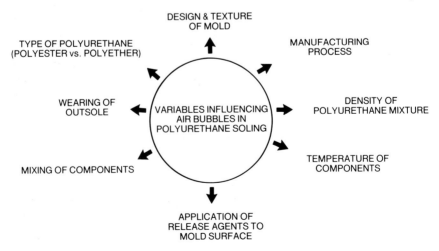

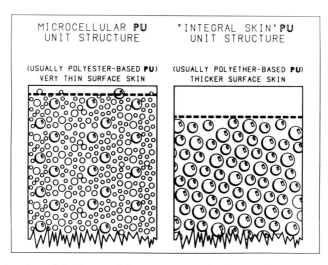

**7.63** A drawing of the integral skin structure of polyester-based and polyether-based PU.

**7.64** Two mixing screws used to mix the components of PU. One mixing screw is clean and will mix the components more efficiently while the other has been covered with hardened PU and will be less efficient.

**7.65**  Enlarged picture of PU samples. The light one on the right, taken while a clean screw was in the mixing chamber, contains more air in it. The darker one on the left was taken while a dirty screw was in the mixing chamber.

The amount of air in sample B is considerably less than in A (Music DK and Bodziak WJ, 1988).

*Physical.* Because the PU becomes viscous and then solid within seconds after injection, as the PU expands and flows through the mold, air is trapped against the mold's surface and suspended in the hardened PU mixture. The physical nature of the mold pattern, i.e., sharp edges, corners, deep pattern designs, and other variously shaped pattern elements, provide ideal areas for air entrapment. Other factors, such as the mold texture, stippling, mold release spray, and contaminants in the mold will also influence the air entrapment and the particular location of air bubbles. The place where the PU is injected, i.e., the heel, the toe, or the bottom of the sole, will also influence the points of air entrapment. Because these factors in the mold are consistent and because almost exactly the same amount of PU is injected in precisely the same manner each time, the air bubbles that are trapped against the pattern on the mold surface tend to be very similar in their size and position from shoe to shoe. These bubbles are referred to as *pattern-influenced* bubbles. The bubbles that are merely suspended in the hardened PU and

**7.66** A PU outsole that has air bubbles that favor the peaks of the herringbone pattern and the top (toe end) of the circular design.

have not touched the mold pattern are *suspended bubbles* (Music DK and Bodziak WJ, 1988).

*Pattern-related bubbles.* Figures 7.66 and 7.67 depict two herringbone design outsoles also having a circular design element. The bubbles in one have favored the peaks of the herringbone design and the toe end of the circular design (Figure 7.66), while the bubbles in the other have favored the valleys of the herringbone design and the heel end of the

**7.67**   A PU outsole that has air bubbles that favor the valleys of the herringbone pattern and the bottom (heel end) of the circular design.

circular design (Figure 7.67). This is attributed to the point of injection (heel, toe, or bottom) and the resultant flow and direction of expansion of the PU.

Although inspection of many successive outsoles from the same mold show there is a tremendous amount of similarity between the pattern-related bubbles, there is still some diversity. In examinations,

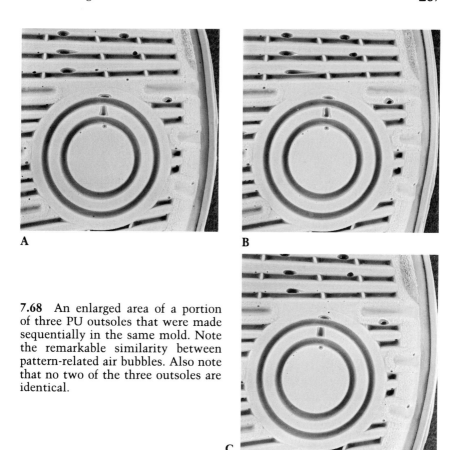

A

B

**7.68** An enlarged area of a portion of three PU outsoles that were made sequentially in the same mold. Note the remarkable similarity between pattern-related air bubbles. Also note that no two of the three outsoles are identical.

C

there are limitations in the number of bubbles that can be observed, as well as the specific clarity of each. Figure 7.68 shows an enlarged area of three PU outsoles that were injected sequentially. There is a remarkable duplication of some bubbles, yet there is also some variation among the outsoles. There is danger in using pattern-related bubbles as the only basis for positive identification, even if a large number of clearly visible bubbles corresponding in both the questioned impression and the known shoe exist. This is because of the possibility that more than one outsole may have a bubble pattern that is indistinguishable from that in the questioned impression. However, numerous pattern-related bubbles can assist in distinguishing any outsole from most others (Music DK and Bodziak WJ, 1988).

*Suspended bubbles.* As the outsole is worn down, the air bubbles that were not originally exposed will appear. Figure 7.69 shows an outsole that has two slices cut through it to reveal large air bubbles beneath the outsole surface, which would appear after the shoe outsole

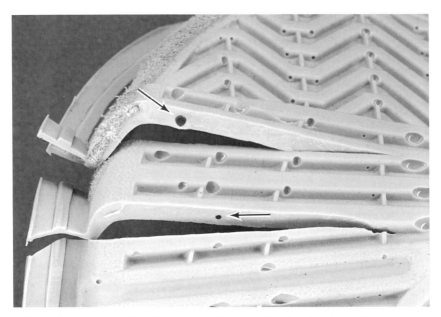

**7.69** A PU outsole, like the ones in Figure 7.68, that has been sliced in two areas, revealing air bubbles that have been suspended in the PU, not trapped against the pattern of the mold.

**7.70** A worn PU outsole that has numerous air bubbles, particularly in the toe area, that were not on the outsole surface when this shoe was new but have been exposed as a result of wear.

**7.71**   This outsole contains large air bubbles trapped in most of the design. Note the glossy nature of the bubbles.

wears considerably. Figure 7.70 depicts the toe area of a well-worn PU outsole that contains many small air bubbles. Those bubbles, unlike the pattern-related bubbles, were not trapped in corners of the design as the expanding PU moved across the mold's surface. Instead, they are random, free-floating bubbles that were trapped and remained suspended in the PU as it hardened. These air bubbles would carry more weight toward the identification of the shoe. In a case like the shoe in Figure 7.70, the suspended bubbles that are now exposed in the toe area would be unique to that shoe (Music DK and Bodziak WJ, 1988).

Air bubbles in the finished outsole are readily visible and have a glossy surface, as can be seen in Figure 7.71. They occur in a variety of sizes, both on the surface of the outsole, where they were trapped against the mold surface, as well as freely suspended in the outsole. The air bubbles can be very large and aspherical or can be very small, such as those in Figure 7.72, which were trapped in the bottom of each stipple.

Polyurethane is mixed in a variety of densities. A density of 1 would be the most dense mixture while a density of 0.38 would be an example of a low density. The lower-density PU outsoles are more likely to contain air bubbles, while the more dense PU outsoles may not contain any.

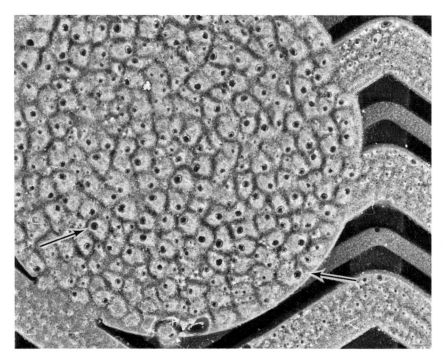

**7.72**   Air bubbles are also trapped in the low spots of stippling in a mold.

## Open-Pour Molding

An increasingly popular method of producing unit soles made of PU is the open-pour process. This method involves the pouring of freshly mixed PU into an open mold. The amount of PU poured into the mold will not initially fill the mold cavity; however, the PU mixture is still expanding and will fill that cavity in a matter of seconds. Before the PU expands, the top of the mold is closed. Any excess PU will escape between the two halves of the mold and form flash. Figure 7.73 depicts an operator in a factory pouring the PU into an open mold. In this particular mold, a unit sole will result.

Although open-pour molding is primarily used for unit soles, it is also possible to produce a direct-attach shoe with this process by attaching a lasted shoe upper to the top of the mold. When the top is closed, part of the shoe upper will be immersed in the PU, which will harden around it.

Another modification of the open-pour PU method is the combination of a preformed rubber outsole with an open-pour PU midsole (Figure 7.74). This process permits the combination of different densi-

**7.73**   Operator pouring PU into an open mold. The top of the mold will then be closed. In this operation, a unit mold will be formed.

ties, materials, and colors in the resulting molded unit outsole. An example of this method would include the use of a compression-molded rubber outsole that is placed into the bottom of a mold cavity, which then has PU poured over it. The PU will adhere to the rubber outsole and will form a lower-density midsole. The rubber outsole provides the qualities of rubber for that portion of the shoe, while the lower density PU provides a lighter-weight, shock-absorbent midsole. Air bubbles also occur in open-pour PU outsoles.

## Recognition of Manufacturing Methods

It is important to be able to accurately recognize the manufacturing method and correctly evaluate the significance of that method in a particular examination. Although the manufacturing characteristics are not always significant in an examination, in some cases, not using this information can result in a loss of important information that in turn may impact the overall examination and conclusion. However, it is also important not to misinterpret or overvalue the manufacturing characteristics in a shoe in relation to an examination.

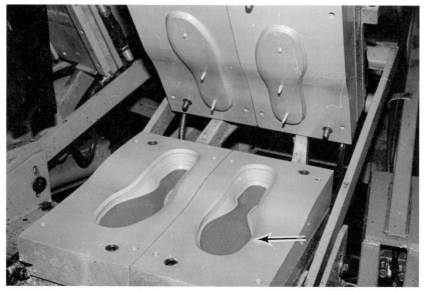

A

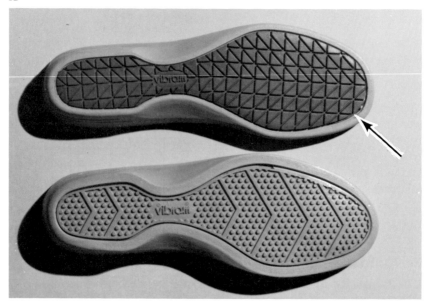

B

**7.74** The qualities of both rubber and PU can be combined. In this operation, rubber outsoles, molded separately in a compression molding machine are placed into a special mold **(A)**. PU is then poured over those outsoles. The result is a rubber outsole with a PU midsole like the shoe in **B.**

The footwear examiner can obtain some training and exposure to the manufacturing methods in several ways. First, there is footwear industry literature and footwear impression examination literature that explains manufacturing methods, terminology, and materials. This can be useful in providing initial exposure to footwear manufacturing and how it relates to footwear impression examination. Second, tours of manufacturing facilities where outsoles are made on the premises can be helpful. Third, one can receive training from a footwear examiner who is knowledgeable in manufacturing methods and how they can be significant in the examination of footwear impressions.

# Known Shoes of Suspects and the Preparation of Test Impressions

8

## Obtaining the Known Shoes from the Suspect

### Discretion Regarding Footwear Evidence

Most suspects are not aware of the existence or the potential of footwear impression examinations. If they become aware that their footwear constitutes important evidence either because an investigator wants to look at or take impressions or photographs of their shoes, through failed attempts to seize their shoes, or through the news media's coverage of footwear evidence at a crime scene, they will be likely to destroy or discard their shoes. For this reason, no mention of an evidentiary interest in shoes or shoe impressions should be made to the public or to the suspect until the shoes have been permanently seized. Revealing this interest seriously jeopardizes the existence of footwear evidence.

### Importance of Obtaining the Actual Shoes

Over the years, I have received several cases where only inked impressions and/or photographs of the suspect's shoes were submitted. In some of those cases, the investigators made test impressions and/or photographs of the shoes and then returned the shoes to the suspect, thinking that the shoes themselves were not essential for making a comparison. In other cases, test impressions and/or photographs of the suspect's shoes were taken because the court would not allow the seizure of the suspect's shoes or because the investigator did not feel obligated or on safe enough legal ground to permanently seize the shoes.

The primary objective in most footwear examinations is to compare the characteristics in questioned impressions with those present in the known shoes of one or more suspects. In order for this examination to take place, it will be necessary for the examiner to have the actual shoes of the suspect(s). Examiners who attempt to conduct footwear impression examinations with only impressions or photographs of the suspect's shoes will usually be severely limited in the conclusions they reach. The investigator should *always* obtain the actual shoes as soon as they can be legally and permanently seized.

## *Multiple Pairs of Shoes Owned by a Suspect*

In cases where shoes are seized from a suspect within a very short time after a crime is perpetrated, only the pair of shoes the suspect is wearing may need to be considered. The suspect would simply not have had the time or opportunity to have changed footwear. However, in many cases, the suspect is not located until several hours, days, or even months later. Whether the eventual seizure of the shoes is incident to an arrest, a search warrant, or an interview, the suspect may or may not be wearing the same shoes that were worn at the crime scene. Consideration must therefore be given to the possibility that the suspect owns more than one pair of shoes and that shoes other than the ones currently being worn by the suspect could be the shoes worn at the crime scene.

More often than might be expected, individuals will have two or three pairs of shoes of the same general design. For instance, a person who owns a pair of basketball shoes having a certain design that are becoming worn is very likely to purchase a second pair of the same or a similar design. I have been the recipient of several cases in which a suspect actually possessed three or four pairs of shoes of the same or a very similar design. In instances such as these, there is an even greater possibility that the investigator will seize the wrong pair of shoes. Doing so, of course, would result in nonidentification of the shoe with the questioned impression and could easily produce results that might be erroneously used as exculpatory evidence. It would also encourage and enable the suspect, after the wrong shoes were seized, to discard the actual shoes that were worn at the crime scene.

Figure 8.1 shows four pairs of shoes that were obtained from a suspect in a homicide case. The two pairs in Figures 8.1A and 8.1B are the same make, size, color, and design. Their outsoles, however, are easily distinguishable to a footwear examiner on close examination because they were die cut from a premolded sheet of outsole material. The other two pairs of shoes are a similar herringbone design, but are more easily distinguished from the first two pairs. Fortunately, in this case, the investigator seized all four pairs with a search warrant. The pair de-

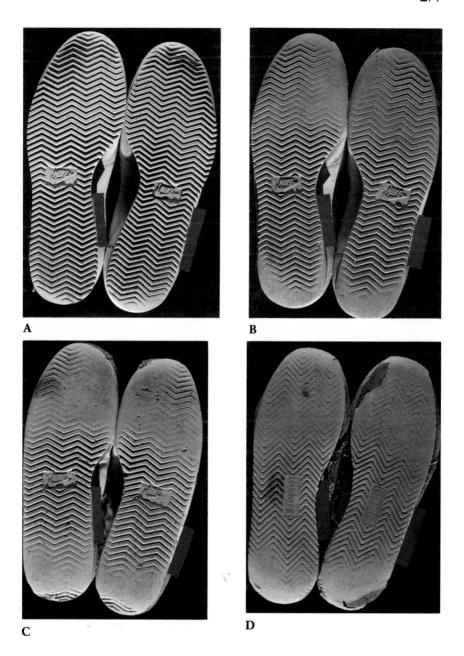

**8.1** Four pairs of shoes of a generally similar design that were obtained from one subject. The pairs marked A and B are identical in brand, size, and color but can still be distinguished based on variations in the way their outsoles were cut.

picted in Figure 8.1A was identified with the crime scene impressions. Imagine the results if one of the other pairs was the only one recovered.

## Similar Shoes Owned by Different Suspects

Investigators should also consider that more than one suspect in a case may have shoes of a similar design. A good example of this was a case involving two suspects and several questioned impressions that were left on two envelopes that had fallen on the floor during a burglary. An enhanced photograph of these envelopes is shown in Figure 8.2. All of the questioned impressions had a herringbone design, some with a concentric circle pattern in the ball area of the shoe. A superficial look at the impressions, particularly before they were photographically enhanced, would lead the average observer to believe that all of them were made by the same shoe. A close comparison of the impressions with the shoes of one suspect revealed that only one of those impressions was made by that suspect's shoes. The other impressions on the envelopes,

**8.2**   Several impressions on two envelopes that appeared to have been made by one suspect's shoes. Only one impression, indicated by the arrow, was identified with the first suspect's shoes. It turned out that the second suspect also had shoes of the same brand and design and that the other impressions were made by the shoes of the second suspect.

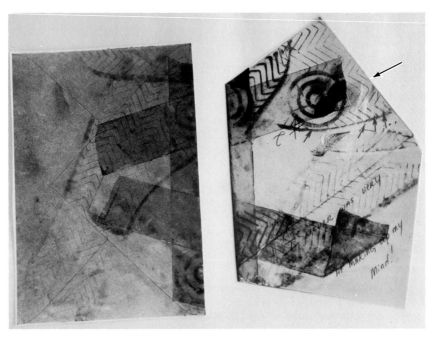

although extremely similar in general design, could be positively eliminated with the first suspect's shoes because there were minor differences in the design, indicating that the shoe outsole originated from a different mold. On contacting the investigator in the case, it was learned that no attempt had been made to seize the shoes of the second suspect. After seizing the first suspect's shoes, the investigator had, in fact, believed those shoes had made all the impressions. On receipt of the examination results, he advised that he would obtain the shoes of the second subject as well. A few weeks later, the investigator had determined that the second subject also had shoes of the same make and design. Confronted with this, both suspects subsequently confessed to the burglary.

## The Need to Obtain Both Shoes

When any suspect's shoes are seized, both the left and the right shoe should be obtained. Footwear impressions can be both positive and negative. They can be lifted, photographed, reversed, cast, and transferred. In addition, partial impressions are sometimes very difficult to visually attribute to the right or left shoe without first making some test impressions and conducting a preliminary examination. It is therefore easy for an investigator to innocently mistake an impression made by a right shoe for one made by a left shoe and vice versa. In addition, it is helpful to the examiner to have both shoes while conducting the examination. Having both shoes will assist in the interpretation and identification of the manufacturing processes and in the interpretation of the changes on the outsole due to wear.

## Dating and Initialing the Shoes

The date on which the shoes are seized should be noted and provided along with the evidence. One good way to do this is to place your initials and the date on each shoe or evidence tag at the time the shoes are seized. It is both necessary and important for the examiner to know whether the shoes were obtained relatively soon after the crime, thus having very little additional wear, or if the shoes were obtained days or months later, in which case they would be expected to be in a more advanced condition of wear.

## Treatment of Known Shoes Relative to Other Examinations

In many cases involving footwear examinations, other forensic examinations are also requested. These include examinations for serologic, soil, glass, hair, and fiber evidence. The integrity of those types of evidence must be maintained from the time the shoes are seized, in the event those other examinations are later requested. Ordinarily, the footwear impression examination is the last to be made, after other forensic examinations have been conducted or considered. If the shoes themselves are wet or contain wet mud, blood, or body fluids, they should be allowed to air dry thoroughly prior to being packaged. The shoes should never be dried in a clothes dryer or by any other artificial means. Plastic bags should not be used to package the shoes. A large, sturdy paper bag, with the top folded over several times and taped or stapled, is sufficient. Each shoe or pair of shoes should be packaged so that there is no chance of leakage or contamination of the other forensic evidence. Shoes that are believed to contain blood or other body fluids should also be kept under refrigeration, but only after they are completely air-dried and packaged.

## Collections of Shoe Designs

Many years ago, before the athletic footwear boom and before there were a large number of footwear imports, it was not too difficult to keep a representative sampling of most athletic footwear designs. There were, relatively speaking, only a few major athletic shoe designs, and those were made by only a few companies. A large portion of the remaining population of shoes were leather shoes with rubber heels. The task of obtaining samples of heel and outsole designs from the limited number of domestic manufacturers was relatively easy.

Collecting a representative sampling of the existing footwear designs is no longer a simple task. Today there are literally thousands of different shoe designs in what is now a worldwide footwear market. These designs are constantly being supplemented and replaced due to the marketing competition, demands of the consumer, and technological changes in footwear manufacturing.

Some of the outsole designs are old standards and will be used by the manufacturer for several years. Because of the investment a manufacturer may have in a set of molds, or because of the popularity of a particular design, the manufacturer may occasionally change the color or design of the upper of the shoe and may even rename the shoe, but the outsole design will remain the same. On the other extreme, some outsole designs are made for just one or two production runs, never to be used again. In addition, many manufacturers produce only the outsoles and then sell those outsoles to several other manufacturers. For that reason, an outsole design that has originated from a single manufacturer can appear on a variety of shoes of different brands.

Today, over 80% of the footwear in the United States is imported. Many of the major footwear companies that sell large percentages of the

**8.3**   The FBI's computerized footwear reference collection.


athletic footwear in this country publish a catalog once or twice each year. These catalogs, in most instances, feature pictures of the bottoms of the shoes as well as the upper designs. For the remaining athletic shoes and other shoes sold in this country, there are very few catalogs, pictures, or samples available. As a result, maintaining a complete collection of *all shoe designs* for the law enforcement community has become an impossible task. In addition, it has become very common-place for small footwear companies to manufacture footwear with out-sole designs that closely resemble those found on other name-brand shoes. This must always be considered when trying to associate a particular impression with a particular brand of shoe.

   Nevertheless, there is often a need in the law enforcement commu-nity to be able to determine the make and manufacturer of footwear that left an impression at a crime scene. If impressions that are plainly visible at a crime scene can be associated with a particular make, style, and color of shoe, it can often assist in the identification of the perpetra-tor of that crime.

   In this country, the Federal Bureau of Investigation (FBI) laboratory maintains a footwear reference collection, shown in Figure 8.3, which consists of the designs of athletic shoes sold by the major footwear companies, as well as photographs of outsoles and shoes collected from other sources. Since the vast majority of footwear impression evidence in criminal cases in this country results from athletic footwear, the reference collection is very successful in identifying the make and/or manufacturer of the shoe. Similar footwear design reference collections are maintained and used by local law enforcement agencies in this country and in several other countries, including England, Australia, and Canada.

## Test Impressions of Known Shoes

### Photographing the Shoes

Prior to making test impressions of the shoes, they should be photographed. Photographs provide a record of the shoe outsole, supply a good reference in your notes, and are of assistance in providing graphic testimony if your results are needed in court. To photograph the shoes, use a black-and-white film having an ISO of 400, such as T-Max 400. Use a low-angled oblique light source. Fill lighting should also be used for shoes with deep tread designs. In order to get sufficient depth of field, the appropriate f-stop and a longer exposure time should be used.

### The Need for Test Impressions

When a shoe makes an impression, that impression usually represents only a portion of the shoe's outsole. For instance, most athletic shoes have designs of varying depths. Whether they are new or worn, they will leave a two-dimensional impression on a hard surface that represents only portions of their design. As the tread pattern of a newer shoe is worn down and changed during the life of the shoe, the impression it leaves will change as well. Figure 8.4 depicts a two-dimensional impression of a worn shoe. The impression reflects only part of the outsole; the other areas of the outsole are not being impressed against the surface.

Regarding more specific details, Figure 8.5 illustrates why the visual examination of a shoe outsole cannot alone show how a feature or characteristic will appear in an impression. Notice how the precise shapes of worn and damaged areas in the test impression do not print exactly the same way the corresponding areas and defects appear on the shoe itself.

### Two-Dimensional Impression Methods and Materials

It is both beneficial and necessary to have adequate materials for and knowledge of several test impression methods. In some instances, two-dimensional impressions are suitable for comparison with the questioned impression. In other instances, test impressions require a tech-

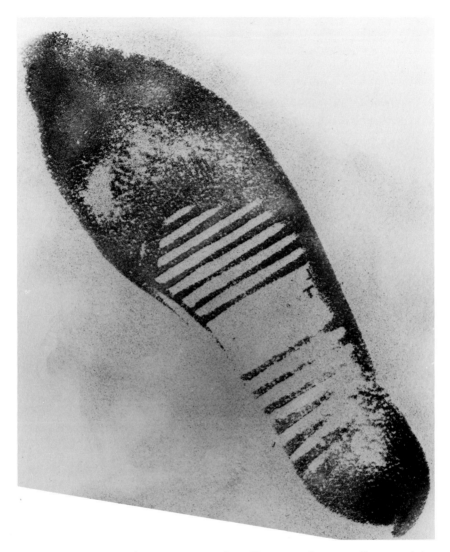

**8.4** An impression of a worn tennis shoe illustrates that not all areas of the outsole are represented in a footwear impression.

nique that approximates what occurred during the making of the questioned impression. For example, if the questioned impression was made on a hard, smooth surface, then it may be necessary to make the test impressions on a hard, smooth surface. If the questioned impression was made in soil and was photographed, then some of the test impressions may need to be three-dimensional. An exact duplication of the materials and conditions that occurred in the actual questioned impression is not necessary. Once an examiner is familiar with several ways of

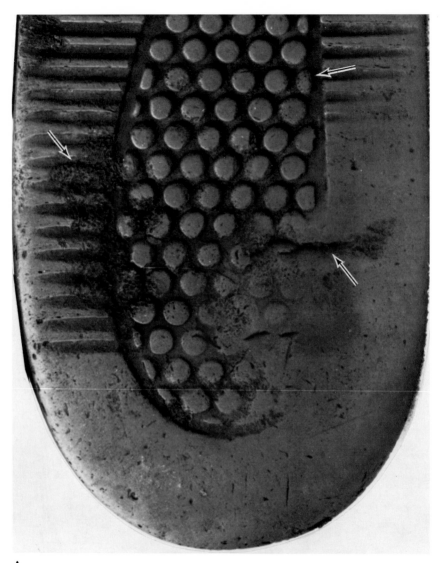

**A**

**8.5** The worn and damaged areas of a shoe (**A**) do not always print in the impression (**B**) exactly the way they appear on the shoe. The arrows point to just a few corresponding areas that print differently than the respective part of the

making test impressions, she or he will usually favor one or two as preliminary methods and use the other methods as needed.

Many of the test impression methods discussed in this chapter require wearing the shoes while making the impressions. It may be desirable to wear gloves and plastic foot covers for this procedure. The fear of

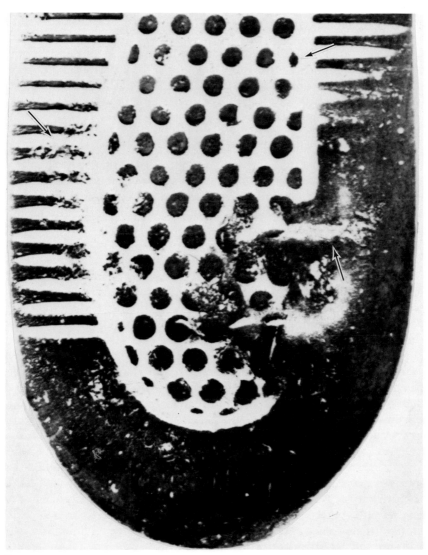

**B**

shoe appears. It should be obvious, after closely comparing each corresponding part of the shoe with its impression, why a known impression of a shoe is needed.

health risks or other personal reasons that might otherwise discourage an examiner or assistant from actually wearing another person's shoes to make those impressions can thereby be overcome.

Test impressions provide a recording of the characteristics already present on a shoe. It is not necessary to have impressions made by a person who is the same size or weight as the suspect whose shoes are being tested.

There are many ways in which a test impression of an item of footwear can be made. In the following pages, descriptions of several methods are offered, along with illustrations of some of them; however, there is no substitute for actually trying these methods and experiencing the results each can give.

When making any test impression, it is a good idea to mark or otherwise identify which shoe was used to make it. For instance, if a right shoe that is being referred to as *item 5* is being used to make a series of test impressions, each impression of that shoe should be marked "#5 right shoe." In this way, there will be a permanent record of which shoe was used to make each impression and, if the impression is on a transparency, it will always be possible to determine from which side the impression was made.

*Ink and tracing paper impressions.* The use of ink and tracing paper provides a quick and relatively inexpensive way of producing several test impressions. In some cases, these may be the only test impressions needed to conduct the examination. If not, this method will provide test impressions for a preliminary examination.

The materials used consist of quality tracing paper, usually found in art or paper supply stores, water-based ink, and a large (6 × 12-inch) ink pad. Ink pads like the one shown in Figure 8.6 can be custom made if necessary, but they are usually commercially available in this size. If the ink pad is kept covered and clean, it will last for thousands of impressions. The ink pad may have to be reinked each time it is used in order to obtain a suitably dark impression.

First, fresh water-base ink should be applied to the ink pad. While the ink is soaking into the pad, the tracing paper can be placed on a hard, smooth surface, such as a tile floor. If a softer surface is desired, a pad of paper can be placed between the tracing paper and the floor. The individual making the impressions should place the shoe on his or her foot and step several times on the ink pad. The multiple stepping on the ink pad will help distribute the ink evenly over the pad and the shoe. The first impressions made after applying fresh ink to the pad will usually contain excess ink; however, after the ink pad is used for a few impressions, their quality will improve. A series of impressions can then be made on several sheets of tracing paper, reinking the shoe after each impression. After the impressions are taken, the ink can be easily rinsed from the shoe with water. The tracing paper test impressions will dry in a few minutes and can be used for preliminary comparisons with the questioned impressions and for an assessment of what additional impressions, if any, are needed. The translucent nature of the tracing paper, particularly if used with a light box, will allow for its use as an

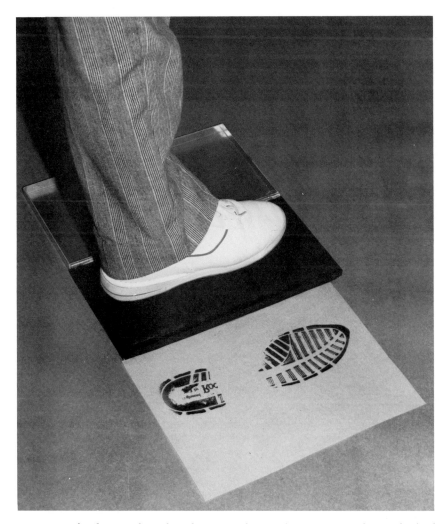

**8.6** Use of a large ink pad and a water-base ink is one simple method of obtaining test impressions of a shoe.

overlay material with photographs of the questioned impressions. In some cases, the tracing paper impressions are all that is needed and actually give sufficient information for the comparison process. Plain white paper can also be used to provide an impression with slightly more contrast.

*Ink and treated acetate impressions.* A second process involves the same procedure as the ink and tracing paper process described above; however, a material known as *treated acetate* or *prepared acetate* is used in lieu of the tracing paper. This material is clear acetate that has been treated so it will accept ink with minimum beading or running and it can be found in most art stores. This enables a test impression to be made on the clear acetate in the same manner as on the tracing paper. The advantage of using this material is that it provides a transparent overlay as soon as the ink dries.

Because this material is more costly than tracing paper, it is most efficiently used in conjunction with tracing paper or other paper. When the inking on the paper becomes uniform and the test impressions are reproducing well, the treated acetate can be substituted, and quality impressions can be obtained with minimal or no waste. This method is more successful when the shoe is being worn because it is easier to apply even and steady pressure to the shoe while it is being worn than when it is hand held and therefore avoid slippage.

*Inkless methods.* A relatively new method of taking impressions uses materials produced by the Identicator Corporation.[1] Until recently, this method has been used primarily for fingerprint impressions; however, it is also useful for obtaining quality footwear impressions. The inkless method employs a flat, padlike dispenser, depicted in Figure 8.7A, that contains a sensitized solution. It is used in conjunction with treated paper that, when it comes in contact with the sensitized solution, turns black. To obtain the impressions, wear the footwear and step on the dispenser pad several times to ensure that the shoe outsole is completely covered. Then step on the treated paper. The impression will immediately appear like black ink and will contain exceptionally fine detail. A test impression using this method is featured in Figure 8.7B.

*Fingerprint powder and clear adhesive impressions.* Sometimes, even if the shoe is worn while a test impression is made, portions of its outsole may not print in the test impression although they appear in a questioned impression. This may be due to the differences between the suspect's feet and the feet of the person making the test impressions, or due to the manner in which the impression was made as well as for other reasons. The following method, which involves black fingerprint powder and a clear adhesive sheet, provides a full representation of the outsole of the known shoe.

The fingerprint powder should be a fine, aluminum-based powder. Black powder is usually used; however, silver or other colored powders can be used as needed. Magnetic powders I have tried do not adhere well

---

[1] Identicator Corporation, Marina Del Re, CA.

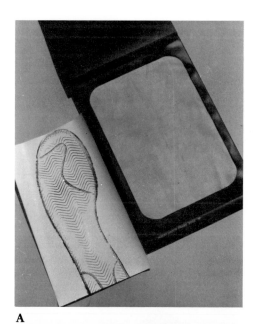

**8.7** A pad (**A**) containing a special solution and treated paper can be used to obtain a quality impression (**B**) having high contrast and excellent detail.

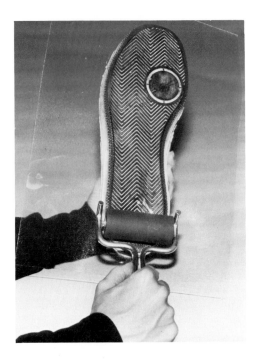

**8.8**   A clear adhesive sheet can be applied to a shoe outsole that has been dusted with fingerprint powder to provide a transparency of the entire surface of the outsole.

to the shoe outsoles and therefore do not produce a dark impression. If magnetic powders are preferred, a 50-50 mixture of magnetic and non-magnetic powder may help. The clear adhesive material should be a quality product that has an accompanying transparent polyester cover-sheet. To prepare the shoe for making an impression, its outsole, which must be thoroughly dry, should be evenly dusted with the fingerprint powder. The shoe should be tapped on its side to shake off any loose or excess powder. The protective cover of the clear adhesive material can be removed, and the clear adhesive portion can be laid on a table surface with the adhesive side up. To make an impression, the outsole of the shoe should be carefully pressed against the adhesive surface, taking care to avoid slippage. The shoe can then be lifted with the adhesive sheet adhering to the bottom of it. As shown in Figure 8.8, by using either a clean fingerprint roller or your fingers, the adhesive sheet can be pressed onto all of the remaining areas of the outsole. If too much powder is used, the adhesive material may not adhere well to the shoe, making it difficult to obtain a full impression of the outsole without some distortion or slippage of the adhesive sheet. After the full outsole is reproduced on the adhesive material, the adhesive sheet should be carefully removed by peeling it away from the shoe from one end to the other. The adhesive sheet should then be laid down with the adhesive side containing the impression facing up. The transparent polyester cover sheet can then be placed over the adhesive material by touching one end of it first to the adhesive sheet and then, using a clean finger-print roller, rolling the remaining portion of the cover over the adhesive sheet. This will permanently cover and protect the impression. The use of a fingerprint roller will help to prevent air bubbles from being trapped between the two sheets.

Like the other methods, this method can also be used while the shoe is being worn. The adhesive material should be laid on the floor. The shoe, after being dusted with powder, is carefully placed on the foot and is then pressed against the adhesive sheet, beginning with the heel and completing the impression as if one were taking a step. The shoe is then removed carefully and turned over with the adhesive sheet still at-tached. Any areas that have not registered against the adhesive can be carefully pressed with a finger or roller against the outsole to give a complete impression. The additional pressure of the shoe against the adhesive when it is being worn assists in preventing the adhesive mate-rial from slipping and becoming dislodged. If the adhesive sheet will not remain stuck to the shoe outsole, there may be too heavy a layer of fingerprint powder on the outside surface.

*Fingerprint powder and roller transport film impressions.* Another method that produces both an excellent test impression and an excel-lent transparency, involves the use of a photographic product known as roller transport film (Petraco N et al., 1982). This film is a clear photo-graphic film with a gelatin coating on each side, which becomes soft when wet. The method involves dusting the shoe outsole with a me-dium to heavy coating of fingerprint powder. After the shoe is dusted, it should be tapped firmly on its side to remove any loose fingerprint powder, but with care to avoid touching the dusted outsole surface. The shoe should then be placed on its side until needed. A sheet of roller transport film should be cut to the proper size to accommodate the impression. The film should be placed on a clean, dry surface. A sponge that is dripping wet with water should then be lightly passed over the film so that the entire surface of the side of the film facing up has been wetted thoroughly. It is important to note that the sponge should completely cover the film with water and that no streaks, such as those that might result from a damp sponge instead of a dripping wet sponge, should be on the film. It is permissible to pass the sponge over the film a second time; however, the sponge is not to be used to scrub or wipe the film but merely as a controlled means of covering one side of the film with water. It is also permissible to simply run water over the surface of the film instead of applying water with the sponge. Immediately after this has been done, a squeegee should be used to make a single pass over the film to remove all of the water from one side of it. A good squeegee and technique must be used here, both to avoid streaking and to remove all of the water with one pass. A clean automobile windshield sponge-

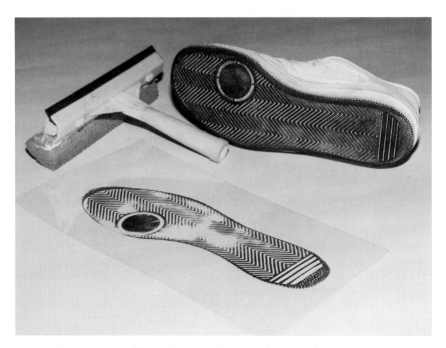

**8.9**   Roller transport film, when its gelatin surface is softened with water, will retain an excellent impression made with a powdered shoe.

squeegee combination, as pictured in Figure 8.9, works well for this procedure.

After the water has been removed, the film should be placed on a clean, smooth, firm floor surface. The gelatin will remain soft for a minute or two. The dusted shoe should now be carefully placed on the foot. The impression is made by stepping on the film. The powder that was on the outsole of the shoe will become imbedded in the soft gelatin coating of the film. The film can then be set aside and allowed to dry for a couple of minutes. The impression can be made lighter or darker by varying the amount of fingerprint powder used. Although black fingerprint powder is usually used, silver or colored powder may be used if it will provide better contrast over a particular questioned impression. The advantage offered by this method is that it provides an instantly available and very clear transparency that has been produced while wearing the shoe, and it reproduces the finest detail from the shoe with the maximum contrast.

*Using fingerprint or talcum powder with gelatin lifting products.* The fingerprint powder and clear adhesive method can be repeated for the purposes of obtaining a higher contrast impression. A clear gelatin lifter used with a powdered shoe will provide a quality

**8.10** An impression made with white talcum powder and a black gelatin lifting film.

impression that can be used as a transparency. The white and black gelatin lifters, used with black or silver powders, respectively, provide test impressions of high contrast. The qualities of the gelatin lifting materials, such as their flexibility and softness, allow for a more thorough recording of the detail of the known footwear. If necessary, a photographic transparency can be made of these impressions. It is usually not necessary to use more than a light coating of fingerprint powder when using these materials. Figure 8.10 depicts an impression made on a black gelatin lifter after dusting the shoe with white talcum powder.

*Carbon paper or black chartboard and talcum powder impressions.* Carbon paper or chartboard can also be used in conjunction with talcum powder. To make impressions this way, dust the shoes with talcum powder or white fingerprint powder and then make the impression on black carbon paper or chartboard. As shown in Figure 8.11, this will provide a light-colored positive impression on a dark background.

**8.11**    An impression made with white talcum powder and black chartboard.

*Using iodine-sensitized paper.* Iodine-sensitized paper can also be used for making test impressions. The sensitized paper is made by fuming paper with iodine, which can be done by hanging it in an iodine chamber. The chamber can consist of any small tank or container that will safely confine iodine fumes. Iodine crystals are then heated in a small dish placed in the chamber. Heating the iodine crystals will produce iodine vapor in the chamber. The iodine fumes will be absorbed by the paper, which can then be removed from the chamber. To make a test impression with this paper, the outsole of the shoe should be evenly dampened. The impression of the damp shoe on the treated paper will result in a purplish color where the damp shoe has contacted the paper. The contrast obtained with this method is not as great as with methods employing fingerprint powder. Impressions made in this way are usually dried first and then stored in an airtight plastic bag. If left out, they will deteriorate.

*Oil residue impressions dusted with fingerprint powder.* Yet another method involves spraying the outsole of the shoe with silicone spray and then stepping on paper, leaving an oil print. A magna brush is then used to develop the oil print test impression on the paper. The color of the paper as well as the color of the fingerprint powder can be changed to provide different combinations of color or contrast. One disadvantage of this method is that the impression will smear if it is touched.

*Negative impressions.* The above methods all involve making positive impressions, in which the raised areas of the shoe outsole, i.e., the portion that contacts the surface, deposits a material onto the surface. In negative impressions, the raised areas of the shoe outsole remove material from the surface. It is not necessary to compare a negative questioned impression with a negative known impression. It may be helpful, though, to have the knowledge of how an original negative impression can be made.

One excellent method of making a true negative impression that I recently discovered involves the use of a light gray spray product called *dulling spray.* This product, usually found in photographic specialty stores, can be evenly sprayed across a smooth, nonporous item, such as a piece of aluminum, plastic, formica, or other smooth surface. After it dries (1 to 5 minutes), it is easily removed by wiping but also by an object, such as a shoe, making contact with it. The areas removed will expose the material beneath the spray. Thus, as a piece of black formica is sprayed with dulling spray, it will be colored light gray. A shoe impressed on its surface will remove the gray dulling spray where the raised areas of the shoe come in contact with the formica. This will reveal the black finish in those areas, resulting in a true negative im-

**8.12**   A negative impression made by spraying a colored surface with dulling spray, which is removed in the areas touched by the shoe outsole during the impression-making process.

pression. This type of impression is pictured in Figure 8.12. Although the impression can be smeared, I have not yet found another method that produces a true negative impression as well as this.

As a better way of illustrating the minor differences of the different methods, parts A, B, and C of Figure 8.13 depict greatly enlarged portions of the impressions in Figures 8.10, 8.11, and 8.12, respectively. Note the variation between the positive impression made on the soft gelatin material with that made on the harder chartboard. Also note the opposite effect of the negative impression compared with the positive impressions. A reversed photograph of the respective portion of the shoe outsole used to make these impressions is provided in Figure 8.13D.

## Three-Dimensional Test Impressions

Often, it is essential to make a three-dimensional test impression of a shoe in order to effectively compare that shoe with a three-dimensional questioned impression. Three-dimensional questioned impressions contain characteristics of both the raised and depressed surfaces of the outsole. If the impression is sufficiently deep, it can also contain impressions of the side of the outsole, the side of the midsole, and sometimes even the upper of the shoe. If those areas of the shoe are recorded in the questioned impression, they can contain characteristics that are as valuable as those found on the bottom of the shoe. It is therefore important to have the materials and knowledge to provide good quality three-dimensional test impressions.

Three-dimensional impressions that are received in the laboratory for comparisons can be either photographs of questioned three-dimensional impressions or casts of those impressions. Since casts are a positive likeness of the shoe that made the impressions, they are best compared directly with the known shoe. For three-dimensional impressions represented by photographs, three-dimensional test impression methods can be used. If necessary, the test impression can be photographed using a light source at a similar height and position as the lighting in the photograph of the questioned impression. A transparency can also be made from the photographs of the test impressions, if needed.

*Impressions in sand and similar materials.* Sand impressions are obtained by placing about $\frac{1}{2}$ inch of fine sand in a tray. Brown sand is sometimes favored over white sand for photographic reasons. Sand impressions can be made using dry sand; however, dry sand usually fills in and does not retain the detail very well. For that reason, it is usually necessary to wet the sand in order for it to retain the detail.

Attempts to move trays full of wet sand will often cause the test impression to break apart. It is therefore easier to make the impression where it will be photographed. The sand in the tray should first be made level and smooth by using a straightedge or ruler. After the sand is smooth, it should be sprayed liberally with a fine mist of water until it is completely wet from the surface to the bottom. If the sand is only wet on the surface, the impression will break apart when the footwear is impressed into the dry sand beneath. For that reason, several sprayings of the sand should be made to ensure that enough water has been used to penetrate and wet all of the sand evenly. The test impression can now

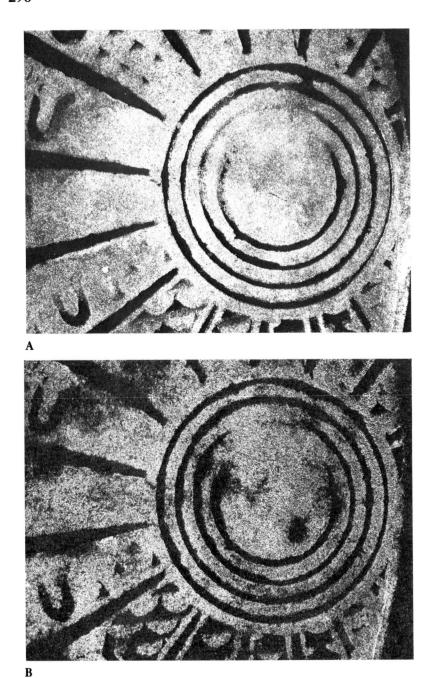

A

B

**8.13** Close-up of a small portion of the impressions in Figures 8.10 (**A**), 8.11 (**B**), and 8.12 (**C**) and a reverse photograph of the same area of the shoe (**D**) used to make those impressions.

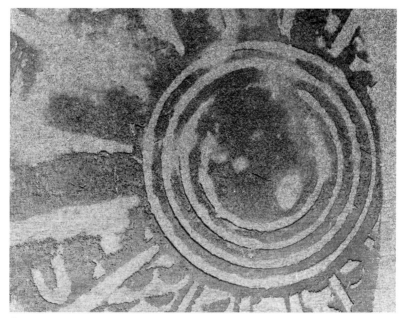

C

D

be made. The shoe should be worn when making the impression. The person wearing the shoe should control the amount of weight to provide a test impression that is similar in depth and other characteristics to the questioned impressions.

After the test impression is made, it should be photographed with a scale and a shadow indicator before it dries out and begins to deteriorate. Remember to place the scale on the same plane as the bottom of the impression. If the test impression is successful, both photographic prints and transparencies can be made to maximize the usefulness of the sand impression. Refer to Figures 2.11 and 2.13 for examples of photographs of sand impressions.

*Cleansing powder and fingerprint powder impressions.* Test impressions can also be made in a variety of other similar materials. One method (Van Rummelhoff J, 1981) suggests the use of cleansing powder and fingerprint powder. By mixing cleansing powder with a small quantity of gray fingerprint powder, and placing that mixture in a small tray, three-dimensional test impressions can be made. Whereas impressions made in the sand mixture are best made by wearing the shoes, these impressions are best made by holding the shoes. This is because the cleansing powder–fingerprint powder mixture is so fragile that the weight of the shoe itself is almost sufficient to make the impression. Once made, these impressions are suitable for photographing. Drawbacks to this method are that it is very messy and the impressions are extremely fragile.

*Impressions in clay.* Modeling clay can occasionally be of use in making test impressions, particularly when attempting to reproduce a particular area of a shoe or the edges of the shoe. It is sometimes necessary to warm the clay slightly to facilitate working with it; this can be done quickly by heating it in a microwave oven. The clay should be laid out and flattened and should be smooth and free of air bubbles. Before any test impression is made, the shoe outsole should be sprayed with a silicone releasing agent to prevent the clay from sticking to the shoe. The impression can be made by holding or wearing the shoe. The clay impression is easily preserved for photographing and can be saved in a shallow box, if desired. If not, the clay can be reused for future impressions.

*Biofoam impressions.* Another deformable material that can be used to obtain three-dimensional standards is a material called Biofoam.[2] This material is a fragile foam material that deforms under minimal

---

[2] Smithers Biomedical Systems, Kent, OH.

**8.14**   An impression in Biofoam.

pressure to conform to the shape of the object deforming it. It is usually used to take anatomical impressions of the feet; however, it can also be used to take impressions of footwear. Figure 8.14 shows a Biofoam impression of a shoe.

*Silicone casts.* One of the best and most successful methods for making a three-dimensional test impression of a shoe involves the use of silicone casting material. In order to do this properly, a compressed air source with a regulator and some silicone casting material are needed. Some shoes, for various reasons, may be curled slightly and may require the placement of a shoetree in them to hold the outsole straight. Figure 8.15 shows the silicone casting procedure. The inverted

**A**

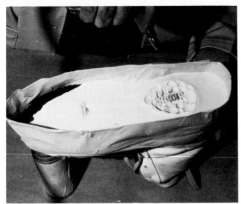

**8.15** The silicone impression process. The shoe is dusted with powder, inverted, and then wrapped with masking tape to build up an area to hold the silicone. The silicone is mixed with the catalyst and poured, $\frac{1}{4}$ inch at a time onto the shoe (**A**). Regulated air pressure is used to spread the silicone over the shoe and to eliminate air bubbles (**B**). The silicone is allowed to cure for 24 hours. When removed, a quality impression of the entire outsole results (**C**).

**B**

**C**

shoe must first be taped with masking tape to create an area to contain the silicone material over the outsole. The shoe should then be secured with the bottom facing up and level. The bottom of the shoe and the tape surfaces that will be exposed to the silicone should be sprayed with a silicone releasing agent.

A pint of silicone casting material should then be thoroughly mixed with the proper amount of catalyst so that the silicone does not harden too fast. The mixing is best done with an electric mixer of some sort. It is almost impossible to achieve homogeneity when mixing this quantity of silicone by hand. Pour a small amount, but no more than $\frac{1}{4}$ inch of silicone onto the bottom of the shoe. Using the compressed air source, adjust the regulator so that only a very slow stream of air is coming out. Direct this air carefully onto the bottom of the shoe, using the air as a means of spreading the silicone over the shoe bottom and into all of the cracks and crevices of the outsole design. This procedure is shown in Figure 8.15B. It may be necessary to use a toothpick or other similar device to assist in popping some stubborn air bubbles or in forcing the silicone into deep areas. Next, add another $\frac{1}{4}$ inch of silicone, and continue to spread the material over the shoe bottom with the compressed air. Add yet another $\frac{1}{4}$ inch of silicone and spread it over the surface of the shoe bottom with the air source. When the surface of the outsole of the shoe is covered completely, add the remaining silicone to the surface of the shoe bottom. Again, use the compressed air to spread the material out over the surface of the shoe and to eliminate any visible air bubbles.

The shoe and casting material should then be allowed to sit undisturbed for 24 hours in order to cure properly. Afterwards, the tape and cast can be removed from the shoe. The silicone cast will provide the maximum detail that the shoe could leave in its three-dimensional impression. A silicone cast of a shoe that has been dusted first with fingerprint powder is pictured in Figure 8.15C.

To obtain a silicone cast of this type, the outsole of the shoe can first be lightly dusted with black fingerprint powder. The powder will be removed with the cast and will highlight the detail in the impression. The fingerprint powder that remains on the shoe after making some of the aforementioned two-dimensional impressions is usually sufficient to highlight the cast. If the shoe has too much powder, it will not highlight the detail in the shoe but will reduce the contrast by simply coloring the entire surface black. The highlighted cast can be photographed to provide a photographic print or transparency.

## Variations in Test Impressions of Known Shoes

Variations will always occur from one test impression to another, just as variations occur between the impressions a shoe leaves at a crime scene. Although this is to be expected, the examiner should be aware of this variation and of the fact that there may also be minor discrepancies that occur between test impressions made holding the shoe versus those made wearing the shoe.

## Photographic Transparencies of Test Impressions

Mention has been made of preparing photographic transparencies of certain test impressions. These can be made by first taking a photograph of the test impression with fine-grained black-and-white film. The negative should then be exposed onto fine-grained positive film, which, when developed, will provide a transparency. A black impression on a white background will provide a black impression on the transparency. A flat scale should be included so that the transparencies can be enlarged accurately to a natural size.

## Copy Machine Transparencies of Test Impressions

Some copy machines allow for the production of transparent copies. It should be noted that minor distortions and size discrepancies occur in transparencies made on certain copy machines. Copy machine transparencies of known impressions of shoes may, in some cases, be satisfactory as a preliminary comparison convenience. Their poor resolution and accuracy does not encourage their use as a final or highly detailed comparison aid.

## Summary

Questioned impressions can be made in many ways and can be found on many surfaces. The knowledge and experience of making test impressions in a number of ways will help the examiner select those best suited for a particular case. For comparison standards of known shoes, one or more of the aforementioned methods of making test impressions should prove to be sufficient. Occasionally, an improvised method must be devised for a particular impression.

Test impressions are made as a comparison aid for use both during the examination and as a demonstration aid in court, if needed. The dynamics and variables involved when a suspect makes an impression on a particular surface are never going to be duplicated exactly. In addition, many questioned impressions contain distortion or slippage beyond those expected variables. As a result, there may be slight disagreements between the dimensions and characteristics of impressions made by the same shoe. Likewise, it is expected that there will sometimes be slight disagreements between the dimensions and characteristics of a questioned impression and that of a test impression made from the same shoe. The examiner must distinguish among a true difference, one caused by a different shoe, and a slight disagreement caused by the usual variables in the impression-making process. Experience in making a variety of both two- and three-dimensional test impressions will help.

# Wear Characteristics

# 9

The interpretation of and value applied to wear characteristics on the surfaces of shoe outsoles varies considerably among examiners. Very little has been written and few forensic studies have been conducted on the topic.

Two factors can be observed in a footwear examination with regard to the wear of a shoe. They are the *position of wear* on the shoe and the *degree of wear* at that position. The position of wear on a shoe is a product of the qualities of the individual who wears it, the extent and use for which it is worn, and a number of other influencing factors. The degree of wear of a shoe at any particular position on the outsole is also a significant factor in the examination, since the degree of wear on that shoe is constantly changing.

## Definitions

The following definitions are being offered as they relate to footwear impression comparisons.

*Wear* on shoe outsoles may be defined as the erosion of the outsole due to frictional and abrasive forces that occur between the outsole and the ground.

*Wear characteristics* are changes in the surface of the outsole that are observable in the impression and/or known shoe and reflect the erosion of the surface of the outsole. These changes have resulted in the current condition of the outsole in contrast to its original condition.

The *wear pattern* or *position of wear* can be defined as an arrangement or pattern of wear characteristics that stands out against areas of relatively less or greater wear. The wear pattern is largely influenced by the shape, size, bone structure, and biomechanics of the wearer's feet.

The *degree of wear* refers to the extent that a particular portion of the shoe is worn.

*General condition* refers to the overall condition or general amount of wear, i.e., unworn, severely worn, slightly worn, and so forth.

## Influences on the Wear of Shoe Outsoles

When a shoe is new, it is not destined to wear in a particular manner. The way and the extent to which it wears are due to a number of influencing factors that act in combination. Some of these factors include a person's foot type and function, occupation, habits, body type, the last the shoe was built on, the shoe style, the shoe materials, and the surfaces on which that shoe passes over as it is worn. Although these factors are independent of one another, most, if not all, influence the wearing of a shoe outsole simultaneously.

### The Human Foot

As pressure is exerted by the foot within the shoe, the areas of the outsole directly beneath the weight-bearing areas of the foot will wear more quickly than other areas. This is because there will be greater frictional forces beneath the weight-bearing areas. In fact, the entire shoe will adapt to the foot according to the foot's form and function. Some basic knowledge of the foot, of various foot types, and of the foot's mechanics during walking is helpful in providing a general understanding of why the shoes of one person may wear in a different way than the shoes of another.

The human foot consists of 26 bones. They are grouped in three different areas: (1) the hindfoot, comprising the talus (ankle bone) and calcaneus (heel bone); (2) the midfoot, composed of five tarsal bones; and (3) the forefoot, which includes the five metatarsal bones and 14 phalanges. These are illustrated and labeled in the dorsal view of the foot pictured in Figure 9.1. In addition, as evident in the medial view of the foot in Figure 9.1, two small bones called sesamoid bones normally occur beneath the head of the first metatarsal.

In the hindfoot, the talus and calcaneus act together to join the foot to the lower leg. The joint formed by the talus and the lower leg together with the subtalar joint, which is the joint formed by the talus and calcaneus, allow the foot to move.

The tarsal bones of the midfoot form the arch of the foot and help

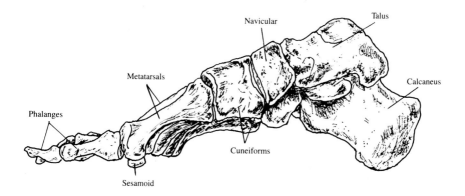

**Medial View**

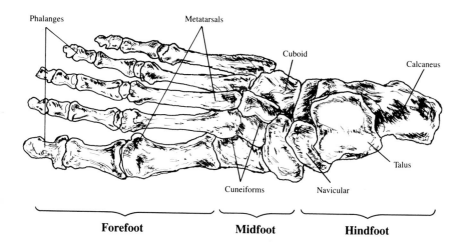

**Dorsal View**

**9.1**   Dorsal and medial views of the bones of the human foot.

transmit the weight of the body through the foot. They include the cuboid, the navicular, and the three cuneiform bones.

In the forefoot, the five metatarsal bones and the 14 bones of the toes, called phalanges, allow more flexibility, help the foot adapt to uneven surfaces, and provide leverage for propulsion. Note that the great toe, also known as the hallux, contains only two phalanges while the other toes each contain three phalanges.

The precise lengths, sizes, and shapes of these bones are initially determined genetically; however, the growth of these bones and their resulting size and shape are further influenced and changed accordingly by the stresses and demands placed on them throughout a person's life. The result is a foot that is unique to each individual.

## Function of the Foot

In addition to being familiar with the bones of the foot, it is also of assistance to the footwear examiner to have some general knowledge of what occurs within the foot during the walking cycle.

The foot can move in four directions. It can extend itself by pointing the toes downward (plantar flexion) or flex itself by pointing the toes upward (dorsiflexion). It can also turn inward (inversion), which it does during supination, and outward (eversion), which it does during pronation. Plantar flexion and dorsiflexion occur in the ankle joint between the lower leg bones and the upper part of the talus. Inversion and eversion obtain their motion in the subtalar joint, between the calcaneus and the talus. The ability of the foot to perform the four basic motions is essential for normal function. When the ability to perform any of these motions is reduced, the foot will be unable to function as it should.

In a normal, nonweight-bearing foot, the tibia and fibula of the lower leg and the talus and calcaneus in the hind foot should line up straight. The center of gravity will ideally pass equally through the bones in that neutral position, as illustrated in the right foot in Figure 9.2.

In the walking cycle, the subtalar joint of a normal foot will be in the neutral position as the heel strikes the ground. The foot will sense the surface, and the subtalar joint will pronate. During pronation, the other joints in the foot become loose, allowing the foot to be flexible and able to adapt to the surface it is stepping on. During the pronating motion, the forefoot rolls inward, flattening out the arch and distributing the weight throughout the foot. At the point where the weight of the body is centered over the foot and when the ball of the foot has contacted the ground, the subtalar joint will begin to supinate. During supination, the foot will become more of a rigid lever, allowing the foot to more efficiently push off from the supporting surface. By the time the foot returns to the ground in the next heel strike, the subtalar joint should have returned to the neutral position. Very rarely does a foot begin or end this cycle with the subtalar joint actually in the neutral position, however. Instead, for most persons, it is still slightly in the supinated position.

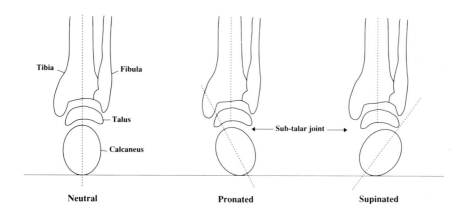

Tibia

Fibula

Talus

Calcaneus

Sub-talar joint

Neutral

Pronated

Supinated

*(Viewed from the back of foot)*

**9.2**   The calcaneus and talus bones of the non-weight-bearing foot are lined up straight in the neutral position. Movement in the subtalar joint allows the foot to pronate and to supinate.

*Forefoot wear.* Most persons also have a condition in which the forefoot, in a *non-weight-bearing state,* is not parallel to the ground when the subtalar joint is at the neutral position. Rather, it is either in the "forefront varus" or the "forefoot valgus" position.

In the condition known as forefoot varus, when the subtalar joint is in the neutral position, the non-weight-bearing forefoot will have the first toe higher than the fifth toe. As the foot strikes the ground, in order to bring the first toe down to the ground, the subtalar joint must pronate to compensate for the forefoot varus condition (Figure 9.3A). As a result of this happening, the weight is slightly shifted to the inside of the foot and is also spread over a broader area of the forefoot. Wear on the shoe will therefore be spread out in a wider area beneath the forefoot and, in some cases, on the medial side of the shoe. The person with forefoot varus will usually have a long, straight, flat foot and will have difficulty fitting into a shoe that has been built on a curved last.

In the condition known as forefoot valgus, when the subtalar joint is in the neutral position, the non-weight-bearing forefoot will have the fifth toe higher than the first toe. As the foot strikes the ground, the subtalar joint must compensate by supinating in order to bring the fifth toe down to the ground (Figure 9.3B). In a foot where this happens, the weight is slightly shifted to the outside of the foot. The foot, when it supinates, is in a contracted position. The toes are more drawn back, which places the weight over the metatarsal heads. The wear on shoes of persons having this condition will often be more localized beneath

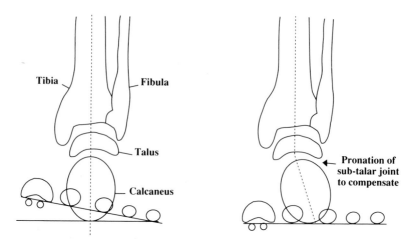

**Forefoot Varus (Flat Foot)**

*(A.) (Viewed from the back of the foot)*

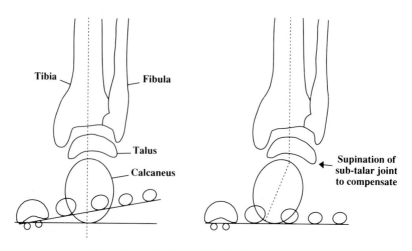

**Forefoot Valgus (High Arch Foot)**

*(B.) (Viewed from the back of the foot)*

**9.3** In the forefoot varus condition (A), the non-weight-bearing forefoot has the first toe in a higher position than the fifth toe. In order to compensate for this and to bring the first toe to the ground when foot bears weight, the subtalar joint must pronate. In the forefoot valgus condition (B), the non-weight-bearing forefoot has the fifth toe in a higher position than the first toe. In order to compensate for this and to bring the fifth toe to the ground when the foot bears weight, the subtalar joint must supinate (right foot).

the first toe, which strikes the ground first, beneath the metatarsal heads, and to the lateral side of the outsole. A high-arch foot usually remains more supinated than pronated.

The resulting wear patterns of the extreme forefoot varus and forefoot valgus conditions can be seen in Figures 9.4 and 9.5. These examples of forefoot varus and forefoot valgus are presented in a simplified way to provide one example of how foot functions influence the position of wear. Real life examples include numerous degrees of these conditions,

**9.4** A typical wear pattern on a shoe belonging to a person with forefoot varus condition whose foot bears weight in a more pronated position. The wear is beneath the medial side of the foot, with little wear on the lateral side.

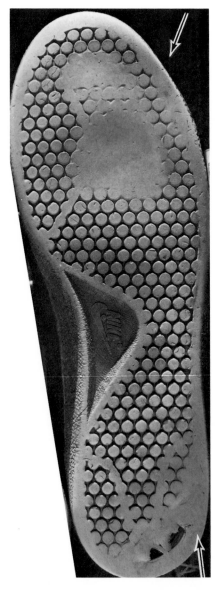

**9.5** A typical wear pattern on a shoe belonging to a person with forefoot valgus condition whose foot supports the weight in a more supinated position. The wear is beneath the lateral side of the foot and the metatarsal heads, with little wear on the medial side.

which are also influenced by the other biomechanical factors in each individual.

*Heel wear.* Because in most individuals the heel is the first part of the shoe to strike the ground and absorb a great deal of the shock and weight, the wear on the heel or heel area of a shoe is perhaps the most noticeable and easiest to recognize. There are several factors that influence the position and angle of heel wear. One of those is the previously discussed degree of supination or, less frequently, pronation of the subtalar joint when the heel strikes the ground during the walking cycle. The amount of supination or pronation of the subtalar joint, and therefore the shoe, influences the degree to which the heel is tilted in or out relative to the ground (Figure 9.6).

Another factor is the amount of "toe in" or "toe out" that the person has. Most people have feet that toe out; fewer have feet that toe in. Feet that toe out result in an angle of wear across the outside of the heel that is directly related to the angle of toe out. Likewise, feet that toe in have an angle of wear across the inside of the heel that is directly related to the degree of toe in (Figure 9.6). The degree of toe-in or toe-out is often not the same on both feet. The combination of the heel being either supinated or pronated at heel strike and the amount of toe-in or toe-out, along with lower leg flexibility, ankle flexibility, and other factors, all contribute to the specific location and angle of wear on the heel of each shoe.

## *Habits, Activities, and Personal Features of the Wearer*

Just as shoe wear is influenced by a person's foot type and function during normal walking or standing, the other activities and habits in a person's daily life, as well as her or his personal make-up, are also factors in the acquired wear on the shoe.

The weight of the person wearing the shoes has a great deal of influence on the rate at which a pair of shoes wear, simply because the wearer's weight is passed on through the shoes to the areas between the outsole and the ground. The more a person weighs, the greater the frictional forces are between the outsole and the ground.

The manner in which a person walks also influences the wear on the shoe. Different gaits and walking peculiarities can result in different areas of the shoe striking the ground first. People who regularly scuff their feet between steps or drag their toes after they push off will have shoes that wear in those areas. Any significant foot problems or disabilities will also affect a person's walking and therefore the wear on the shoe.

The sex and body type of the wearer also can play a role in the wear of a shoe. Factors like the width of a person's hips, the flexibility in the lower legs, any unevenness in the lengths of the legs, and the leg swing will have an influence on shoe wear.

The occupation and/or habits of the wearer can also have a great impact on shoe wear. Some occupations or habits cause excessive contact of parts of the shoe with the ground. For instance, a delivery person or salesperson who might pivot on one foot as he or she gets in and out

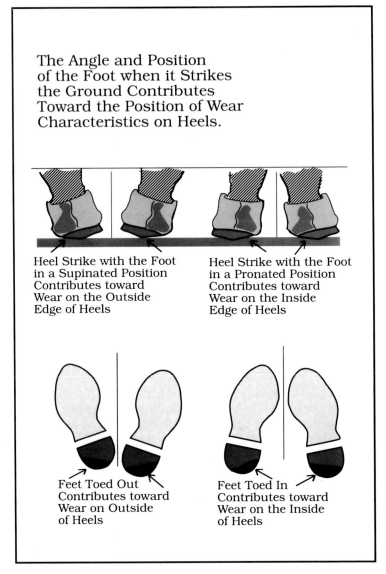

**The Angle and Position of the Foot when it Strikes the Ground Contributes Toward the Position of Wear Characteristics on Heels.**

Heel Strike with the Foot in a Supinated Position Contributes toward Wear on the Outside Edge of Heels

Heel Strike with the Foot in a Pronated Position Contributes toward Wear on the Inside Edge of Heels

Feet Toed Out Contributes toward Wear on Outside of Heels

Feet Toed In Contributes toward Wear on the Inside of Heels

**9.6**  The angle and position of the foot when it strikes the ground contributes to the position of the wear characteristics on the heels.

of a vehicle many times each day, will begin to accumulate added wear in that area of the shoe. A motorcyclist who uses one foot to change gears hundreds of times each week will cause additional wear on specific parts of that shoe. And a person who works in a carpeted office all day will not wear shoes out nearly as fast as one with an occupation that requires a considerable amount of outdoor activity such as a construction worker or a mail delivery person.

Hypothetically, if three different persons having very similar foot types and foot functions were to wear the same exact type of tennis shoes and if they all were to wear those shoes only for routine daily usage, then the wear patterns and characteristics on the outsoles of those three pairs of shoes could be somewhat similar. However, if those three persons, in addition to their usual walking and standing, also took part in additional specialized activities, the shoes would receive additional wear in different positions. For instance, if the first person played basketball frequently, the second person spent a great deal of time bicycling, and the third person played tennis, then additional wear in certain areas of each of their shoes would be caused by those activities. The position of additional wear would vary in the three examples, relative to those activities.

Life's daily experiences that influence the wearing of shoes are not as simple as the above hypothetical example. Although each person has a particular foot type and biomechanics and may even use her or his shoes for a specific function, the exact wear on one's shoes at any point in time is the result of the sum of all the influencing factors up to that time. The sum of those factors can never be duplicated. If a person were to buy two identical pairs of shoes and wear them equally, the wear on those shoes, although probably extremely similar, would never be *exactly* the same. Although in theory, the wear characteristics could never be duplicated, this is not to imply that wear could, in itself, evidence uniqueness. Wear on different shoes could be so close that, given the reduced detail and variations found in questioned impressions and the fact that the wear is constantly changing, two shoes, at some time during their life, could have indistinguishable wear characteristics.

## Design and Manufacturing Influences on Wear

Whether a shoe is made on a straight last or on a curved last can affect the position of wear in the shoe. For instance, a foot will be positioned differently over the outsole of a shoe built on a curved last than it would in a shoe built on a straight last. The differences in the precise position of the foot in the shoe and thus, over the top of the outsole will affect the position of wear on the outsole.

Some outsole materials or combinations of materials, particularly in today's athletic shoes, result in some shoes wearing down faster than others. Microcellular materials like expanded ethyl vinyl acetate and low-density polyurethane, although excellent for cushioning and shock absorption, wear more rapidly. Dense rubbers and high-density polyurethanes resist wear and last much longer.

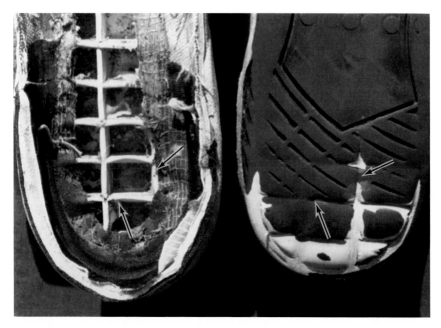

**9.7** The honeycombed or latticelike patterns on the upper side of some molded outsoles transmit a greater amount of weight through the shoe directly beneath those areas, resulting in wear that reflects the pattern.

Certain other manufacturing characteristics can also influence the wear position and pattern. Figure 9.7 depicts the heel area of the outsole of a well-worn shoe. Apparent in the wear on the heel is a grid pattern. This is attributed to the honeycomblike area found on the opposite side of the molded outsole, also pictured in Figure 9.7. The grid of the honeycomb design transmits more of the weight to the outsole than do the void areas causing additional wear directly beneath the grid areas.

Another example can be seen in the siped shoe, pictured in Figure 9.8 in both its new and worn condition. Note the sharp points of the peaks and valleys of the siped herringbone design in the unworn shoe. As the shoe flexes during walking, these peaks and valleys protrude. The result is that the pointed areas wear down to a more rounded herringbone pattern, with several of the points actually being torn away. The wearing effects on siped shoes as they relate to the manufacturing characteristics are also discussed in Chapter 7.

Yet another example would occur when the upper material of a shoe or boot is tucked and glued beneath the lasted shoe, resulting in a bulge of material at that point. A soft, calendered, unvulcanized outsole placed over the bulging material may result in a bulge in the outsole at

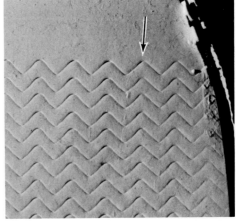

**9.8** The peaks of the herring-bone pattern of a siped shoe protrude when the shoe is flexed, resulting in those areas becoming rounded or being torn off. The precise pattern of the shoe before it is worn (**A**) may change slightly after some wear (**B**) and may appear more rounded.

A

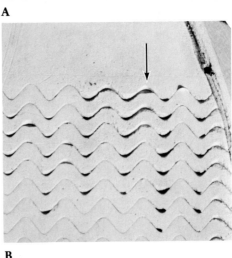

B

that point. Any part of the outsole that bulges or protrudes will be likely to wear faster than other areas of the outsole. For that reason, it is not uncommon to see wear appear first beneath the areas of an outsole that contain the tucked upper material.

## Differences Between Wear in Left and Right Shoes

The numerous factors that influence the wearing of shoes will not be exactly the same in both the left and right feet of individuals. Therefore, the precise position and degree of wear will not be identical in a person's left and right shoes. Figure 9.9 depicts portions of two pairs of shoes that

**A**

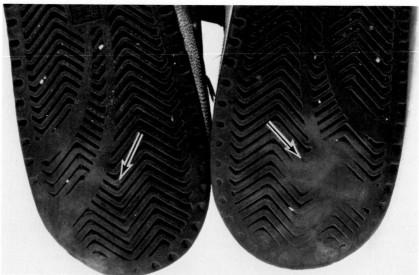

**B**

**9.9** The shoes of a person's left and right feet do not wear exactly alike. This is reflected in the two pairs of shoes in both the forefoot areas (**A**) and the heel areas (**B**).

are typical inasmuch as they exhibit different wear on the left and right shoes.

## Considerations of Wear Characteristics During Examination

The wearing of a shoe is a continuous process that is constantly changing the outsole of the shoe. The degree of wear at various positions on a shoe on one day may be changed significantly 2 weeks or a month later, as that wear spreads out. It is important in the comparison of footwear impressions that the degree of wear and the position of wear on a shoe are in agreement with those reflected in the questioned impression. If they are not in agreement, this does not necessarily denote a lack of identification. A shoe obtained 2 months after the crime could have a much more advanced degree of wear.

### Degree of Wear

*When the specific degree of wear is identical.* The wearing down of a shoe causes portions of its design to undergo change. As this happens, the overall appearance of those portions of the shoe outsole will also change. When the degree of wear in an area of the shoe is at a specific point on both the questioned impression and the shoe, then those areas can be said to correspond in the *specific degree* of wear. This is often the case if the shoes were obtained shortly after the crime. The presence of stippling and other finely detailed patterns in certain shoe designs makes the comparison of the specific degree of wear easier than on shoes that have no design or a more durable or rugged design. Figure 9.10 shows a questioned impression and a known impression that agree in specific wear characteristics.

*When the degree of wear on the shoe is more advanced.* When the degree of wear on a shoe is in a more advanced stage than that exhibited in the questioned impression, consideration must be given to the time that has elapsed between the crime when the impression was made and the seizure of the shoe. If the shoes were not recovered until a long time after the crime, several possibilities could exist. The suspect may have worn the shoes in question either very little or not at all, in which case the condition of the shoes and degree of wear could be virtually the same as if they had been recovered shortly after the crime. If the suspect had worn the shoes continuously during that time, the wear would likely be in a more advanced condition, unless the outsole was of a very durable substance and/or the shoes were not subjected to harsh wear during that time.

**A**

**9.10** The specific degree of wear in an impression (**A**) which corresponds precisely with the known shoe (**B**).

**B**

Figure 9.11 depicts an enlarged area of a cast of a boot impression made in snow. An enlarged photograph of the same areas of the boot, which was obtained 1 month later, is also featured in Figure 9.11. The position of the wear is centered in the same area, but the degree of wear has advanced outward slightly in the shoe beyond where it is reflected in the cast. This would be expected if the boots had received additional wear.

If the condition of wear in a pair of shoes is significantly more advanced than the wear that is evident in the questioned impression, considering the time lapse between the crime and the seizure of the shoes, it may be possible to eliminate those shoes from having made the impression. *Extreme caution must be used in this type of situation.* It is very hard to estimate how much time it would take for a particular person to wear down a particular pair of shoes. Only when there is no doubt that the additional amount of wear could not have in any way taken place should a positive elimination be considered. As an example, I can recall a case where the crime scene impressions were made by a jogging shoe in practically new condition. The detail in the design elements was crisp and clear and showed virtually no wear, except on the extreme outer edge of the heel. A pair of shoes was seized with a search warrant 14 days after the crime. The shoes were not being worn by the suspect at the time. Although the physical shape and design of the suspect's shoe corresponded with the questioned impression, the condition of the suspect's shoes was one of extremely advanced wear. The shoes simply could not have been worn down that much in 2 weeks, even if the suspect covered 20 to 30 miles a day.

Figure 9.12 is a series of three photographs of the heel of a jogging shoe, taken over a period of three months. The shoe was worn on a daily basis. The degree of wear increases and the position of wear expands from its original position as the heel surface is worn down.

*When the wear in the shoe is less than that in the questioned impression.* If the wear in an area of the shoe has not yet reached the degree of wear evident in the questioned impression, then obviously the shoe could not have made the impression. Caution should be used before reaching a conclusion such as this, due to several factors. The differences between the questioned impression and the known shoe should be clear and confirmable. The examiner should be aware of the variables that can be expected to occur in the impression-making process and that often misrepresent wear. One example would include an outsole filled in with dirt or snow, which leaves an impression that appears as if that area of the shoe was worn down (Figure 9.13). Another example would be an outsole which, because it contained large amounts of blood, squeezed out the excess blood while making the impression. The blood that was squeezed out, if in sufficient quantity, would flow back into and fill in the patterned areas, thus giving the appearance of those areas being worn smooth. In addition, some questioned impressions simply do not record well and leave only an outline or very general

**A**
**9.11** An enlarged area of a cast in snow depicts a specific wear pattern (**A**). the boot, obtained a month later, contains wear centered in the same areas but somewhat expanded (**B**). Thus the position of wear corresponds, but the boot

detail of the shoe. The absence of specific detail should not necessarily be used to conclude that the design had been worn from the shoe.

## Position of Wear (Wear Pattern)

*Position of wear* or *wear pattern* may refer to the wear on the entire shoe or just a portion of the shoe. The term *wear pattern* is used by the examiner to compare wear on shoes and impressions, not to denote the

**B**
now contains a slightly greater degree of wear, which has spread out from the
original areas.

pattern of wear associated with a particular individual. The position of
wear on a sole or heel will change during the life of a shoe. When a shoe
is new, it does not contain a wear pattern. As it begins to receive wear,
some areas will wear at a faster rate than others. When these areas of
greater or lesser wear differ sufficiently to distinguish them from one
another, a wear pattern becomes evident. As the shoe continues to
wear, the initial wear pattern can change substantially, in the sense that
it can spread out. This is because, as areas of the outsole that were

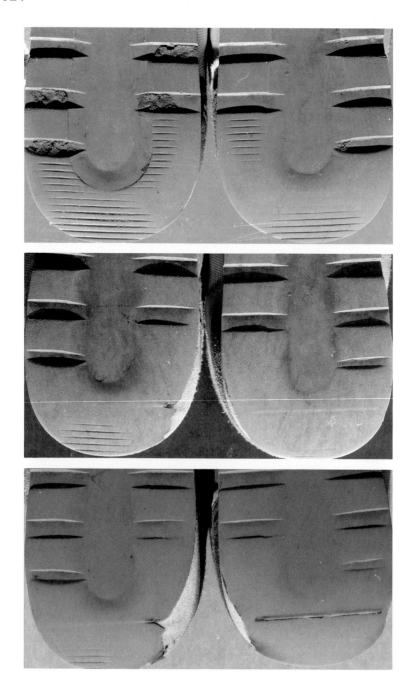

**9.12**  The wear on the heels of a pair of jogging shoes changed considerably over a period of three months.

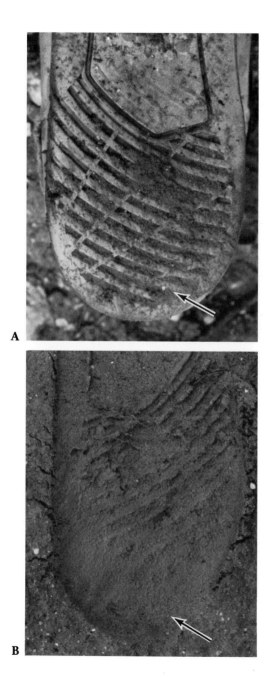

**9.13** A shoe outsole (**A**) that is packed with mud, soil, or snow can often leave an impression in which the design characteristics are obscured. The impression (**B**) appears to have been made by a shoe that was worn considerably in that area.

initially supporting the shoe become worn down, the adjacent areas of the shoe must support more weight and therefore begin receiving more wear themselves. This spreading out effect will change the appearance of and expand the wear pattern areas as the shoe continues to be worn (Figures 9.11 and 9.12).

If the position of wear on a shoe is reported to correspond, it means that the position of wear on the shoe is in agreement with that in the questioned impression. This is common in cases where little time had elapsed between the crime date and seizure of the shoes and in cases where the shoes have not received much additional wear for one reason or another.

In other cases, where more time has elapsed and the wear on the shoes is in a more advanced condition, the comparison must consider the additional amount of time and wear. The examiner must decide whether the additional wear is merely an advancing condition and spreading of the wear from the same areas as those reflected in the questioned impression or whether it constitutes wear centered over different positions.

The wear on some persons' shoes will actually reflect some shape and size characteristics of their feet, particularly in the toe area. This wear pattern is sometimes referred to as an anatomical wear pattern (Figure 9.14C). It is reflected in both plain-bottomed shoes and shoes having a designed pattern. The pattern will not be evident during the initial stages of wear on the shoes. During the later stages of wear, it may possibly spread out or become less obvious. For that reason, certain shoes may contain some degree of an anatomical wear pattern, while other shoes belonging to the same person may not.

## Studies Concerning Wear Characteristics

There are a few forensic studies that have addressed the subject of wear and wear patterns on shoes. One study (Davis RJ and DeHaan J, 1977) surveyed 650 pairs of used men's footwear and examined the position of wear on the heels. The shoes were in various stages of wear, ranging from almost new to well worn, and included all varieties of dress shoes, boots, and athletic shoes. A transparent grid was superimposed over the heels of these shoes as a means of measuring the position of wear. The study concluded that the majority of shoes had wear that fell somewhere within a 60-degree arc on the outside of the heel. This same study also concluded that observing wear in other areas of the heel or in multiple areas of the heel was much less common. This finding is consistent with the observation that the feet of most persons are slightly supinated and toed out during the heel strike phase of the walking cycle, as previously discussed in this chapter.

In another study concerning wear (Cassidy MJ, 1980), 97 separate shoes and test impressions taken from those shoes were individually intercompared. The shoes were of police recruits and consisted of only two different designs. The shoes were worn for identical periods of time within a very confined geographical area. Some conclusions of that study were that (1) "the chances of general wear being accurately duplicated decreased in proportion to [the length of time shoes were] worn (e.g., 74% of the shoes 2 months old had similar wear compared with 18% of 5-month-old shoes)"; (2) "the value of wear . . . becomes more significant as the shoe becomes worn"; (3) "identification of footwear should not be based on general wear alone"; and (4) "minor disagreements of wear should not constitute a bar toward identification."

### Using Wear to Determine or Rule Out Identification

*Identification. Wear characteristics alone are not accepted as a means of positive identification.* Although in theory, no two shoes are worn exactly alike, the extremely minute differences in the wear of some shoes, the fact that the wear is continually changing, and the presence of variation in the recording of the wear characteristics in a questioned impression, all prevent a positive identification of a shoe based on wear alone. In other words, the possibility exists that shoes of different persons can contain wear, which, given the detail and variables in questioned impressions, may be indistinguishable. Nevertheless, both the degree of wear and the position of wear, particularly when these are in specific agreement in the shoe and the impression, can contribute immensely toward the positive identification of a shoe.

Although wear characteristics are not sufficient to make a positive identification, in those cases where the wear is so extreme that a hole in the shoe has resulted, random characteristics associated with those holes, such as ragged edges (Figure 9.14A and B), are random identifying characteristics that make the shoe unique and can be used to identify it.

*Nonidentification.* Although a positive identification cannot be made on wear characteristics alone, *it is possible to eliminate a shoe based on characteristics of wear alone.* As previously stated, this is possible in cases where the questioned impression reflects wear characteristics that are advanced well beyond that of the shoe outsole that is later recovered. Caution must be used for impressions made by shoes whose design may have become filled in with materials like soil or blood or whose detail may not have been recorded well, thus leaving an impression that may appear similar to one made by a shoe of greater wear.

**A**

**B**

**9.14** The shoes depicted in **A** and **B** are from one person and contain a similar degree of wear in similar positions on the outsole. Note that the holes that have worn through the outsole contain ragged edges that are random and are therefore identifying characteristics. The shoes depicted in **C** and **D** belong to a

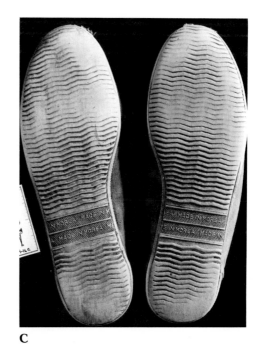

C

second person. They do not reflect specific similar wear characteristics because of the different materials and different degree of wear. The shoes in **C** have an anatomical wear pattern. The shoes in **D** are of a more microcellular material, and the degree of wear is more advanced and has spread out.

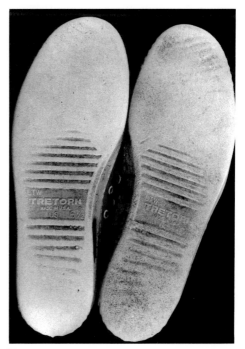

D

A nonidentification is also possible in cases where the degree of wear of the shoes is greater than that reflected in the impression, and the shoes are recovered within a short time after the crime was committed. In this case, nonidentification would be based on the opinion of the examiner that the shoes could not have in any way received sufficient additional wear between the time of the crime and the time the shoes were seized to account for the differences. Again, caution must be used when making a nonidentification of this type.

### The Value of Wear When the Shoes Are Not Recovered

There have been occasions when distinctive wear patterns were reflected in questioned footwear impressions, yet the suspect had discarded the actual shoes that made the impressions. Other shoes belonging to the suspect, which had a similar wear pattern, were compared with the wear pattern of the questioned impressions. This kind of examination, because of the number of factors that influence wear characteristics, is very limited and is usually of minimal value. It should be emphasized that, just as in a direct comparison of wear characteristics with the shoes believed to have made those impressions, wear characteristics do not alone constitute a basis for a positive identification. To attempt to reach an opinion using this kind of comparison is extremely dangerous and can easily result in a mistaken identification or mistaken nonidentification.

Figure 9.14 illustrates how the wear reflected on two pairs of shoes belonging to one person may be similar and on two pairs of shoes worn by another person may appear different.

# Class and Identifying Characteristics

# 10

The outsoles and other areas of footwear that can be involved in the impression-making process contain a large variety of features. Some of those features represent "class" characteristics while others represent "identifying" characteristics. The understanding, recognition, and proper valuation of both class and identifying characteristics in the comparison of footwear impression evidence is important.

## Class Characteristics

### Single Class Characteristics

The term class characteristic is used in many forensic disciplines. Definitions of class characteristics more specifically aimed at footwear impression evidence have been provided by many authors. Cassidy (1980) states that "in footwear these [class characteristics] would be size, shape, style and pattern design." In his 1984 work, C. W. Cooke elaborates: "Class characteristics are those characteristics which all similar items have in common. . . . The size (i.e., length and width) of a shoe sole impression and the general pattern design of the tread are class characteristics." And Osterburg (1967) offers the following: "Class characteristics are the more obvious, gross features distinguishable in an object. . . . With evidence involving impressions such as those left by shoes, . . . the general dimensions, design and contour of the imprint constitute the class characteristics."

As applied to footwear, I would define a class characteristic as *an intentional or unavoidable characteristic that repeats during the manufacturing process and is shared by one or more other shoes.* Class characteristics of shoes would include such features as specific shape, dimensions, specific design, and any other characteristics that typically repeat during the making of a quantity of shoes. It would not include those that happen rarely simply through chance or coincidence. Obviously, in the vast majority of cases, any single class characteristic will be shared by many other shoes.

## Combined Class Characteristics

Shoe outsoles and other parts of the shoe involved in the impression-making process often contain many features, not just one. Those features may each constitute a single class characteristic, because other shoes also have that identical feature. The combination of two or more independent class characteristics will usually result in a shoe that can be distinguished from the majority of other shoes of that same make, size, and design. Several examples of this have already been illustrated in this book. Shoes, like the classic Converse Chuck Taylor All-Star, of a particular size and design that (1) can originate from any of several distinguishable molds, (2) have a foxing strip that varies in position as well as the manner in which it overlaps itself, and (3) contain other variables such as a toe bumper guard and heel label, offer a perfect example of *combined class characteristics*. Each of these single class characteristics are shared by many of the shoes in the total number made in that size and design. However, with each specific class characteristic that is added, the number of shoes that share those exact combined characteristics is rapidly reduced.

To illustrate this further, an example of two outsoles of a particular size and design is offered as follows. The outsoles are cut from a sheet of outsole material to a specific size with a specifically sized and shaped die. In the cutting process, because of the pattern in the design, the outsoles are die cut in a variety of positions, most of which result in outsoles that are not exactly like the others. Parts C and D of Figure 10.1 show the impressions of the heel areas of two die-cut outsoles cut from the same design of outsole material. If the questioned impression was partial and limited, like the one shown in Figure 10.1A, and could not be referenced to the perimeter or some other reference point, then, within the limitations of that comparison, both outsoles shown in Figure 10.1C and D would have to be considered as possibly sharing class characteristics with the outsole that made the impression in Figure 10.1A. Neither outsole could be eliminated. At this point, only one class characteristic, the general pattern of the design, is involved, and both shoes contain this pattern. If the impression were to include a portion of the perimeter, such as the impression in Figure 10.1B, then it could be determined that only one of those outsoles, that in Figure 10.1D, would share the two combined class characteristics reflected in that impression. That outsole still shares the general class characteris-

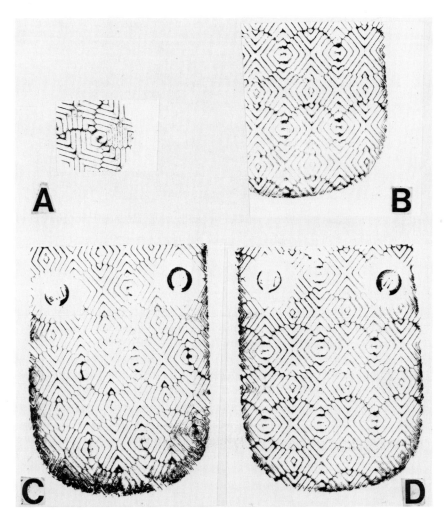

**10.1**   Impressions of the heel areas of two outsoles (**C** and **D**) from shoes of the same size and brand that have been die cut from a sheet of the same patterned material. If the questioned impression were only to include a limited area like that represented by **A**, both outsoles **C** and **D** would be candidates for sharing the class characteristics with the shoe that made the impression; however, if the questioned impression were to include the area represented by **B**, only outsole D could have made the impression, because it is the only outsole that shares the two combined class characteristics of design and precise cut.

tics of the design pattern with all of the other outsoles cut from that material, but it shares the *combined* two class characteristics with a much smaller number of shoes, i.e., only the outsoles that happened to be both of that design and cut in precisely the same position.

Each of the class characteristics reflected in one shoe outsole design

**10.2**   An enlarged area of three size 13 outsoles from shoes of the same brand and style, but originating from three different molds. Notice the difference in the stippling design and in the relationship of the position of the herringbone pattern relative to the logo area.

should be exactly alike in any other shoe in order for those shoes to be considered to share the same combined class characteristics. It would not be correct to state that three different shoes of the same make, size, and general design, but originating from three different molds shared identical design class characteristics if there were distinguishing features between each of the molds. Figure 10.2 depicts a small portion of three outsoles, all from a size 13 shoe and from the same manufacturer. As can be seen in the photographs, they are all easily distinguished, even though they are the same make, manufacturer's size, and general design. There are variations in the stippling and the relationship of the herringbone pattern to the other design elements. This is very typical for footwear. These three size 13 shoes of the same make, model, and manufacturer's size *do not* share class characteristics with regard to their combined design features. Only if the three molds were *exactly* the same or if all three shoes came from the same mold would they truly share the class characteristic of design.

   To further illustrate how combined class characteristics can rapidly reduce the number of shoes sharing those characteristics, the following simplified example is offered and is summarized in Figure 10.3. Ten thousand pairs of compression-molded basketball shoe outsoles in size 10 must be molded as part of a total order of 75,000 pairs of shoes. In order to meet production demands, it is necessary to have four pairs of size 10 hand-engraved molds manufactured. Because of the mold manufacturing method, each of the four molds for both the left and right outsoles are easily distinguishable in many areas, as were the molds for the outsoles in Figure 10.2. During the production of the 10,000 pairs of size 10 outsoles, 2,500 left outsoles and 2,500 right outsoles are molded in each of the four mold cavities for that size. Because there is a general

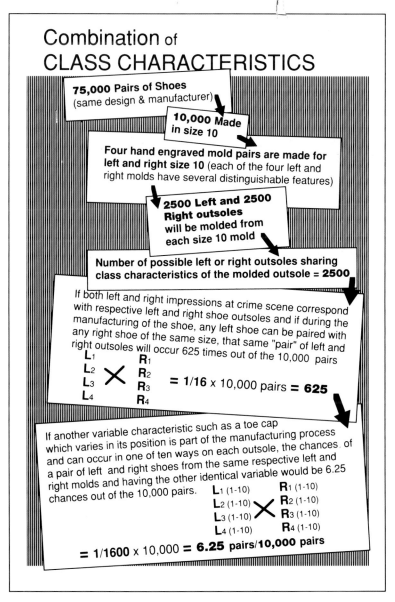

**10.3** A simplified example of how combined class characteristics can reduce the possible number of shoes that could have made an impression.

similarity between the molded outsoles, it might be stated that all of the size 10 outsoles shared class characteristics with *all* of the other outsoles of that size. This is not correct. It would, however, be correct to state that any of the left or right outsoles shares class characteristics with regard to the outsole design with only 1/4 (2,500 out of 10,000) of the left or right outsoles produced in size 10. If, in the procedures of this particular factory, any left outsole was combined randomly with any right outsole in size 10, then only 625 pairs (out of the 10,000 pairs) of shoes would contain the *combined* left and right shoes from the same respective left and right molds.

The presence of other variable class characteristics could further reduce the number of shoes or pairs of shoes that shared those additional combined class characteristics. A variable such as the beginning and ending point of a toe cap or toe bumper guard, which, for purposes of this example could randomly occur in each shoe in ten different distinguishable positions and which would be reflected in the impression, could further reduce the number of single shoes sharing this characteristic from 2,500 (out of 10,000) to 250 (out of 10,000). The combined occurrence of left and right shoes from the same respective left and right molds and having the toe bumper guards in the same respective positions on both the left and right shoes would be approximately 6 pairs of shoes out of 10,000.

The above examples and discussion are not to suggest that shoes or pairs of shoes can be presumed to be so unique in their combined class characteristics as to allow for the positive identification of footwear impressions based on those characteristics alone. Although in some cases where several class characteristics are involved, the shoes or pairs of shoes could theoretically be unique, it must be understood that each of those specific class characteristics can occur repetitively, and therefore the presence of those combined class characteristics *does not, by itself, evidence uniqueness.* The understanding and recognition of the potential for the presence of combined class characteristics and their resulting value can, however, contribute significantly to the overall examination results.

## Identifying Characteristics

In the examination of footwear impression evidence, identifying characteristics are *characteristics that result when something is randomly added to or taken away from a shoe outsole that either causes or contributes to making that shoe outsole unique.* Cuts, scratches, tears, rocks wedged in the outsole, gum, shoe-patching material, holes, and air bubbles are all examples of identifying characteristics, provided that they occurred with some randomness. The term random infers that the *size, shape, and/or position of the characteristic depends, to some degree, on chance.* Figure 10.4 illustrates several examples of identifying characteristics resulting from (1) items being added to the outsole, such as hardened tar or gum on the outsole and rocks wedged in the sole design, or (2) portions of the outsole being lost through cuts, gouges, scratches, or areas of the design being randomly torn away.

Although identifying characteristics usually occur through the use of the shoe after the shoe is purchased and worn, some identifying characteristics, such as random air bubbles, damage, or incomplete formation of the outsole material, occur in shoes during the manufacturing process and either contribute to or result in a shoe's individuality before it is ever worn. These were discussed in the chapter on manufacturing.

Identifying characteristics, because of their independent and countless possible origins, can range from the tiniest, almost obscure, pinpoint-size characteristic to one having tremendous distinctness and uniqueness. Figure 10.5 depicts a small sampling of the countless variety of random cuts on a small area of a shoe. Some of those are very small and almost without shape, while others are larger and contain both shape and direction.

When identifying characteristics of sufficient value or number are present in both the impression and the shoe outsole, the outsole can be positively identified as having made the impression. Several things must be considered by the examiner in order to determine the value that each identifying characteristic contributes to identification. Those considerations include (1) the clarity of the characteristic, (2) its reproducibility in the impression of the known shoe, (3) its confirmation as a random occurrence in the shoe, and (4) its degree of uniqueness.

## Clarity of the Characteristic in the Questioned Impression

Characteristics must be *sufficiently clear* in the questioned impression to correlate with the corresponding characteristics in the shoe outsole. The term *sufficiently clear* does not necessarily denote the crispest and sharpest detail possible, but rather a reasonable amount of clarity to adequately correlate the size, shape, or some detail of the characteristic in the questioned impression with the known shoe. A characteristic that is clear and correlates well with the known shoe will carry far more value in the examination than one that is not as clear.

In those instances when characteristics are not clear enough to correlate well with a known standard, consideration must be given to the possible or known reason for the limited clarity. Some clarity problems occur due to reproduction problems and can be recognized as such. Impressions in certain surfaces such as coarse soil and dry sand usually do not enable good reproduction of, nor do they retain, fine detail. Impressions in wet materials may squeeze excess material into the characteristics, either filling in or changing the shape of those characteristics. In addition, some characteristics that have been reproduced

**A**

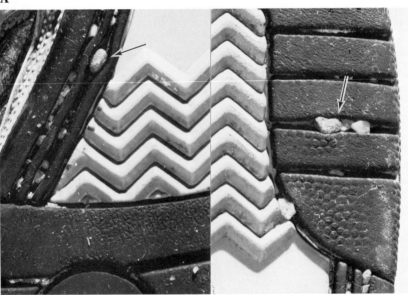

**B**

**10.4**  Examples of different random characteristics include those that have been randomly added to the shoe outsole, such as gum or tar (A) or rocks wedged in the outsole (B), and those that have resulted when something has been randomly removed from the outsole such as in the case of cuts, scratches, chunks, or tears (C) or when void areas of the outsole have randomly resulted during the manufacturing process, as in the case of air bubbles (D).

C

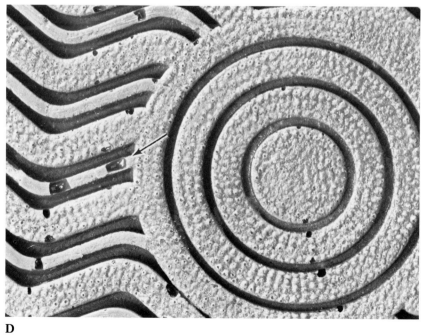

D

A

10.5   Reverse photograph of an enlarged area of a portion of a shoe (**A**) containing a variety of shapes and sizes of random identifying characteristics and an impression of that area of the shoe (**B**). Notice the immense variety of shapes and sizes of the random characteristics.

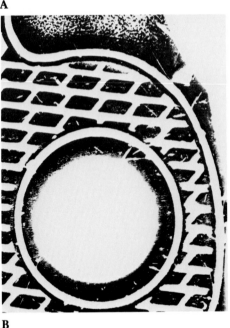

B

well in the impression may lose detail, may be partially obscured, or may be totally lost in the retrieval process.

If the presence and position of a characteristic on the outsole and in a questioned impression are the same, but the detail is of limited clarity, the characteristic may still be of some value regarding some of its features. Characteristics of such limited clarity that they appear only as a possible disturbance in the questioned impression, even if they are in the same precise spot, are of even less, and possibly no, value in the examination. The examiner must be as objective as possible in associating identifying characteristics on a shoe with characteristics in the questioned impression. *There must be some degree of association between the random characteristics on the shoe and the characteristics in the questioned impression before that characteristic can be used in the comparison.* The degree of association, however slight it may be, must still be clear enough to be demonstrable.

Figure 10.6 depicts four impressions of a small area of the same shoe. Three characteristics (arrows) are visible in three of the four impressions, but with different degrees of clarity. In the fourth impression, the characteristics appear very minimally or not at all. Inked impressions of the same area of the shoe are shown in Figure 10.7. A reverse photograph of the portion of the shoe used to make these impressions is featured in Figure 10.8.

## Reproducibility

The reproducibility of a characteristic in both the questioned impression and the known impressions often enters into the assessment of detail in a characteristic. Any characteristic will vary slightly in its reproduction, even under very similar circumstances. Although the exact conditions and materials that went into the questioned impressions can never be precisely duplicated, a good way to assess how a characteristic can reproduce is by making several test impressions of the known shoes. Figure 10.7 depicts three successive inked impressions of the same small area of the same shoe that was used to prepare the impressions in Figure 10.6. Even under extremely similar circumstances, i.e., the same person making the impression, the same surface, the same ink pad, etc., there is still some slight variation in the precise manner in which a characteristic reproduces. The precise reproduction of characteristics will vary in questioned impressions as well.

## Confirmation of the Characteristics as Random

Each identifying characteristic being considered in the examination must be confirmed as random. Random characteristics that have been *added* to the outsole will be composed of foreign matter such as rocks, gum, nails, tacks, etc. and can be recognized and verified as such. Random characteristics that are a result of the loss of part of the outsole (cuts, scratches, gouges, etc.) will be recognizable under magnification. Figure 10.8 depicts an enlarged and reversed photograph of the same small area of the shoe used to make the impression in Figures 10.6 and

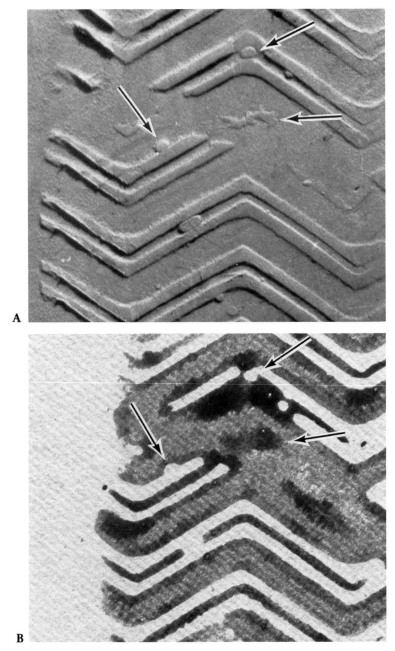

A

B

**10.6** Characteristics from the same area of the same shoe as in Figure 10.7 will reproduce with a variety of clarity, depending on the materials they are made in. Some impressions will contain a clearer reproduction of those characteristics, as depicted in **A** and also in Figure 10.7; some may contain less clarity due to

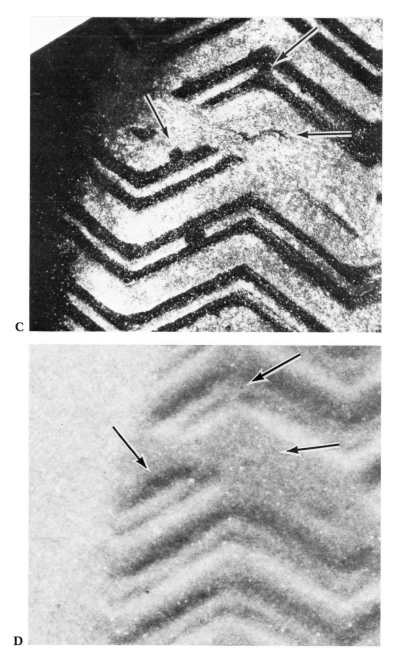

factors such as the squeegee effect in a blood impression (**B**) or the fragile nature of some dust impressions (**C**). The impression in loose sand (**D**) failed to reproduce the same three characteristics with sufficient clarity to be of value.

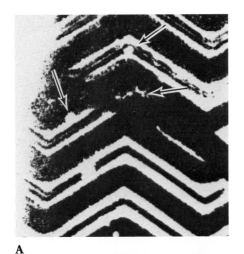

A

B

**10.7** Reproducibility of characteristics. Characteristics such as those marked vary in the precise way they reproduce. In this example of three sequential inked impressions from the same shoe, the amount of ink, the pressure, and other subtle variables contribute to variations of those characteristics.

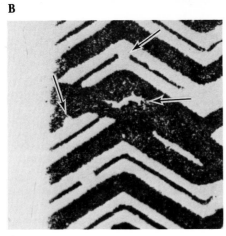

C

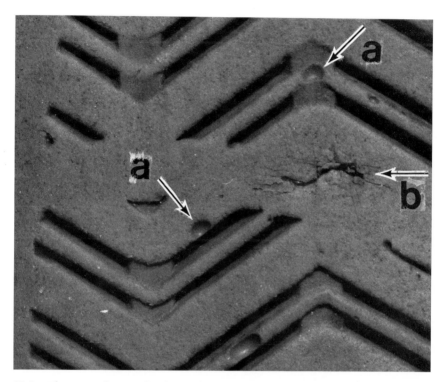

**10.8**   The typical smooth, glossy features of the air bubble **(A)** is easily distinguished from the rough and torn features of the random cut **(B)**.

10.7. The two glossy holes (A) are air bubbles, while the torn area (B) represents random damage to the shoe. Areas representing coded manufacturer's marks (Figure 10.9A) or damage to a mold, as discussed in the chapter on manufacturing and class characteristics, will appear as raised areas of the shoe outsole and not areas that have been randomly removed. Examiners should be familiar with recognizing these different characteristics. If a piece of debris or rubber should be left in or fall into the mold, a depression or disturbance in the outsole would result as pictured in Figure 10.9B.

## The Value of One Confirmable Random Characteristic

In considering whether another characteristic of an identical size, shape, and position on one shoe could occur on a second shoe, a general understanding of the probability of that exact characteristic being duplicated in another shoe is needed. The probability example provided here is only for discussion purposes and is not meant to imply that mathematical probabilities could be devised in actual case examples.

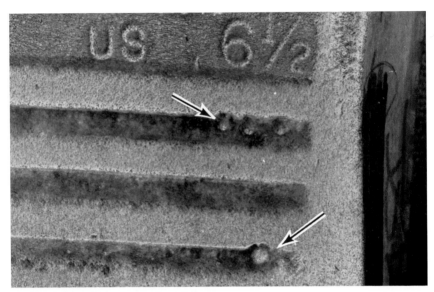

A

B

**10.9** Intentional marks placed in the mold by the manufacturer or damage to the mold itself will be in the form of a depression on the mold surface and therefore a raised area on the shoe outsole (**A**). When a foreign object such as a piece of rubber, flashing, or debris falls into a mold and a shoe is molded over it, a depression in the surface of the outsole will result (**B**).

Probability can be defined as the number of ways something can occur divided by the sum of the number of ways it cannot occur and the ways it can occur. Thus, if the numbers 1 through 10 are placed in a hat, the chances of drawing the number 5 would be one in ten and could be expressed as:

$$\text{Probability of drawing } 5 = \frac{1 \text{ (the number of ways of selecting 5)}}{\substack{9 \text{ (the number of ways of not selecting 5)} \\ + 1 \text{ (the number of ways of selecting 5)}}}$$

which equals 1/10 or one out of ten chances.

In the above example, it is easy to define the number of possibilities for the occurrence of each number and then the probability of each number being drawn. With regard to random characteristics that occur on shoe outsoles, the problematic assessment is far more complicated. In fact, for all practical purposes, there is an unlimited number of different random characteristics that could occur on a shoe, any of which could be on any part of the outsole. The importance of just one confirmed characteristic on a particular part of a shoe outsole is demonstrated by the following example:

For the purpose of discussion and to illustrate the value of a single random characteristic, one examiner (Stone R, 1984) offered the following example. Assume that the smallest random characteristic is a small, simple, pinpointlike cut that can be contained in the space of 1 mm$^2$. For discussion purposes, this cut will be treated as having no other descriptive features, such as variable size, shape, or orientation on the outsole. Placing a metric grid over the shoe in this example, a size 8A, revealed that it contained over 16,000 mm$^2$ of surface area on its outsole. Thus, on the shoe outsole there are 16,000 different possible places that a small, random characteristic, such as a pinpoint cut, could occupy. The chances of that one pinpoint cut appearing on any particular point in the outsole can be calculated to be one in 16,000.

$$\text{Probability} = \frac{1}{15,999 + 1} = \frac{1}{16,000}$$

A cut of this type and the space it occupies, compared to the number of possible positions on the outsole, is illustrated in Figure 10.10.

If *more than one* random characteristic is present on the bottom of the shoe, then the chances of another shoe having those *combined characteristics in the same positions* can be expressed as follows:

$$C = \frac{N!}{(N - R)! \, R!}$$

where C is the chance of the combined occurrence, N is the number of available spaces, and R is the number of random characteristics.

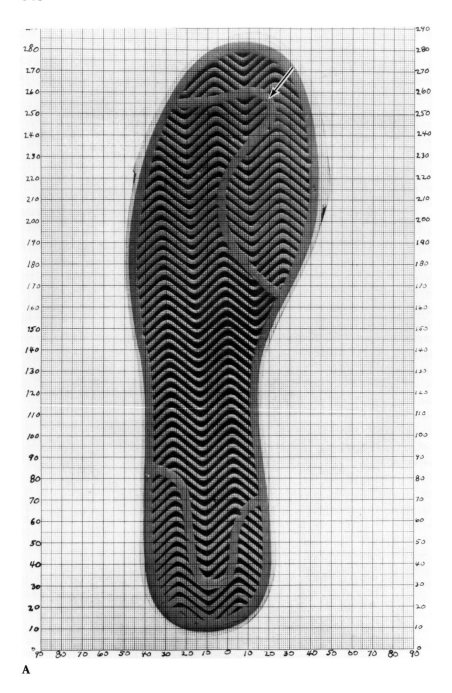

A

**B**

**10.10**  A metric grid placed over an average-size outsole (**A**) can divide that outsole into approximately 16,000 square millimeters, each of which can hold a pinpoint characteristic, such as the one shown by the arrow. The enlarged area depicts that characteristic (**B**).

| Number of Characteristics | Chance of Combined Occurrence | Number of Characteristics | Chance of Combined Occurrence |
|---|---|---|---|
| 2 | 1 in 127,992,000 | 7 | 1 in 53 septillion |
| 3 | 1 in 683 billion | 8 | 1 in 106 octillion |
| 4 | 1 in 2.7 quadrillion | 9 | 1 in 189 nontillion |
| 5 | 1 in 8.7 quintillion | 10 | 1 in 300 decillion |
| 6 | 1 in 23 sextillion | | |

Thus, the chances of a second shoe containing the same two pinpoint characteristics in the same two positions is one in 127,992,000; for three characteristics, the chances are one in 683 billion; and so forth.

Remember that these simplified statistics are for confirmed simple, small, nondescript pinpoint cuts of independent origin. They do not take into account the shoe design, shoe size, wear characteristics, or other variables. More importantly, they do not account for the particular descriptive features that may be associated with each random characteristic such as size, shape, and orientation, i.e., the uniqueness of the characteristic itself.

Statistics are used here only to generate an appreciation of the importance and significance of random identifying characteristics and are not intended to represent actual statistics or circumstances that might surround a specific case. Nevertheless, the tremendous weight that a *confirmed random characteristic* on the outsole of a shoe can have is clearly shown by this example.

## Uniqueness of the Characteristic

The uniqueness or unusualness of the characteristic must also be considered. Some characteristics are extremely unusual in their shape and size while others, like the pinpoint characteristic used in the prior example are a minimal representation of a random characteristic. Figure 10.5 depicts a shoe outsole that contains various examples of identifying random characteristics. The minimal characteristic, perhaps best described as a pinpoint characteristic, is valued more for its position in the outsole than it is for any size or shape features. On the shoe outsole, there are many ways a pinpoint characteristic could have occurred, although it would still be extremely rare to find another one in the identical position on another shoe of the same size and design. The weakness of a limited characteristic of this type lies in the difficulty of specifically associating it with the corresponding characteristic in the impression. It would be difficult to deny the possibility that what appears as a single pinpoint characteristic in a questioned impression could have occurred for other reasons or be attributable to contamination or coincidence.

In Figure 10.7 the three impressions were made by the same shoe. Yet there are numerous pinpoint-size characteristics that appear in one of those impressions but not in the other two, due to the contamination of the outsole. Some of those characteristics were due to particles of grit that had temporarily adhered to the outsole. The grit had prevented contact of the outsole with the surface in that area, therefore preventing a recording of the outsole at that point. In many instances, it would not be possible to determine whether the resulting void area in the impression was attributable to contamination or to damage to the shoe. Any one of those void areas could coincidently be at the location of a pinpoint cut in a suspect's shoe. Of course, if two or three or more of these characteristics were present in both the impression and the shoe, then they collectively would become more valuable, since contamination or coincidence in the same multiple points becomes very unlikely. When assessing the value of these characteristics during an examination, the focus is on the likelihood of a characteristic of this size and shape occurring in the same exact position on another shoe of the same type.

As a characteristic begins to take on more size, shape, and orientation qualities, as do many of the features in Figure 10.5, it becomes more unlikely that another characteristic of the same size and shape would be found in the same precise position and orientation in another shoe outsole of the same size and design. Thus, if such a characteristic is found in both a shoe and an impression, it becomes increasingly unlikely and very quickly impossible, as the complexity of the characteristic increases, that this event could be coincidental or due to contamination.

## Making a Positive Identification

A positive identification occurs when the questioned impression and the known shoe share confirmed random characteristics that, by virtue of their features and placement on the shoe outsole, in the opinion of a qualified footwear impression expert, could not be repeated on another outsole sharing the same class characteristics. The positive identification means that no other shoe in the world could have made that particular impression.

### Number of Characteristics Required for Identification

The question has often been asked, "How many points of identification do you need in a footwear impression to make a positive identification?" Obviously, this question has arisen from the public's familiarity with counting "points" of identification in a fingerprint examination.

In a fingerprint, there are three general features: the bifurcation, the

ending ridge, and the island. These three characteristics occur repeatedly on the fingers of all persons and appear in patterns such as arches,
loops, and whorls. When one of these features appears in both the
questioned and known print, it is referred to as a point. In contrast,
there are literally thousands of designs of shoes, each coming in a large
variety of sizes, any of which could be distinguished. And even within
one specific design and size, there can be distinguishable manufacturing variables that will further decrease the total number of possible
shoes of a particular size and design that could have made the impression. Add to that the wear characteristics present in the shoe, and the
shoe is already approaching uniqueness. As summarized in Figure
10.11, the features used to identify a fingerprint and those features used
to identify a footwear impression are not exactly the same, although
both are based on the randomness of the occurrence of certain characteristics and the positioning of those characteristics.

With regard to random identifying characteristics in footwear, there
is no way to ever determine the statistical probability of any single
identifying characteristic's occurrence. The innumerable possibilities
of accidental cuts, gouges, tears, or other identifying random features of
varied size and shape is so staggering that many of those characteristics,
by virtue of their features alone are unique. One single characteristic
may have many points, or features, about it. Taking into account both
the random placement on a particular outsole's surface and the characteristic's points or features, the chance of a recurrence of that characteristic on another shoe, in many cases, is simply not conceivable or
possible.

The results in any comparison that concludes that a shoe positively
made an impression must always take all of the features and areas of
comparison into consideration. Identifications may be made with only
one random identifying characteristic, if that characteristic is confirmable; has sufficient definition, clarity, and features; is in the same
location and orientation on the shoe outsole; and in the opinion of the
experienced examiner *could not occur again on another shoe.*

Parts A and B of Figure 10.12 depict the heel of a shoe and its impression, which reflect one characteristic in common. The characteristic,
marked 1, is not strong enough to establish a positive identification due
to its limited size and shape features. Notice that in the questioned
impression there are other characteristics that are not represented in
the shoe. These are due to contamination. They were caused by pieces
of grit on the shoe or surface that interfered with the impression
process, leaving a void area.

In Figure 10.12C and D the shoe contains a random characteristic
that has several features of size and shape. It contains sufficient size,
shape, and orientation characteristics to conclude that it could not be

## FINGERPRINTS

—Contain 3 types of characteristics–
bifurcation, ending ridge and dot,
which occur over and over again
on the fingers of all persons, from
the embryo stage until
decompostition after death

—Whereas these characteristics
occur repeatedly on the fingers of
all persons, they appear in patterns,
namely arches, loops and whorls,
but in different frequency and
relative position to one another

—The frequency and unit
relationship of these
characteristics combine to form
a fingerprint that is truly unique

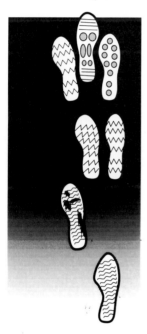

## FOOTWEAR IMPRESSIONS

—Represent only one of many
thousands of possible designs,
each of which is available in a
wide variety of possible sizes

—Can have manufacturing
variables and characteristics
within that size and design

— Can have wear
characteristics, which relate
to both the degree of wear
and the position of wear, and
which are changing throughout
the life of the shoe

—Can have randomly acquired
characteristics which, based on
the presence, location, shape,
and size, can make that shoe
outsole unique.

**10.11**   Comparison of fingerprints and footwear impressions are often made.
Both rely on the randomness of the occurrence of certain characteristics and the
positioning of those characteristics. Footwear impressions can also be unique,
but the uniqueness is the result of slightly different criteria.

mistakenly due to coincidence or contamination and could have originated only from that shoe. Identifications with just one characteristic
are not common and should be made only when the characteristic in
the questioned impression has more than one unique feature and, by
virtue of those unique features, is convincingly the result of the corre-

**A**

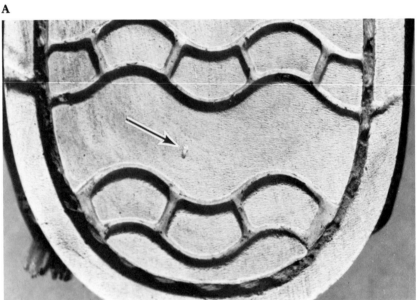

**B**

**10.12**  An impression (**A**) and shoe (**B**) containing only one small, hardly distinguishable characteristic, like that pointed out, would fall short of uniqueness,
due to the limited value of that characteristic alone. More than one characteris-

C

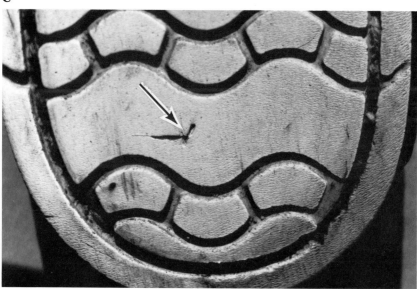

D

tic of this size, shape and quality would be needed for identification. However, if that one characteristic contained several distinct features, the impression (C) could be positively associated with the shoe (D).

sponding random characteristic on the shoe. Each case must rest on its own merit.

According to Zmuda and Brodie (undated),

> The question commonly asked by the neophyte is specifically "what number of characteristics is necessary for an identification and what quality must these characteristics have?" The answer depends upon the uniqueness and individuality of the characteristics themselves and the number felt necessary in the examiner's judgement.

In his 1985 presentation on footwear evidence, Roger Davis discussed the importance of the size and number of outsole features:

> Random characteristics . . . are the blemishes that the working surface of shoe acquires constantly while being worn: cuts, nicks, gouges, scratches, dents, burns, holes, and so on. Most random wear marks are acquired purely by chance and it is the combination of these and other things (like general wear) that give a shoe its unique character. Random wear characteristics can be very large or minutely small. A scientist would attach much greater significance to a large characteristic than to a small one, so the difference between footwear and fingerprint identification should be obvious. *One good 'characteristic', taken with other factors like pattern, etc., can be sufficient to identify a shoe conclusively.*

Regarding factors affecting the number of random characteristics needed, Cassidy (1980) stated, "A number of factors enter in the number of accidental characteristics required before a positive identification can be established, the most important of which are the examiner's experience, the impression's clarity, and the uniqueness or significance of characteristics."

It should be emphasized that a full recording of the footwear is not necessary in a questioned impression in order to make a positive identification. In fact, it is not unusual to make positive identifications of partial footwear impressions that represent only a small fraction of the outsole surface. The identification is not based on the size or completeness of the impression, but on the quantity and quality of random identifying features in the questioned impression that correspond with the respective portions of the known shoe.

## Case Identifications

Figure 10.13A illustrates a residue footwear impression that has been enhanced with high-contrast photography. Figure 10.13B is a test impression of the same area of the known shoe. There are many random accidental characteristics on the shoe that are reflected in the known impression. Several of those characteristics also reproduced well in the questioned impression; others reproduced with less detail or not at all.

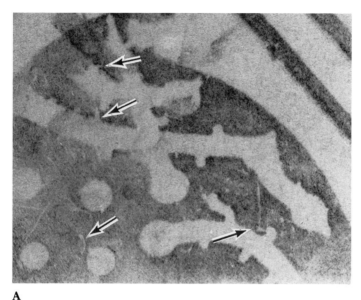

A

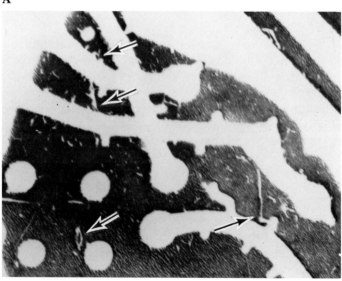

B

**10.13** A positive identification based on numerous random characteristics. Although not all of the random characteristics that appear in the known impression (**B**) also appear in the questioned impression (**A**), sufficient characteristics in common do permit identification. The characteristics present in the known impression and not in the questioned impression either occurred after the questioned impression was made or did not reproduce in the questioned impression. The arrows point to just a few of the identifying characteristics.

This is to be expected because the residue on the shoe at the crime scene is not evenly distributed and cannot provide the quality of reproduction that a powdered or inked impression provides. In addition, some of the characteristics may have worn off prior to seizure of the shoes. Of the various characteristics in Figures 10.13A and 10.13B, some might be sufficient for a positive identification alone, while others would only contribute to an identification.

Figure 10.14 depicts a partial impression in blood as well as a test impression of the known shoe. The arrows point to a number of random characteristics. The unevenness of the blood was evident and resulted in some areas of the impression recording more accurately than others. The blood was squeezed or flowed into many areas, obliterating the detail. In this case, there were still sufficient identifying characteristics to positively identify the known shoe as having made this impression.

## Changes in Identifying Characteristics as Shoe Wear Continues

When a random identifying characteristic occurs on a shoe outsole, it can change as the shoe receives additional wear. How drastically it changes and how long some recognizable part of the characteristic remains on the shoe outsole depends on a number of factors, including the depth and shape of the characteristic itself, the position that it occupies on the shoe (heel, arch area, toe, etc.), and the amount of wear the shoe received. Some features will change considerably in their appearance as the shoe is worn down, while others will stay similar in appearance.

Figure 10.15 depicts impressions of a small area of the center of a heel that were taken in March, May, and September of a single year. Some random characteristics present in the original impression are still present in the most recent impression. Other characteristics have been acquired since the first impression.

When a characteristic such as the cuts in the shoe in Figure 10.15 changes in its appearance, its value can be affected in the following ways:

1. It can still be directly and positively associated with the questioned characteristics, in which case its value will not be affected or diminished.
2. It cannot be positively associated with the identifying characteristic but could be a remnant of that characteristic and is in the same position in the shoe. Its value will be reduced accordingly.

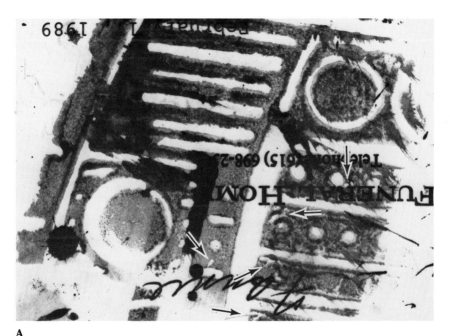

A

B

**10.14**  A questioned impression in blood (**A**) and a known impression (**B**) reflect several random identifying characteristics in common. Other characteristics have been obliterated by excess blood.

**A**

**B**

**C**

**10.15** Impressions of a small central portion of a rubber heel of a shoe, taken in March (**A**), May (**B**), and September (**C**) of the same year. Some random characteristics, visible in March, although slightly changed, are still present in September. Other characteristics have disappeared and still others have been newly acquired since the March impression. The shoe was worn almost daily.

3. It cannot be associated in any way with the characteristic. It will no longer have any value in the comparison.
4. It can be a new characteristic acquired between the time the questioned impression was made and the time the known shoe was seized.

Although it would be ideal to obtain the suspect's shoes as quickly as possible after the crime's occurrence, obtaining the shoes months later does not always prevent the possibility of an identification. Random identifying characteristics will still be present on areas of the shoe, such as the area beneath the arch of the foot, which usually does not receive much wear, or on entire shoes that, for whatever reasons, are not receiving much additional wear. I have been involved in cases in which the shoes were not obtained until months after the crime. In one particular case, $1\frac{1}{2}$ years elapsed prior to the recovery of the shoes, and in another case, 9 months elapsed before the recovery of the shoes. Yet in both cases, positive identifications were still possible, and many random identifying characteristics were still present on the shoe outsoles.

# Comparison of the Questioned Impression with Known Shoes

# 11

The methods of comparing questioned footwear impressions with known shoes, like many other forensic examinations, cannot be treated in a cookbook fashion. Each case has its own evidence and requires different considerations and approaches. While it is recognized that every laboratory and examiner has individual preferred procedures, the following discussion contains some suggestions for the basic treatment and preliminary examination of footwear evidence.

## Treatment of the Evidence

### Receiving the Questioned Impressions

When receiving footwear impression evidence, be certain that all casts, negatives, lifts, and original impressions have been provided. It is not uncommon to find that contributors select only certain photographs and certain casts or lifts of the impressions for examination, thinking they are submitting the best ones or only the portion of the impression evidence that is required. You should also determine, if not already known, the date on which the questioned impressions were made, which is usually the same as the date the crime was committed.

Since other comparisons are likely to be performed on some of this evidence, appropriate consideration should be given to that possibility when you receive the evidence. Care should be taken to ensure that items that will be examined for soil, hair, fibers, glass, or body fluids have been received in an uncontaminated condition and that they will continue to receive treatment that will preserve them as such.

Once the evidence has been inventoried, a worksheet should be prepared that contains a listing of the evidence and can accompany any notes that are made during the course of the examination. A general example of a worksheet is featured in Figure 11.1. The examiner should initial the evidence and place identifying marks on each item of evidence that coincide with those used on the worksheet.

Depending on what form the footwear impression evidence is in, i.e., casts, photographs, lifts, or the actual impression itself, certain steps must be taken to prepare the case for examination.

**11.1** An example of a worksheet containing a description of the footwear evidence.

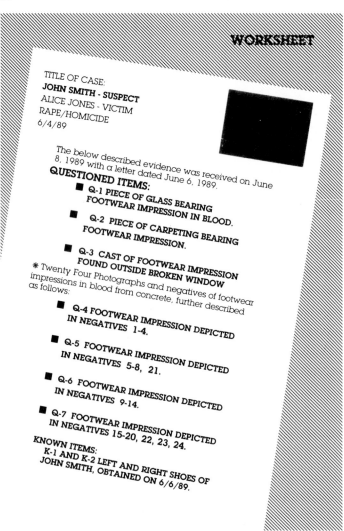

WORKSHEET

TITLE OF CASE:
JOHN SMITH - SUSPECT
ALICE JONES - VICTIM
RAPE/HOMICIDE
6/4/89

The below described evidence was received on June 8, 1989 with a letter dated June 6, 1989.
QUESTIONED ITEMS:
■ Q-1 PIECE OF GLASS BEARING FOOTWEAR IMPRESSION IN BLOOD.
■ Q-2 PIECE OF CARPETING BEARING FOOTWEAR IMPRESSION.
■ Q-3 CAST OF FOOTWEAR IMPRESSION FOUND OUTSIDE BROKEN WINDOW
* Twenty Four Photographs and negatives of footwear impressions in blood from concrete, further described as follows:
■ Q-4 FOOTWEAR IMPRESSION DEPICTED IN NEGATIVES 1-4.
■ Q-5 FOOTWEAR IMPRESSION DEPICTED IN NEGATIVES 5-8, 21.
■ Q-6 FOOTWEAR IMPRESSION DEPICTED IN NEGATIVES 9-14.
■ Q-7 FOOTWEAR IMPRESSION DEPICTED IN NEGATIVES 15-20, 22, 23, 24.
KNOWN ITEMS:
K-1 AND K-2 LEFT AND RIGHT SHOES OF JOHN SMITH, OBTAINED ON 6/6/89.

## Photographs

Whenever examining a footwear impression in a photograph, it is necessary to have the original negatives. If the original negatives have not been provided, you should insist on having them. *There should be no exception to this.* From the original negatives, at least two natural-size enlargements should be made, which should be custom printed to best enhance the footwear impressions depicted in them. As previously covered in the chapter on photography, a natural-size photograph is one in which the print is enlarged until the scale in the photograph equals its true size. A photograph of an impression having a 12-inch ruler next to it would be enlarged until the ruler depicted in the photograph measured 12 inches. If, for some reason, there is not a scale in the photograph, then a print 8 × 10 inches or larger should be made to allow the examiner to more easily evaluate the content of that particular exposure. If only photographic prints, even those enlarged to a natural size, and not the negatives are received for comparison, the examiner cannot fullfill his or her responsibility to ensure that all the evidence on the entire negative has been examined or that the best photographic prints of that evidence have been obtained.

The full frames of the original negatives should be printed if any footwear impressions contained in them run into the edges of those negatives. Figure 11.2A depicts a photograph that was submitted as evidence to be compared with the known shoes of a suspect. Figure 11.2B depicts a full-frame photographic print of the same impression. If only the photograph in Figure 11.2A and not the negative were provided, the examiner would not have had an image of the entire questioned footwear impression and would not have been aware of the other impression that was recorded on the film. Examination of original negatives assures the examiner of having all the evidence. There have been instances when valuable characteristics in the footwear impressions were overlooked because they were depicted on the negative's edge and were lost in the printing process. Once the photographic enlargements are made or obtained, they should be checked for accuracy with an appropriate scale and should also be checked for any perspective problems.

Whenever possible, the enlarged photographs should be arranged so that multiple exposures of the same impressions are grouped together. This not only avoids possible confusion in the examination and in the reporting of results, but also ensures that the examination will benefit from all the exposures of each impression. An example of this is provided and is incorporated in the description of the questioned impressions in Figure 11.1. Twenty-four exposures were taken of four different footwear impressions at a crime scene. Negatives numbered 1 through 4 were of impression 1, negatives 5 through 8 and 21 were of impression

A

B

**11.2** A regular print, as submitted to a laboratory, depicting a questioned footwear impression (**A**). A full-frame print (**B**) made from the same negative depicts additional areas of the impression in **A** and also reveals a portion of a second impression.

2, negatives 9 through 14 were of impression 3, and negatives 15 through 20 and 22 through 24 were of impression 4. Rather than describe them as questioned impressions numbered 1 through 24 in order by ascending negative number, they may be described as follows:

Questioned impression 1: negatives 1–4

Questioned impression 2: negatives 5–8 and 21

Questioned impression 3: negatives 9–14

Questioned impression 4: negatives 15–20 and 22–24

The photographs can then be marked with the above impression numbers. One copy of these photographs can then be used for comparison, while the other can be returned along with the report to the contributor. This ensures that the contributor is aware of the descriptive numbers assigned to the photographic evidence and makes clear what you are referring to in the examination results in your report. The examination photographs that you retain can also be used to note specific characteristics and features that are observed during the examination. Organizing the photographs this way also makes convenient the cumulative use of several photographs of one impression during the examination. At the conclusion of the examination, it may also be desirable or necessary to have additional enlargements made of some of those negatives to be used in court in the event testimony is anticipated.

## Casts

Despite repetitive instructions on the use of proper casting materials, casting techniques, and the proper handling of casts, casts seem to show up in the laboratory on a regular basis in a variety of conditions. Some are received dry and others, wet; some are received in one piece, while others are in several pieces. Further, some are received with soil still on their surface, as it should be, while others show evidence of already being cleaned. Ideally all of the casts you receive will be made of dental stone, will not have been cleaned, and will have been thoroughly air-dried prior to being properly packaged.

As previously covered in the chapter on casting, dental stone casts should be cleaned in the laboratory with a saturated solution of potassium sulfate. If a plaster cast is received, it will have to be cleaned separately and as cautiously as possible to avoid the loss of detail. When the casts have been cleaned, they should be photographed with a scale and with the proper amount of oblique and fill light to provide a high-contrast recording of the detail on them. Casts that are received broken should be pieced back together as carefully and accurately as possible and photographed as if whole. At least two natural-size photographic prints should be made, so that one copy can be returned with the evidence and one can be used and retained by the examiner.

## Lifts

Electrostatic lifts taken at the crime scene and then transmitted to you should be carefully checked in a totally dark room with a high-intensity, oblique light. This will allow a determination of the content and potential value of that item of evidence. If an impression is on the lift, it should be photographed with a scale and a strong, oblique light source. When viewing an impression on an electrostatic lift (black side up), you will see a positive image of the footwear that made it. A regular photographic print of that lift could be compared directly against the outsole of the shoe. However, since the lifted impression is a two-dimensional impression and will most likely be compared against a two-dimensional test impression, it may be more desirable to have reverse photographic prints made of the electrostatic lifts.

Gelatin or adhesive lifts should be photographed in the same manner, with a scale and using high-contrast and/or oblique-light photography, which will best enhance the impressions on them.

## Original Impressions

The most desirable evidence for an examiner to have is the original impression itself, whenever that is possible. Objects such as paper, pieces of tile floor, carpet, and numerous other objects that contain the original impressions require a variety of treatments. The treatment will depend on the surface, the nature of the impression, the contrast between the impression and the surface, and whether it was a dry or wet impression when it was made. The original impression should first be photographed using a scale and the type of forensic photography that will best enhance the impression and capture as much detail as possible. In many cases, this simply involves high-contrast and/or oblique-light photography combined with a high-contrast printing process. However, the use of ultraviolet and infrared photography, as well as filters, other light sources, and specialized films, can often enable a forensic photographer to capture far more detail than is visible in the original impression. Additional treatment of original items of evidence after photography is covered in the chapter on enhancement.

## Receiving the Known Shoes

Known shoes, like questioned impressions, are often submitted for other examinations in addition to the footwear impression comparisons. If they are to be examined for other evidence, such as hairs, fibers, glass, soil, and body fluids, the appropriate cautions should be taken to ensure that they do not become contaminated. The date on which the shoes were seized should also be ascertained, since comparisons of known shoes that have been obtained months after the crime can necessitate additional considerations over comparisons of shoes obtained a short time after the crime. The outsoles of the known shoes should be photographed with a scale. The photographs provide an aid during the examination, as well as a record of the shoe. They can also be used for court presentation.

## Variation and Distortion

Both variation and distortion must be considered in the interpretation and examination of the footwear impression. Variations are the slight distinctions that exist between different footwear impressions made from the same item of footwear. Repetitive impressions of the same item of footwear will never result in two impressions that are *exactly* the same in every respect. Whether known or questioned, impressions will vary slightly from one another. These variations are due to many things, including the surface receiving the impression; the weight distribution in the footwear; the resilience of the outsole material; the location and quantity of residue, ink, or other materials on the outsole surface; and the possible interference of foreign matter between the footwear and the surface.

Another reason for variation between impressions is distortion. In some cases, distortion can be so minor and subtle that it is neither observable nor significant in an impression. It is merely a factor in the expected variation from one impression to another. In other cases, the distortion is more extensive and results in changes in the impression that go beyond the extent of ordinary variation. Distortion of the more extreme type includes slippage, double (or ghost) impressions, twisting, and other unnatural movements of the footwear. Distortions of these types are usually recognizable, but still cause concern in the interpretation of a footwear impression.

### Variation in Impressions of the Same Shoe

Variations are subtle differences between repetitive impressions of the same shoe. Examiners, in their experience and training, must learn to understand and recognize what constitutes a variation and what constitutes distortion so that they do not mistake either for differences that indicate that a different shoe made the impression.

Variations occur both in making the questioned impressions and in preparing known impressions for use in the comparison process. It is important to understand that these variables are, in fact, expected and simply part of the dynamics of the impression process. The variables occur for a number of reasons, a few of which are listed below:

1. Variations in the precise way in which the footwear strikes the surface. During each step that is taken, the precise angle of strike, the precise point of initial contact of the footwear with the surface, the amount of weight, and the distribution of that weight exerted by the foot through the shoe will not be exactly the same from one impression to the next.
2. In the case of a shoe depositing a residue impression, the amount of residue on the shoe, the condition of the receiving surface, how it receives the residue, and other marks or extraneous matter that may be between the footwear and the surface influence each impression and cause it to vary from other impressions.
3. In the case of a three-dimensional impression, the consistency, evenness or unevenness, presence of debris, and composition of the surface will cause variables from one impression to the next.
4. Distortion during the impression-making process.

## Distortion in Questioned Impressions

Distortion, as it applies to footwear impressions, could be defined as an unclear or inaccurate representation of the shoe outsole in the impression due to anything that prevents or interferes with a true recording of characteristics during the impression-making process or its subsequent retrieval.

There are several things that can prevent a clear representation of a shoe in its impression when it strikes a surface, resulting in some distortion. Causes of distortion in the actual impression-making process would include abnormal movement of the footwear during the impression-making process, interference of other matter, and unevenness or angulation of the footwear relative to the surface.

1. Abnormal movement of the footwear would include slippage, twisting, pivoting, rotation, or any movement of the footwear during the impression-making process that deviates from the movement in a normal impression. Slippage can occur in both two-dimensional and three-dimensional impressions. Slippage occurs when the footwear does not hold fast on the surface it is striking and thereby slips across or through it. It also occurs when the surface moves or gives way as a result of the footwear coming in contact with it. One example of slippage is that of a heel strike in soft soil, sand, or snow. The heel does not grab hold of the surface and continues to press down and forward into the surface, sliding forward until there is sufficient friction to stop it.

2. Interference of other matter refers to material that may become entrapped between the footwear and the surface as the impression is being made. This material can include sticks, rocks, pebbles, trash, and virtually anything that could come between the footwear and the surface on which the person is stepping.

3. Unevenness of the surface or angulation of the footwear relative to the surface could occur on uneven surfaces that might give way, change shape, or stretch during the making of an impression. The surface of the human body is a good example of this type of surface, and this kind of distortion is apparent in some contusion impressions. Snow, sand, and soil surfaces are occasionally uneven or give way during the impression-making process. The angle at which the foot strikes the surface can also result in a distortion of its features during the impression-making process.

## Distortion in Photographs of Impressions or Casts

Although photographic distortion does not occur in the impression-making process, it is commonly encountered in footwear comparisons. Photographic distortion can occur in many ways, but the most common type encountered in footwear impression evidence is the perspective problem that occurs when the film plane is not parallel to that of the impression. Other photographic distortions can result from the use of an improper lens or in the photographic printing process; however, these occur less commonly.

Photographic perspective problems occur when the plane of the film in the camera is not parallel to the plane of the footwear impression. As discussed in the chapter on photography, it is necessary to use a tripod so that the camera can be adjusted to and held in a parallel position. Unfortunately, many photographs are not taken in this manner. If the camera is hand held over top of the impression or if the camera is not positioned properly on the tripod, there will be in all likelihood some degree of perspective problem. In some cases, perspective problems are very noticeable; in other cases, they are sufficient to interfere slightly with the comparison process but are not obvious because they are so minimal.

Photographs of uneven surfaces, even if the film is parallel to the overall impression, will result in yet another distortion problem. This was previously discussed and illustrated in Chapter 2. This distortion is commonly found in photographs of deep impressions in sand, soil, and snow. It occurs when an uneven footwear impression is photographed and therefore transferred from a three-dimensional impression in more than one plane to a flat, two-dimensional image of the impression. The dimensions within the actual impression may not be accurately represented by the photograph. Although it is the unevenness of the surface causing the problem and not the photography, it is a problem encountered when interpreting footwear impressions in photographs.

The use of wide-angle or other improper lens choices can also cause a visual distortion of the image of the footwear impression. The use of a lens that is considered to give a normal image for a particular camera, such as a 50-mm lens for a 35-mm camera, should prevent this problem.

Photographic printing is usually not the source of distortion in photographs of footwear impression evidence, but distortion can occur if the printing easel and the negative are not parallel or if the negative is not flat within its holder.

## Distortion in Casts

Most casting materials have such minimal shrinkage or expansion that it is totally insignificant in the casting of footwear impression evidence. Most dental stones have less than 0.05% expansion on setting. Some casting materials that do have a real shrinkage problem are materials containing hydrocolloid alginates, which can shrink as much as 30% when they dry. Fortunately, they are rarely encountered. If there is ever a question concerning significant size differences between a cast impression and a known shoe, the examiner may wish to check with the individual who prepared the cast to ascertain the type of casting material that was used.

Distortion or size discrepancy between a cast and a shoe occasionally occurs when impressions are made in certain types of wet, oversaturated soils. When a person steps into soil that is totally saturated with water, the impression may close itself up slightly as the person removes her or his foot. This is particularly common in supersaturated clay soil, in marshy areas, and in the bank of a river or creek. Distortion can result, since it is unlikely that the overall size will be accurately represented or that the impression will close up evenly. Casts and photographs of these impressions will reflect this distortion.

## Variation and Distortion in Casework

As discussed above, there are many forms of and causes for variation and distortion during the making and retrieval of footwear impressions. While some of these can be severe and restrict the comparison process, very few of these are significant enough to prevent a successful comparison. I have seen many examiners make comparisons of a questioned impression with the shoe that in fact made the impression, and yet, because the impression and shoe did not superimpose perfectly with one another, the examiners severely restricted their opinion and in some cases even determined that the impression was not made by the shoe. They expected the impression left by a shoe to always perfectly superimpose with the test impression later made with that shoe. This does occur in some comparisons, but due to all of the factors of variation and distortion that can and do occur in the impression of the shoe against a surface, a certain amount of variation from one impression to the next, as well as possible variations between a questioned impression and a test impression, is expected.

## Examination of the Questioned Impression

### Preliminary Examination of the Evidence

Two of the accepted methods of comparison regarding footwear impression evidence are (1) "side by side comparison" and (2) "superimposition." Side by side comparison consists of placing the known shoe or known shoe impression alongside of the questioned impression where respective areas of the two can be examined. The use of dividers, calipers, oblique lighting and low magnification are often used to assist in this type of comparison. The second method, superimposition, includes the placement of a transparent known impression over the questioned impression to see the degree of agreement between the respective areas of the impression. Transparent known impressions, placed over either the original evidence or over photographs of the original evidence, often assisted by transmitted light of oblique light, normally are used with this method.

On first comparing a questioned impression with a known shoe, a preliminary visual side-by-side examination should be made. The known shoe and the questioned impression will either appear similar in design and require additional comparison or be a totally nonidentical design and require no additional examination.

For those impressions that need to be further compared, it will be necessary to prepare some test impressions of the shoes. The test impressions along with some other basic comparison aids such as dividers, low magnification, and the photographs of the questioned impressions should now be collected, along with any original impressions, lifts, or casts and the known shoes.

By comparing the impressions alongside each shoe and/or by superimposing the test impressions over the questioned impression, areas of the known shoes that could possibly have made the respective questioned impressions can be located. For purposes of conducting more detailed comparisons, additional test impressions might be required to provide better impressions of certain areas of the shoe or to better simulate what the general conditions were when the questioned impression was made.

Five areas, namely physical shape and size, design, manufacturing characteristics, wear, and random identifying characteristics, should be considered during each comparison.

## Physical Shape and Size

The physical shape and size of an impression refer to just that. They do not refer to the manufacturers size, such as a size 9. If the actual physical size and shape of an impression or a partial impression is in close agreement with the respective portions of the known shoe, then it can be said that the physical size and shape of features in that impression corresponds with the known shoe. This means that the impression, considering the variables of the impression-making process, could have been made by the respective areas of a particular known shoe. If the physical size and shape of an impression is not in close agreement with a known shoe, it is either because the known shoe did not make the impression or because of some other factor, such as distortion. Rarely do just the physical shape and size characteristics of a shoe appear in an impression alone. They are usually present and compared along with the design and other characteristics in the impression. There are some instances, however, in which only size and shape characteristics may appear. Partial or faint impressions of shoes in powdery snow or soft sand, particularly of plain-bottomed or well-worn shoes, often leave physical size and shape characteristics only. Positive identification of a shoe with a questioned impression cannot be made based on physical size and shape characteristics alone. Nonidentification, however, can be affected through absolute confirmable differences between the questioned impression and test impressions of the known shoe. Outsoles of various sizes and shapes are shown in Figure 11.3. One of those known outsoles is the same physical shape and size as the questioned outsole, yet it is distinctly different from the rest. A report of this would read:

> It was determined that the physical size and shape features in the questioned impression correspond with the respective features of the known shoe.

## Design

As discussed and illustrated in the prior chapters on manufacturing and on class and identifying characteristics, design is an exceptionally specific category. To say that the design of a questioned impression corresponds with a known impression means the specific design characteristics of both are in agreement. It pertains not only to a full impression but to any partial impression compared to the respective portion of the

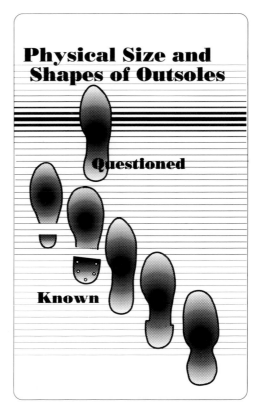

**11.3** The physical size and shape characteristics of an impression can be used to help eliminate known shoes or correlate that impression with known shoes. The questioned outsole depicted here agrees in physical size and shape with only one of the known outsoles.

known shoe. Sometimes a shoe will have several different design elements, which, together constitute the full design of the shoe, but all of them may not be represented in a partial questioned impression. Nevertheless, the comparison can still address whether or not the design elements in the partial impression correspond and are in agreement with the respective portions of the known shoe.

The comparison of the design of an impression with a known shoe goes hand in hand with, and is usually conducted along with, the comparison of the physical shape and size. Although they are in fact two separate areas of comparison, the physical size, the shape of the perimeter of the outsole and the design elements are so interrelated that those features in a questioned impression are usually hard to separate during the comparison. In fact, when using transparencies as a comparison aid, these features should be compared simultaneously. They should, however, continue to exist in the mind of the examiner as two separate areas. This is because (1) the design element size may remain the same but change in quantity within the confines of outsoles of smaller or larger sizes and (2) other designs may be enlarged or shrunk proportionally on larger or smaller outsoles.

Except in rare cases, a positive identification cannot be effected based on both physical size and shape and design alone. In order for design to be a basis for identification, it would have to be a custom-cut outsole or some similar type of unusual shoe. I once saw a case that would be the exception to this. It involved a pair of custom-made sandals. The outsoles of the sandals were individually hand cut from scraps of old tire tread. The design of the tire tread pattern combined with the precise cut of each outsole was unique.

Prior to 1970, there were relatively few choices of shoe designs available. Most shoes sold in this country were still made domestically. Since then, the footwear manufacturing situation has changed dramatically. Changing technology, specialty shoes, and the competitiveness in the footwear industry between domestic and foreign footwear manufacturers has resulted in a continuing and very rapid change in the designs of shoes. Footwear designers and manufacturers are constantly trying to improve the design of their shoes for additional comfort, better fit, improved function, and fashion. As their competitors do the same, the number of designs and the frequency with which they are changing is resulting in a vast number of designs—too many to even comprehend or count.

Although the combination of corresponding physical size and shape and design characteristics of a questioned impression with a known shoe does not normally constitute the basis for positive identification, the agreement of those features between a questioned impression and a known shoe usually carries far more weight than most persons realize. This is because there are literally many thousands of different designs of footwear manufactured in or imported into this country. The Footwear Industry of America's *International Directory of Trade and Brand Names* contains approximately 10,000 different trade and brand names alone. Any examiner who has seriously attempted to gather together pictures or standards of outsoles knows that examples of several hundred different outsoles can easily be accumulated from just a few footwear manufacturers. The point is that a footwear impression of a particular physical size and shape and of a specific design is going to be owned by only a small fraction of 1% of the general population.

In casework, when dealing with a specific outsole, the combined class characteristics of the outsole design and components can often reduce the field even further. The number of possible shoes sharing combined class characteristics can be exceptionally small. Shoe designs that are extremely popular and therefore sold in very large numbers are no exception. Although more popular shoes involve a larger volume of shoes than a less popular one, there likewise will be many more molds from which those shoes are made, and in most cases the molds of different sizes and even within the same size will be distinguishable from one another. For this reason, the number of shoes of a size and specific design is again shared by a very small fraction of 1% of the population.

One exercise that would illustrate this would be to select a particular athletic shoe someone is wearing and then begin to look for another person having a shoe of the same size and specific design, including the same mold characteristics or cut characteristics. You will observe many other shoes and may never be able to find another shoe sharing the same combined class characteristics. Even if you were to look in shoe stores, it may not be possible to find a duplicate. This is *not* to suggest that many other shoes of the same class characteristics do not exist, but is an exercise to appreciate the sparseness of shoes that are alike in precise size and design features.

Rare exceptions such as the tire tread sandal aside, there is no basis for making a positive identification based on size and specific design alone. The significance of the agreement, in specific terms, of physical size and shape and design between a questioned impression and a known shoe is, however, highly significant. A report of this might read:

> It was determined that the questioned footwear impression corresponds in physical shape and size and in design with the respective portions of the known shoe.

## Manufacturing Characteristics

The previous discussion of manufacturing in Chapter 7 not only reflects the many ways in which shoes can be made but the number of variations that can occur in shoes made in certain ways. The examination of manufacturing characteristics can address two areas: The first is whether or not the cut or molded outsole agrees in all characteristics that could vary in a particular manufacturing process, and the second is the amount of any variation that exists in that process and how likely it would be for another shoe to be made exactly like the known shoe.

On examination of a known shoe, the general method of manufacturing should be determined. This should include first, the determination of whether the shoe's outsole was cut or was molded to reach its final condition. Both the left and right shoes should be used when determining what procedure went into the assembly of the shoe, and what, if any characteristics may be variable ones. To someone who is very knowledgeable about manufacturing processes, many manufacturing characteristics and variables, especially those in the cut and wrap processes, can be observed and recognized as such without ever contacting the manufacturer. Extreme caution should be used here if you are not absolutely positive and do not have sufficient experience to make this evaluation. If characteristics that are not known for certain or on which there is speculation are of potential significance in the examination, it may be necessary and possible to determine more about them by either observing other shoes of the same type, design, and brand or by contacting the manufacturer of the shoes.

The manufacturing characteristics of a shoe, if of the variable type and if visible in the questioned impression, can add a significant dimension to the results of the footwear examination. Examiners who are not familiar with manufacturing techniques and are not certain of the variables of a shoe in a particular examination should not factor this information into their examinations until they acquire this knowledge and experience.

Examinations that determine that a shoe possesses characteristics of physical shape and size, specific design, and variable manufacturing characteristics that correspond to a questioned impression, even when lacking wear and identifying characteristics, are still highly significant. Although it is statistically impossible to predict how many shoes will possess the same combined characteristics, it is evident that the number of shoes is significantly smaller than just those sharing the size and general design categories alone. In some cases, manufacturing characteristics do not play a significant role in the comparison. For instance, a molded outsole with just general class mold characteristics that has no additional variables such as air bubbles, foxing strips, etc. would not be a factor in the examination process. In other cases, although the shoes may contain significant manufacturing variables, those characteristics may not be part of the impression or may be insufficiently clear to be of use in a particular examination. A report of this might read:

> It was determined that the questioned impression corresponds in physical shape and size and design with the known shoe. In addition, the known shoe reflects some characteristics that vary in the manufacturing process and that are therefore not present in all of the shoes of this particular size and design. These characteristics are also present in the questioned impression.

In addition, some manufacturing characteristics, including air bubbles that are random and the incomplete formation of outsole material in calendered outsoles, could be of sufficient randomness to allow for a positive identification.

## Wear Characteristics

Wear of the shoe may be defined as the erosion of the outsole due to frictional and abrasive forces that occur between the outsole and the ground. As previously discussed in Chapter 9, two factors in wear are of importance: the position and the degree of the wear on the shoe.

In the continuing examination process, the addition of corresponding wear to the other observed characteristics of physical size and shape, design, and possibly manufacturing variables, further reduces the chances that another shoe or shoes would share the same features. As a shoe wears, all of the characteristics present on the outsole are slowly but constantly undergoing change. The design, due to the wearing of the shoe, can change in its appearance and with considerable wear can even begin to disappear. Some finely detailed characteristics, such as stippling, that were visible when the shoes were new, will also change and eventually disappear, while others, such as air bubbles or the joint of a foxing strip, will change or become more evident both in the impression and on the shoe.

A shoe that corresponds in physical size and shape, design, manufacturing characteristics, and wear characteristics is approaching uniqueness. In some cases, particularly those with both manufacturing variables and specific wear characteristics, the probability of another shoe of that size and design sharing those same characteristics may be very small. Although it may be highly unlikely that another shoe will share those combined characteristics, the presence of those characteristics alone, without random identifying characteristics, in most cases would still not constitute the basis for a positive identification. A report of these features might read:

> It was determined that the questioned impression corresponds in physical size and shape, design, and specific wear characteristics with the known shoe. In addition, the known shoe reflects several design characteristics that vary in the manufacturing process during the assembly of the shoe and that, in combination with one another, would only be present in a small number of shoes of that size and design. These characteristics are also evident in the questioned impression. Although these aforementioned characteristics are not sufficient for a positive identification, it is very unlikely that another shoe would share these same characteristics and also be in the same specific condition of wear.

## Identifying Characteristics

Identifying characteristics occur on the shoe outsole with some degree of randomness. Because of their random nature, they are so unlikely to recur precisely in the same position and orientation on a shoe of the same design, that they can carry or contribute enough weight in the examination to establish positive identity. If both the questioned impression and a shoe contain sufficient identifying characteristics in common, it can be stated without any reservation or qualification that that particular shoe positively made the impression and no other shoe could have made that impression.

A positive identification based on random characteristics does not require the presence of all of the other areas of examination. For example, a footwear impression photographed without a scale but that clearly depicts distinct random characteristics could possibly still be identified, even though no reference of size is present. Another example would be a shoe that is essentially new and hasn't acquired any significant wear characteristics but has acquired some random characteristics. The presence of identifying characteristics would still allow a positive identification. A report of a positive identification would read:

> It was determined that the questioned impression was positively made by the known shoe.

The examiner should remain as objective as possible during the comparison of features shared by both the questioned impression and the known shoe. The examiner should not have expectations of finding all of the characteristics that appear on the known shoe and in the known shoe's impression. On occasion, examiners have detected characteristics on the known shoe or in impressions of the known shoe and then actually visualized those respective characteristics in the questioned impression, even though they were not visible to others. This is not being objective and is improper practice. The characteristics that are used as a basis for the conclusion must be ones that can be reasonably observed. It is better to have a conclusion that is confirmable and within the limits of observable features than to reach a greater conclusion that cannot be fully supported and demonstrated.

## Reporting the Results of the Examination

The statement of the opinion of the examiner in a report is a way of conveying that examiner's observations and conclusions to the person or agency that requested the examination.

The specific format of a report and the amount of detail or elaboration on the results of the examination are often controlled by policies of the agency or person by whom the examiner is employed or by the circumstances of the specific requests made for a particular examination. In most cases, the results can be divided into (1) positive identifications, (2) positive nonidentifications or (3) inconclusive examinations accompanied with additional statements concerning the observations that were made in the examination and why the results could not be more conclusive.

*Reporting positive identifications.* A positive identification can be simply and clearly reported as follows:

> It was determined that the impression represented by the Q-21 cast *was positively made* by the K-4 right shoe.

The word positively was included in the above statement, since there are still those who are not aware that a shoe can be *positively identified* as having made an impression.

*Reporting nonidentifications.* A nonidentification can be simply and clearly reported as follows:

It was determined that the impression depicted in the Q-14, Q-15, and Q-23 photographs *was not made* by the K-8 shoe.

If necessary, the examiner may wish to provide the reason or reasons why the nonidentification was effected.

*Inconclusive results.* Inconclusive results are those that involve comparison between known shoes and questioned impressions and do not result in a positive identification or a positive nonidentification. They include a wide range of opinions, including everything from examinations in which there was insufficient detail to conduct a meaningful examination to those in which it was highly probable a shoe made an impression or highly probable that a shoe did not make an impression.

Three items that are frequently included in an inconclusive report are (1) a statement that the result is not conclusive as to whether the shoe positively did or did not make the impression, (2) a statement of what similarities or differences were noted in the examination, and (3) what factors may have prevented a more conclusive opinion. Some examples of inconclusive findings follow:

It was determined that the questioned impression was too partial and lacked sufficient clarity to enable a meaningful comparison with the known shoes.

It was determined that the questioned impression corresponds in physical shape and size, design, and specific wear characteristics with the known right shoe. Due to the lack of observable random identifying characteristics, it could not be definitely determined whether the known right shoe made that impression or whether another right shoe, also corresponding in physical shape and size, design, and the same specific wear characteristics, made that impression.

It was determined that the questioned impression corresponds in physical shape and size and in design with the known left shoe. Based on those characteristics, that impression could have been made by the known left shoe but could also have been made by other left shoes of the same size and specific design characteristics. The absence of wear and observable random characteristics in that impression precluded a more definite determination.

# The Footwear Impression Examiner in Court

# 12

## Expert Witnesses

### Definition

Rule 702 of Article VII of the Federal Rules of Evidence (Anonymous, 1975) states that "if scientific, technical or other specialized knowledge will assist the trier of fact to understand the evidence or to determine a fact in issue, a witness qualified as an expert by knowledge, skill, experience, training, or education, may testify thereto in the form of an opinion or otherwise." State and local courts have similar guidelines allowing opinion testimony by a qualified expert witness.

An expert is thus defined as a person who has specialized knowledge in a particular area based on her or his experience, skills, training, or education. The judge will rule on whether a person meets the necessary requirements to qualify as an expert in a particular field.

The specific definition of and required qualifications of the expert witness is not further specified or defined by the courts for the various specific forensic sciences. Instead, it is the decision of the trial judge to rule on whether the expert is qualified in a particular case. The balancing factor lies in the fact that the jury can decide the weight, or importance, of each expert's testimony. If the jurors feel the expert is well qualified and knowledgeable, they can apply a great deal of weight and significance to the testimony. If the jurors feel the expert is not very experienced or knowledgeable, they can apply less weight and significance and even choose to ignore the expert's testimony.

### Qualifications of a Footwear Impression Expert

Today, footwear impression comparisons are made by a broad range of persons in several different forensic fields, including examiners of latent fingerprints, documents, and tool marks, as well as those who are described as criminalists, trace analysts, and microscopists. In many cases, these examiners have received very little and sometimes no specialized training to conduct comparisons of footwear impression evidence. They rely mainly on their general training from other forensic disciplines to conduct the examination of footwear impression evidence. In addition, many of these examiners are infrequently requested to make footwear examinations and therefore dedicate an extremely small percentage of their time to matters involving footwear impression evidence. This, of course, does not contribute to their additional experience and knowledge in this field.

Although certain forensic disciplines, such as the comparison of printed and stamped documentary materials, fingerprints, and tool marks, have some relation to either the examination or the retrieval of footwear impression evidence, none are so similar that being an expert in those fields, in itself, qualifies one to conduct comparisons between questioned footwear impressions and known shoes.

It is therefore important that the examiner be afforded specific training and experience in the field of footwear impression examination. That training and experience should include

1. Training under the direct supervision of an experienced and qualified footwear impression examiner. This would include working on cases and practical exercises of sufficient quantity over an extended period of time to enable the training examiner to acquire the necessary skills and knowledge related to this forensic discipline.
2. Reading the available literature in the field of footwear impression examination.
3. Attending specific courses, seminars, and workshops on the various aspects of footwear impression examination that are offered by federal, state and local law enforcement communities.
4. Attending meetings of forensic science societies such as the American Academy of Forensic Science, the International Association for Identification, and others whose educational programs include presentations on various aspects of footwear impression examinations.
5. Touring footwear manufacturing facilities, either in conjunction with a case or to obtain general knowledge of the various methods of manufacturing footwear.
6. Gaining additional experience and insight into this type of evidence and how it is represented in impressions by making impressions of shoes and by casting, photographing, and lifting footwear impressions.
7. If possible, conducting research to acquire more specialized knowledge of particular aspects of this evidence.

Testimony regarding footwear impression evidence and examination has been offered in courts in the United States by many persons other than forensic footwear examiners. Testimony concerning the more general aspects of footwear and footwear impression evidence has been given by police officers, crime scene technicians, shoe salespersons, and others. Although they may have knowledge about footwear, casting footwear impressions, etc., those who have not received forensic training and who do not routinely conduct footwear impression examinations are not qualified to conduct a thorough and accurate comparison of footwear and footwear impression evidence. Their testimony is usually limited to the footwear evidence as it relates to their other responsibilities.

## Courtroom Procedure

### Pretrial Conferences

A pretrial conference should always be held between the expert witness and the attorney who will offer that person as a witness. During the meeting, the following items should be attended to as they relate to the expert's examination of evidence and testimony:

1. Discuss your qualifications and experience. This is especially important in the case of an expert who has never testified before as a witness for this attorney.
2. Review the evidence and check its condition. If considerable time has elapsed between the date of the examination and the trial, or if other experts or witnesses have looked at this evidence, it may be desirable to check and review the evidence the attorney plans to use.
3. Explain the results of your examination and the significance of your opinion. It is important that the attorney understand the full meaning and significance of the results stated in your report. It is also important that any charts or graphic aids you intend to use in court be made available and discussed.
4. Check the courtroom conditions. It is a good idea to be familiar with the layout of the courtroom and to assure that there will be a place to display your charts, place your slide projector, etc.

### Presentation of Examination Results

One of your duties as an expert in court is to successfully demonstrate your findings to the jury so that they understand what examinations were conducted, what observations were made, and what opinion was reached and why. Since features examined in footwear impression comparisons, such as design, size, wear, and random characteristics are easily presented in graphic form, the use of enlarged photographs, charts, or slides to convey your observations and findings is an invaluable resource.

Demonstrative aids such as enlarged photographs, charts, and slides accomplish several things. They recapture the attention of the jury, which sometimes has lessened after long hours in the courtroom. Visual aids are often needed to show and explain evidence and concepts that are typically unfamiliar to a lay person. They also provide tangible evidence that the jury can see and examine and take into deliberation with them.

In addition, research (Illsey C,   ) has shown that graphic arts displays, such as charts and enlarged photographs, present information in a way that enhances clear understanding. In addition, the jury will retain the information provided by testimony with graphic aids longer and more completely than with verbal testimony alone.

*Enlarged photographs.* Enlarged photographs, such as those shown in Figure 12.1, while more expensive and time consuming in their preparation, are preferred by many when demonstrating findings to a jury. They are easier to see and enable demonstration of both general and minute characteristics at the same time. They also offer plenty of room for labeling or marking and provide an entire display that can be seen simultaneously. In addition, an enlarged transparency can be used, when appropriate, to demonstrate the comparison of certain features.

**12.1**  Photograph of an enlarged trial chart that has been labeled and can be used to assist the examiner in testifying.

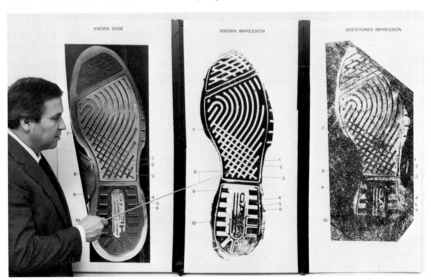

The jury can conveniently review the photographs during their deliberation, should they have a need to do so.

*Natural-size photographs.* If photographic resources are not available to make large graphic displays, a display can be made of the natural-size photographs and known impressions. Natural-size photographs are usually readily available, since they were prepared and used in the examination. They permit the demonstration of general features of footwear impression materials to the jury but are not large enough to use as a display of minute or subtle characteristics. Natural-size transparencies can also be used when needed. If properly prepared and labeled, natural-size photographs are also suitable for review by the jury during deliberation.

*Slides.* Slides can be prepared from the natural-size photographs and known impressions used during the examination. By taking slides of both general and minute features, the jury can see both a general and enlarged view of the pertinent characteristics on which the opinion was based. A roll of film and processing for slides is not a large expense, if cost is a factor that must be considered. The fact that a superimposed known impression cannot be used with slides, the logistics of obtaining a projector and screen and showing slides to a jury, and the unlikelihood of the jury ever looking at the slides in deliberation are some disadvantages of using slides. Slides, combined with the labeled natural-size photographic display, could allow an enlarged demonstration to the jury and offset some of the aforementioned disadvantages.

Any enlarged photographs, charts, or slides should have the major features to be discussed clearly labeled so that they can be specifically referred to in the written court record and so that the jury can more easily locate and review these features later during deliberation, if necessary. For instance, an identifying characteristic such as a cut that appears in both the known impression and the questioned impression should be labeled by affixing an arrow or number next to it (Figure 12.1). In this way, when discussing identifying characteristics in court, they can be clearly referred to.

The preparation for testimony in court actually begins when preparing for the examination. Consideration must be given to obtaining and retaining good photographs and test impressions that can later be used to explain the basis for your opinion.

## Last-Minute Examinations

It is not uncommon to be asked by an attorney to make a last-minute examination of some additional evidence that for some reason had never been submitted for comparison. Even worse is the occasional request to examine an item of evidence while actually in court on the witness stand. These types of requests are difficult to accommodate and often interfere with an accurate and fair evaluation or examination of the evidence. For that reason it is not advisable, nor may it always be possible, to conduct even a limited examination under those circumstances.

# References

Abbott JR. In Germann AC (Ed). *Footwear Evidence.* Springfield, IL: Charles C. Thomas, 1964.

Abbott JR. Reproduction of footprints. *RCMP Quarterly* 9(2):186–193, 1941.

Abbott JR. Reproduction and identification of impressions and marks. *RCMP Gazette* 14:3–8, 1952.

Allen JW. Making plaster casts in snow. *International Criminal Police Review* 89:171–174, 1955.

*American Shoemaking Directory.* Cambridge, MA: Shoe Trades Publishing Co., 1989.

Barnett CH. The normal orientation of the human hallux and the effect on footwear. *Journal of Anatomy* 96(4):489–494, 1962.

Beecroft W. Enhancement of physical develop prints. *RCMP Gazette* 51(2):17, 1989.

Birkett J. *Variations in Adidas 'Kick' and Related Sole Units.* Personal communication. London: Metropolitan Police.

Bodziak WJ. Evidence photography of shoe and tire impressions. *The Professional Photographer* 43–44, 1985.

Bodziak WJ. Manufacturing processes for athletic shoe outsoles and their significance in the examination of footwear impression evidence. *Journal of Forensic Science* 31(1):153–176, 1986.

Bodziak WJ. Shoe and tire impression evidence. *FBI Law Enforcement Bulletin* 53(7):2–12, 1984.

Brabant PR. Developing footwear evidence. *Identification News* 25(9):14–15, 1975.

Bradford WR. Light on the invisible footprint. *Spectrum* 140:1–4, 1976.

Brennan JS. Dental stones for casting depressed shoemarks and tyremarks. *Journal of Forensic Science Society* 23:275–286, 1983.

Bulbulian AH. A professional look at plaster casts. *FBI Law Enforcement Bulletin* 34(9):2–7, 1965.

Bullock JL. Footwear photographic techniques. *AFTE Journal* 15(2):91–94, 1983.

Carlsson K. A new method for securing impressions in snow. *Crime Laboratory Digest* 1–4, 1982.

Carlsson K, Maehly AC. New methods for securing impressions of shoes and tyres on different surfaces. *International Criminal Police Review* 299:158–167, 1976.

Cassidy MJ. *Footwear Identification.* Quebec: Canadian Government Printing Centre, 1980.

Cayton JC. Recent footwear identification innovations reviewed. *AFTE Journal* 16(3):123–125, 1984.

Cayton JC. Procedure for recovery of flooring with shoeprints. *AFTE Journal* 16(3):119–122, 1984.

Chee HW, Wilson SJ. A modified method of plaster casting. *The Forensic Sciences Society Journal* 3:83–84, 1963.

Cheskin MP. *The Complete Book of Athletic Footwear.* New York: Fairchild Publications, 1987.

Cold weather cast. *FBI Law Enforcement Bulletin* 31(4):20, 1962.

Cooke CW. Comparative analysis (footprint and tire identification). *Identification News* 29(4):3–6, 1979.

Cook CW. *A Practical Guide to the Basics of Physical Evidence.* Springfield, IL: Charles C. Thomas, 1984, pp. 101–136.

Cooke CW. Footprint identification. *Fingerprint and Identification Magazine* 57(6):9–10, 1975.

Cooke CW. Footprints and tiretracks. *Identification News* 31(7):7–10, 1981.

Creer KE. Some applications of an argon ion laser in forensic science. *Forensic Science International* 20:179–190, 1982.

Davis RJ. Current perspectives in footwear identification. *Identification News* 36(10):8–11, 1986.

Davis RJ. Footwear training seminar. Presented at the Michigan State Police Footwear Impression Evidence Seminar, East Lansing, MI, June, 1985.

Davis RJ. An intelligence approach to footwear marks and toolmarks. *Journal of the Forensic Science Society* 21:183–193, 1981.

Davis RJ. Notes on the use of chemical reagents for footwear-mark enhancement. Presented at the Florida Department of Law Enforcement Seminar on Footwear Impression Evidence, Tallahassee, FL, 1988.

Davis RJ. Scientific bureau: Electrostatic lifting. *Fingerprint Whorld* 9(36):114, 1984.

Davis RJ. A systematic approach to the enhancement of footwear marks. *Canadian Society Forensic Science Journal* 21(3):98–105, 1988.

Davis RJ, DeHaan JD. A survey of men's footwear. *Journal of the Forensic Science Society* 17(4): 271–285, 1977.

DeHaan JD. Wear and accidental characteristics of men's footwear. Presented to the International Association of Forensic Scientists, Zurich, 1975.

DeHaan JD. Footwear evidence, an update. 1982.

DeHaan JD. Wear characteristics of men's footwear. Presented at the International Association of Forensic Science Meeting, Vancouver, August, 1987.

Eade JF. Frost, fingerprints and photography. *The Police Journal* 27(1):27–30, 1954.

An electrostatic method for lifting footprints. *International Criminal Police Review* 272:287–292, 1973.

Fawcett AS. The role of the footmark examiner. *Journal of the Forensic Science Society* 10(4):227–244, 1970.

Federal Rules of Evidence, 1975, p. 13.

Fischer JF, Green E. A technique for the enhancement of shoeprints by painting with ultraviolet light. *Identification News* 30(3):7–8, 1980.

*The Foot Inside the Shoe.* National Shoe Manufacturers Association, New York, undated.

Footprint and tire impressions. *RCMP Gazette* 15–19, 1965.

Footprint examinations and the FBI rubber footwear file. *FBI Law Enforcement Bulletin* 14(3):2–12, 1945.

Footprints and tire treads. *FBI Law Enforcement Bulletin* 10(8):21–30, 1941.

*FMI Shoe Size Report.* Nashville, TN: Footwear Market Insights, 1986.

Forrest R. Step into the future with polyurethane. *American Shoemaking* 363(5):17–18, 1988.

Fox RH, Cunningham CL. *Crime Scene Search and Physical Evidence Handbook.* Washington, DC: U.S. Government Printing Office, 1973, pp 134–149.

Freels RH. Improved test impressions and prints. Presented at the FBI Technical Conference on Footwear and Tire Tread Impression Evidence, Quantico, VA, 1984.

Gaensslen R. *Sourcebook in Forensic Serology, Immunology, and Biochemistry.* U.S. Department of Justice, National Institutes of Health, 1983.

Geller J. Are we adequately trained in footwear/tire tread identification? *Florida Division International Association for Identification News* 38(3):10–12, 1988.

German ER. A microscopic footwear identification on cloth. *Identification News* 31(1):10–12, 1981.

Groom PS, Lawton ME. Are they a pair? *Journal of the Forensic Science Society* 27:189–192, 1987.

Gross H. *Criminal Investigation.* London: Sweet & Maxwell, 1949, pp 207–242.

Gupta SR. Footprint and shoeprint identification. *International Criminal Police Review* 205:55–61, 1967.

Hague F, Westland A, Kerr FM. An improved non-destructive method for detection of latent fingerprints on documents with iodine-7,8-benzo-flavone. *Forensic Science International* 21:79–83, 1983.

Hague F. Physical developer after 13 years. *Identification News* 37(8):10–12, 1987.

*Handbook of Forensic Science.* Washington, DC: Federal Bureau of Investigation, 1984.

Hamilton D. Traces of footwear, tyres, and tools, etc., in criminal investigations. *The Police Journal* 22:42–49, 128–137, 1949.

Hamm ED. Chemical developers in footwear prints. *Fingerprint Whorld* 9(6):117–118, 1984.

Hamm ED. Enhancement of bloody footwear prints by physical and chemical methods. Presented at the 35th Annual Meeting of the American Academy of Forensic Sciences, Cincinnati, OH, February, 1983.

Hamm, ED. Footwear evidence. July 28, 1982. Presented at 67th Annual Education Conference, International Association for Identification, Rochester, N.Y.

Hamm ED. Footwear and tire track examination in the Soviet Union. *Journal of Forensic Identification* 39(6):367–374, 1989.

Hamm ED. The individuality of class characteristics in Converse All-Star footwear. *Journal of Forensic Identification* 39(5):277–292, 1989.

Hamm ED. Tire tracks and footwear identification. *Identification News* 27(1):3–6, 1973.

Hamm ED. Track identification: An historical overview. *Journal of Forensic Identification* 39(6):333–338, 1989.

Hamm ED. The value of shadow in footwear and tire track evidence recovered by photographic techniques. *Journal of Forensic Identification* 38(3):91–97, 1988.

Hardwick SA. *User Guide To Physical Developer: A Reagent For Detecting Latent Fingerprints.* Sandridge, England: Home Office, Scientific Research and Development Branch, 1981.

Harvey AJ. *Footwear Materials and Process Technology.* New Zealand Leather and Shoe Research Association, 1983.

Hegvold AE. Relationships between document and footwear examinations. Presented to the American Academy of Forensic Sciences, Washington, DC, 1976.

Hempling SM. The application of ultraviolet photography in clinical forensic medicine. *Medicine Science and the Law* 21:3, 1983.

Hickman GM. Iodine sensitized paper technique for test impressions. Presented at the FBI Technical Conference on Footwear and Tire Tread Impression Evidence, Quantico, VA, 1984.

Hirschi F. Tell-tale soles. *International Criminal Police Review* 240:219–222, 1970.

Hofstede JC. Convicted by his shoes. *RCMP Gazette* 27:6–11, 1965.

Hussain JI, Pounds CA. The enhancement of marks in blood. Part 1. 5-Sulphosalicylic acid: A convenient and effective fixative for marks made in blood. Berkshire, England: Central Research Establishment, Home Office Forensic Science Service, 1988.

Hussain JI, Pounds CA. The enhancement of marks in blood. Part II. A modified amido black staining technique. Berkshire, England: Central Research Establishment, Home Office Forensic Science Service, 1989.

Hyzer WG, Krauss TC. The bite mark standard reference scale: ABFO No. 2. *Journal of Forensic Sciences* 33(2):498–506, 1988.

Hyzer WG. Scales and perspective revisited. *Photomethods* 10–11, 1988.

Illsley C. "Juris, fingerprints, and the expert fingerprint witness." Presented to the International Symposium on Latent Prints, FBI Academy, Quantico, VA, July, 1987.

*Instructions for Operating the Brannock Scientific Foot-Measuring Device.* Syracuse, NY: The Brannock Device Company. *International Directory of Trade and Brand Names.* Footwear Industry of America.

The International Directory of Footwear Brand and Trade Names, published by Footwear Industries of America, Arlington, VA 1986.

Iten PX. Recovery of shoe and fingerprint impressions by means of electrostatic transfer. *Kriminalistik* 10:468–470, 1986.

Jay C, Grubb MJ. Defects in polyurethane soled athletic shoes: Their importance to the shoeprint examiner. *Journal of the Forensic Science Society* 25:233–238, 1984.

Jay DR. A method for preparing high resolution test impressions for footwear comparison. *Identification News* 23(10):5, 1983.

Johnson R. Casting methods. Presented at the Shoe Print and Tire Tread Impression Seminar, 1983.

Joling RJ. Shoeprints: Quantum of proof. *Journal of Forensic Sciences* 13(2):223–235, 1968.

Joseph A, Harrison CA. *Handbook of Crime Scene Investigation.* Boston, MA: Allyn and Bacon, 1980, pp 84–93.

Katterwe H. *Forensic-Physical Investigations of Polyurethane Treads.* Wiesbaden, West German: Institute for Criminal Police.

Kearney J. *Tracking: A Blueprint For Learning How.* El Cajon, CA: Pathways Press, 1983.

Keijzer J. *The Identification Value of Imperfections in Shoes with Polyurethane Soles in Comparative Shoeprint Examination.* The Netherlands: Forensic Science Laboratory of the Ministry of Justice, Journal of Forensic Identification, Vol. 40(4):217–223, 1990.

Kirk P. (deceased). *Crime Investigation,* second edition. Edited by John I. Thornton. NY: John Wiley & Sons, Inc., 1974.

Koehler JRG. Footwear evidence. *RCMP Gazette* 48(9):1986.

Krauss TC, Warden SC. The forensic science use of reflective ultraviolet photography. *Journal of Forensic Sciences* 30(1):262–268, 1985.

Lafrance G. Reproduction of impressions. *RCMP Gazette* 38(1):12–13, 1976.

Last: The birthplace of shoe fashion. *Leather and Shoes* 36–42, 1974.

Lee HC. TMB as an enhancement reagent for bloody prints. *Identification News* 34(3):10–11, 1984.

Lee HC, Gaensslen RE. Electrostatic lifting procedure for two-dimensional dustprints. *Identification News* 37(1):8–11, 1987.

LeRoy HA. Physical developer. *RCMP Gazette* 48:7–8, 1986.

Loveridge FH. Shoe print development by silver nitrate. *Fingerprint World* 10(38):58, 1984.

Lucock LJ. Identifying the wearer of worn footwear. *Journal of the Forensic Science Society* 7(2):62–70, 1967.

Lytle L, Hedgecock D. Chemiluminescence in the visualization of forensic bloodstains. *Journal of Forensic Sciences* 23:550–562, 1978.

Major crime scene investigation: Casting. *Law and Order* 1972.

Mansfield ER. Footwear impressions at scenes of crimes. *The Police Journal* 43(2):93–96, 1970.

*Manual of Shoemaking.* England: C&J Clark, Ltd., 1980.

Martin FW. A simple method of taking footprints. *The Police Journal* 9:450–452, 1936.

McBrayer WS. Dust shoe prints on plexi-glass. *AFTE Journal* 13(4):26–28, 1981.

McCaffery JD. The shoe fits. *The Police Journal* 28:135–139, 1955.

McGonigle C. Tracking: An ancient skill makes a comeback. *Law and Order* 36(2), 1988.

Milligan J. Physical developer after 13 years. *Identification News* 37(8):10–12, 1987.

Moran B. Physical match/tool mark identification involving rubber shoe sole fragments. *AFTE Journal* 16(3):126–128, 1984.

Moreau DM. *Fundamental Principles and Theory of Crime Scene Photography.* Forensic Science Training Unit, FBI Laboratory.

Moriarty CC. Taking casts of footprints. *Police Journal* (London) 5:229–232, 1932.

Morton S. Shoe print development by physical developer treatment. *Fingerprint Whorld* 9(34):60–61, 1983.

Murdock JE. Photography of luminol reaction in crime scenes. *The Criminologist* 10(37):14–19, 1966.

Music D, Bodziak WJ. A forensic evaluation of the air bubbles present in polyurethane shoe outsoles as applicable in footwear impression comparisons. *Journal of Forensic Science* 33(5):1185–1197, 1988.

Myers DA. *A Reference Guide for Law Enforcement Personnel.* Beaverton, OR: SOLE Publications, 1982.

Napier TJ, Thompson LR. *Transfer and Back-Transfer of Electrostatic Lifts Between Film and Folder.* 1987.

Nause LA. Footwear impressions on glass. *RCMP Gazette* 47(5):9–14, 1985.

Norkus P, Nappinger K. *New Reagent for the Enhancement of Blood Prints.* Florida Department of Law Enforcement, Vol. 36 (April 1986).

O'Hara CE, Osterburg J. *An Introduction to Criminalistics.* New York: MacMillan, 1949, pp 103–120.

O'Hara CE. *Fundamentals of Criminal Investigation.* Springfield, IL: Charles C. Thomas, 1956, pp 726–735.

Ojena SM. A new improved technique for casting impressions in snow. *Journal of Forensic Sciences* 29(1):322–325, 1984.

Olsen RD. Sensitivity comparsion of blood enhancement techniques. *Identification News* 36(8):5–11, 1986.

Osterburg JW. *The Crime Laboratory,* 2nd ed, 1967.

Owen F. A latent heel impression. *Police Journal* (London) 27:221–223, 1954.

Pagliano J. Last stop: The shoe shop. *Runners World* 20(10):70–71, 1985.

Petraco N, Resua R, Harris H. A rapid method for the preparation of transparent footwear test prints. *Journal of Forensic Sciences* 27(4):935–937, 1982.

Petty CS, Smith RA, Hutson TA. The value of shoe imprints in automobile crash investigations. *Journal of Police Science and Administration* 1–10, 1973.

Pick up the trail from impressions found on firm surfaces. *FBI Law Enforcement Bulletin* 20(6):12–15, 1951.

Pick up the trail with plaster casts. *FBI Law Enforcement Bulletin* 20(5):6–10, 1951.

Preparation for, and casting of, shoe and tire impressions in soil. *Forensic Bulletin* 3(6).

Preservation of impressions in earth. *Ohio Law Enforcement Training Bulletin* 1(1):1959.

Preserving prints of shoes and tires on hard surfaces. *FBI Law Enforcement Bulletin* 30(6):7–10, 1961.

*Professional Shoe Fitting.* New York: National Shoe Retailers Association, 1984.

Puri DKS. Footprints. *International Criminal Police Review* 187:106–111, 1965.

The reproduction of original evidence in the third dimension. *FBI Law Enforcement Bulletin* 5(12):3–9, 1936.

The reproduction of shoeprint and tiretread impressions. *FBI Law Enforcement Bulletin* 16(6):5–11, 1947.

*Retailer's Guide to Footwear Construction.* Kettering, England: SATRA Footwear Technology Centre, 1986.

*Retailer's Guide to Footwear Fitting.* Kettering, England: SATRA Footwear Technology Centre, 1986.

Reynard JN. Footprints: The practical side of the subject. *The Police Journal.* 30–34, 1948.

Robbins LM. *Footprints: Collection, Analysis and Interpretation.* Springfield, IL: Charles C. Thomas, 1985.

Robbins LM. Estimating height and weight from the size of footprints. *Journal of Forensic Sciences* 31(1):143–152, 1986.

Robbins LM. The individuality of human footprints. *Journal of Forensic Sciences* 23(4):778–785, 1978.

Robbins LM. Making tracks. *Law Enforcement Communications* 12(1):14–15, 1984.

Rossi WA. How shoe sizes grew. *Footwear News Magazine* 34–35, 1988.

Russell JR, Matharu SS, Brennan JS. *A New, Portable Device for the Electrostatic Lifting of Marks.* Personal communication. Metropolitan Police, 1985.

Samen CC. Major crime scene investigation: Casting (shoe and tire impressions). *Law and Order Magazine* 52–57, 1972.

Schacter RJ (Ed). *The Dictionary of Shoe Industry Terminology.* Philadelphia: Footwear Industries of America, 1986.

Segura MA. Footprints and tire marks. *Forensic Science Digest* 7(1):1–17, 1981.

*Selection and Application Guide to Police Photographic Equipment.* Washington, DC: U.S. Department of Commerce, National Bureau of Standards Publication 480-23, 1980.

Sharma BR. Foot and footwear evidence. *Journal of the Indian Academy of Forensic Sciences* 9(1):9–13, 1970.

Sharma BR. *Footprints, Tracks and Trails in Criminal Investigation and Trials.* Allahabad, India: Central Law Agency, 1980.

Shoe Allied Trades Research Association: Soling in the 1990's. *American Shoemaking* 362(5):14–16, 1988.

Shoe and tire impression evidence. *FBI Law Enforcement Bulletin,* revised ed, 1986.

Shoe and tire impressions. *FBI Law Enforcement Bulletin* 24(1):15–17, 1955.

Shoe and tire impressions put the suspect at the scene of the crime. *Forensic Bulletin* 4(4):2–4, 1975.

Shoeprint on rug links man to house robbery. *FBI Law Enforcement Bulletin* 30(6):18–19, 1961.

Sodermann H, O'Connell JJ. *Modern Criminal Investigation.* New York: Funk & Wagnalls, 5th ed, 1945, pp 156–168.

The soul of a running shoe. *Science '82* 3(6):104–105, 1982.

Soule RL. Reproduction of foot and tire tracks by plaster of Paris casting. *Identification News* 11(1):8–12, 1961.

Speller HC. The identification of crepe-rubber sole impressions. *The Police Journal* 22:269–274, 1949.

Stone RS. Mathematical probabilities in footwear comparisons. Presented at the FBI Technical Conference on Footwear and Tire Tread Impression Evidence, Quantico, VA, April 1984.

The story of footwear, National Shoe Manufacturers Association, New York, NY, edited by Harold Quimby, 1949.

The story of lasts, National Shoe Manufacturers Association, New York, NY, edited by Harold Quimby, 1948.

Thompson RW. Sulfur casting. *AFTE Journal* 12(2):15–16, 1980.

Tiller CD. Examination of footprints at crime scenes. *RCMP Gazette* 24:12, 1962.

Tips on making casts of shoe and tire prints. *FBI Law Enforcement Bulletin* 32(10):18–22, 1963.

The true story of shoe sizes. Long Island City, NY: Sterling Last Corporation, undated.

*Trace Metal Detection Technique in Law Enforcement.* Washington DC: U.S. Department of Justice, Law Enforcement Assistance Administration, 1970.

Truszkowski GJ. Daylight flash photography of three dimensional impressions. *Journal of Forensic Identification* 38(3):83–90, 1988.

Tryhorn FG. Scientific aids in criminal investigation. Part V. Marks and impressions. *Police Journal* (London) 10:19–27, 1937.

Vandiver JV. Casting materials. *Identification News* 30(12):3–9, 1980.

Vandiver JV. Easier casting and better casts. *Identification News* 30(5):3–10, 1980.

Vandiver JV, Wolcott JH. Identification of suitable plaster for crime scene casting. *Journal of Forensic Sciences* 23(3):607–614, 1978.

Vandiver JV. Silicone rubber casting problems and very few solutions. *Identification News* 31(1):7–9, 1981.

Vandiver JV. Tests of polysulfide, silicone rubber and polyether. *Identification News* 31(2):3–8, 1981.

Van Hoven H. A correlation between shoeprint measurements and actual sneaker size. *Journal of Forensic Sciences* 30(4):1233–1237, 1985.

Von Rummelhoff J. Does the print belong to the perpetrator? *AFTE Journal* 15(2):96, 1983.

Walker SA. *Sneakers.* New York: Scholastic Book Services, 1978.

Walsh KAJ, Buckleton JS. An aid for the detection and correction of inaccuracies in photographic reproduction of shoeprints. *AFTE Journal* 19(3):1987.

Walter E, Wilson D. Joint forces research and resource unit physical developer. *Identification Canada* 8(2):13–16, 1985.

Warren DF, Briner RC, Longwell CR. Visualization of latent shoeprint impressions by the freeze-thaw technique or freeze-thaw III. *Crime Laboratory Digest* 1983.

Warren DF, Lemonds AT, Longwell CR, Briner RC. Photography of footwear latents using ultra-high contrast techniques. *AFTE Journal* 16(3):113–118, 1984.

Warren G. Snowprint-wax casting material information. *AFTE Journal* 15(2):77–78, 1983.

Watson J. The technique of lifting and photographing shoe prints left in dust. *Fingerprint and Identification Magazine* 1–6, 1958.

Webster's Third New International Dictionary. Springfield, MA: Merriam Webster, 1981.

Wojcik RJ, Sahs PT. Reproducing footwear evidence impressions. *Identification News* 34(7):6–7, 1984.

Wolfe JR, Beheim CW. Dental stone casting of snow impressions at sub-zero temperatures. Presented at the Northwest Association of Forensic Scientists Meeting, Spring 1989.

Yeomans RE. A non-classic perspective on footwear identification. *RCMP Gazette* 47(6):10–15, 1985.

Young PA. Electrostatic detection of footprints. *Police Research Bulletin* 21:11–15, 1973.

Zmuda CW. Identification of crepe sole shoes. *Journal of Criminology, Criminal Law and Police Science* 44(3):374–378, 1953.

Zmuda CW, Brodie TG. Limitations in the identification of foot and shoe impressions. Miami, FL: Dade County Crime Laboratory, undated.

Zweidinger RA, Lytle LT, Pitt CG. Photography of bloodstains visualized by luminol. *Journal of Forensic Sciences* 18(4):296–302, 1973.

# Glossary

*Adhesive lifter* Any of a variety of adhesive coated materials or tapes used to lift fingerprints or footwear impressions. They are more suited to lifting powdered fingerprints and are less suited for lifting the larger footwear impressions.

*Air sole* An outsole or midsole having an air cushion incorporated into it.

*Ambient light* the available or existing light that surrounds the object being photographed. Natural light.

*Anatomic* The shape of the body or parts of the body. As it relates to the foot, the natural shape of the foot.

*Ankle* The joint formed at the lower ends of the two leg bones, the fibula and tibia, and the talus bone of the foot.

*Anterior* The forward portion.

*Arch* Portions of the foot that are curved in an arc formation. The main arch is the longitudinal inner arch that runs along the inner border of the foot.

*Arch support* A device made of leather or synthetic material that can be shaped to a person's longitudinal arch and inserted or built into a shoe to give support to that person's natural arch.

*Attenuated light* Supplemental light that is added when photographing luminol enhancements. The light is sufficient to allow for exposure on the film of the object being photographed, but not to significantly interfere with the photography of the luminescence.

*Athletic shoes* Shoes designed for participation in sports.

*Autoclave* An oven or heated pressure chamber used to vulcanize rubber.

*Back strap* A strap of leather or material running down the center and rearmost portion of the heel of the shoe.

*Ball* The part of the foot just behind the large toe.

*Biomechanics* The science that concerns itself with the structure and mechanical movement of parts of the body, such as the foot.

*Blocker* An oversized unit sole made of one or more components that are later die cut or trimmed to size.

*Brannock device* Registered name of a foot measuring device of the Brannock Device Company.

*CAD–CAM* Abbreviation for Computer Assisted Design–Computer Assisted Manufacture.

*Calendering* A process where raw outsole materials are passed between rollers under heat and pressure to produce a textured or designed outsole.

*Casting* The filling of a three-dimensional footwear impression with material that takes on and retains the characteristics which were left in that impression by the footwear. *Also,* a method of making a mold by first making a three-dimensional model of a shoe and then making a series of casts of that model, eventually resulting in a mold from which additional outsoles can be formed.

*Class characteristic* An intentional or unavoidable characteristic that repeats during the manufacturing process and is shared by one or more other shoes.

*Clicker* A name commonly used to describe a machine that cuts through outsole and/or midsole materials in a cookie cutter fashion.

*Combined class characteristic* The combination of two or more independent class characteristics.

*Compression molded* A molding method in which a molding compound is placed into an open mold cavity, after which the mold is closed with heat and pressure applied causing the molding compound to melt and conform to the size and shape characteristics of the mold cavity.

*Court shoe* An athletic shoe used for tennis, basketball, and other court sports.

*Crepe rubber* A lightly colored, natural, unvulcanized rubber used for soles and heels. Most crepe rubber made today is synthetic crepe rubber.

*Cut outsole* An outsole whose final shape and/or size has been affected by cutting or trimming.

*Cutting dies* Steel dies having a sharp edge used to cut shoe parts and outsoles.

*Deformable impression* An impression that causes the surface to deform, either permanently or temporarily. Permanent deformable impressions would include those impressions in sand, soil, and snow, whereas a temporarily deformed impression would include those on skin, carpeting, etc. A depressed mark.

*Degree of wear*  The extent that a particular portion of the shoe is worn.

*Dental stone*  A gypsum product similar to plaster of paris but with different properties due to its manufacturing process. It is far superior to plaster of paris for use in casting footwear impression evidence because of its hardness and durability. It is produced by heating gypsum material in an autoclave under pressure and in the presence of steam.

*Die cutting*  Cutting outsoles or other shoe components by forcing a sharpened steel die through preformed outsole material with the assistance of a "clicker" machine.

*Die stone*  A gypsum product produced like dental stone but normally in the presence of a catalyst. It is slightly harder than dental stone.

*Direct attach*  A process wherein the lasted upper of a shoe is lowered into the mold cavity where the midsole of outsole is molded directly onto that upper.

*Distortion*  An unclear or inaccurate representation of the shoe outsole in the impression due to interference with the impression making process or its subsequent retrieval.

*Dorsiflexion*  Position of the foot with the toes pointed down.

*Dry origin*  A footwear impression that contained no moisture, either from the footwear itself or from the surface, and which has remained free of moisture.

*Dual density*  A term used for a midsole-outsole combination, where the outsole and midsole are composed of materials having different densities.

*Electrostatic lifting device*  A device consisting of a high-voltage supply used with a special conductive lifting film to electrostatically transfer a dry footwear impression from a surface to the film.

*Electrostatic detection apparatus*  A device primarily used to detect indented writing on documents and thin card stock, and can also be used to detect footwear impressions on those items.

*Enhancement*  Rendering an impression more clear or more visible through physical, photographic, or chemical means.

*EVA*  Ethyl vinyl acetate.

*Eversion*  Raising of the outer border of the foot.

*Extension*  Movement of the foot forward and downward.

*Examination quality photographs*  Sometimes called evidence photographs, they are close-up photographs taken of specific items such as footwear impressions in a manner to capture the maximum detail, so that they can later be used in a scientific comparison.

*Fixatives* A spray or powder applied cautiously to a three-dimensional footwear impression just before casting. It assists in the release of the substrate material from the cast.

*Flat foot* A foot without a longitudinal arch.

*Foot stance* Position of the feet while standing or walking. The feet may be turned inward or outward.

*Footwear* Any apparel which is worn on the foot, such as shoes, boots, etc.

*Footwear Industries of America (FIA)* The trade association of the U.S. footwear manufacturers.

*Foxing* A component of the shoe used to reinforce and/or cover the shoe where the outsole and the shoe upper join together. Usually a strip of rubber (foxing strip) wrapped around the lower part of the shoe.

*Gelatin lifter* A gelatin material laid on a pliable backing that can be applied to a surface to lift a footwear impression. The lifters can be white, black, or transparent.

*General condition* The overall condition or general amount of wear (i.e., unworn, severely worn, slightly worn).

*General crime scene photography* General photographs taken at a crime scene to show a broad view of objects and their surroundings.

*Hallux* The large toe of the foot.

*Hand milling* In the mold making operation, the process of routing or milling metal off of a mold blank by hand during the manufacture of a mold, as opposed to the milling operation being directed by a computer.

*Heel* A separate component attached to the rear portion of the outsole; or, in a continuous outsole, a raised area in the rear portion of the outsole. In a flat shoe, the heel area.

*Heel area* In a flat shoe, the area which would normally be occupied by a separate heel component.

*Identifying characteristic* A particular characteristic resulting from something randomly added or removed from a shoe outsole and which causes or contributes to making that shoe outsole unique.

*Impression evidence* Objects or materials that have retained certain characteristics or other objects or materials which have been impressed against them.

*Injection molding* A molding system in which the sole or entire shoe is formed by forcing a midsole or outsole material into a closed mold. Variations of the process include molding outsoles separately and molding outsoles directly onto lasted shoe uppers.

*Insole* A piece of material which is shaped and sized to match the bottom surface of a last and which is between the upper and the outsole of the shoe.

*Inversion* Raising the inner border of the foot.

*Known shoe* A shoe of known origin that is compared to a questioned footwear impression.

*Last* A piece of wood, metal, or synthetic material that has been shaped and sized to simulate a foot. The last serves as a form on which the shoe is built.

*Lasted* A shoe upper on a last awaiting the bottom to be cemented or molded onto it.

*Lift* To transfer an impression from its original surface to a surface having better contrast.

*Logo* A name, design, or pattern that appears on the sides or outsoles of athletic shoes and which is a trademark or the manufacturer.

*Manufacturer's shoe size* The shoe size that a particular manufacturer has assigned to a particular shoe, and is indicated on a shoe and/or shoe box by the manufacturer.

*Microcellular* Made of expanded soling material with small closed cells and a density of less than 0.8.

*Midsole* The component, found on some shoes, that is placed between the outsole and the shoe upper.

*Molded outsole* An outsole which is formed in a mold and whose final size and shape characteristics of a mold.

*Multi-density midsole* A midsole which is composed of materials of two or more densities.

*Oblique light* Light that is positioned at a low angle of incidence relative to the surface being photographed. Also referred to as side-lighting.

*Open pour molding* A method of making outsoles normally utilizing Polyurethane (PU). The mold is filled by pouring the PU into the mold cavity and then closing the mold. Single unit sole, direct attached soles, and combination outsoles can be made utilizing this process.

*Outsole* The outermost sole of a shoe. The portion of the shoe that contacts the ground and is exposed to wear.

*Plaster of paris* A gypsum casting material produced by heating crushed gypsum in an open oven at high temperatures. Although used for years as a casting material for footwear impressions, it is no longer regarded as the best material, due primarily to it softness.

*Polyurethane (PU)* A family of resins produced when di-isocyanate reacts with organic compounds containing two or more active hydrogens. It is used in both the outsole and midsoles of shoes.

*PVC* Polyvinyl Chloride. A thermoplastic polymer used in shoe outsoles

*Plantar* Pertaining to the sole of the foot.

*Plantar flexion* Position of the foot with the toes and the foot bent back toward the leg.

*Porous* A material or surface having pores.

*Posterior* The rear portion.

*Random characteristic* One in which the size and/or shape and/or position of the characteristic depend, to some degree, on chance.

*Ritz stick* A foot measuring device used primarily for heel-to-toe and ball width measurements.

*Rubber* A material made from the extract of the rubber plant or synthetic versions of the same material.

*Running shoe* A shoe specifically designed for jogging or running.

*Sequenced enhancement* A series of two or more enhancement procedures arranged so that none adversely affect the success of the next.

*Shoe upper* The components of the shoe excluding the outsole and/or midsole.

*Sneaker* An athletic shoe with a fabric upper and rubber sole having the characteristic foxing strip around the upper-outsole joint.

*Snow print wax* Registered name of an aerosol product used to assist in the casting of footwear impressions in snow.

*Sprue* The piece of material formed in the feed channel through which the material is injected in an injection molding process and which remains attached to the shoe when the molding operation is finished.

*Sprue mark* A mark left on the surface of an injection molded shoe after removal of the sprue.

*Stippling* Small raised designs sometimes placed on the otherwise smooth surfaces of a midsole or outsole mold. The stipple pattern is placed on the mold through individual strikes of a die containing the stipple pattern. A hand-struck stipple pattern is unique to the mold it is on.

*Stitching* The use of a tool to help join the various unvulcanized parts of a shoe together prior to vulcanizing. It is associated primarily with shoes made utilizing unvulcanized rubber soles, foxing strips, and rubber upper components. *Also,* the application of thread through the bottom (bottom stitched) or side (side stitched) of a shoe to help join the bottom to the upper.

*Texture* A rough surface of shallow design added to otherwise smooth surfaces of a mold. Texture can be applied mechanically and chemically. The texture is reproduced in shoes made in that mold. Texture differs from stippling in that it is more shallow and is not applied in the same fashion.

*Test impression* An impression made utilizing a known shoe for the purposes of comparing it to a questioned footwear impression.

*Toe bumper guard* A thick strip of rubber that is placed around the front perimeter of the shoe surrounding the toe area.

*Toe cap* A piece of rubber or material placed across the top of the toe area or vamp of a shoe to increase the durability and strength of the shoe in that area.

*Tongue* A strip of material covering the instep of the foot lying beneath the shoe laces.

*Three-dimensional impression* An impression with the dimension of length, width, and depth.

*Thermoplastic rubber (TR)* A polymeric material that maintains rubber-like properties.

*Two-dimensional impression* An impression, which for all practical purposes, has only the dimensions of length and width and not depth.

*Unit sole* A molded heel-sole unit of a predetermined size. It must be glued and/or stitched to the upper.

*Variations* Those variables or subtle differences that normally exist between repetitive impressions of the same shoe.

*Vulcanization* An irreversible process in which a rubber compound is heated under pressure resulting in a chemical change in its structure. The process to which shoes with raw rubber components are subjected in order to permanently bond the components together.

*Wear* The erosion of the outsole due to frictional and abrasive forces that occur between the outsole and the ground.

*Wear characteristics* Changes in the surface of the outsole that are observable in the impression and/or known shoe and that reflect the erosion of the surface of the outsole.

*Wear pattern* The position of wear on a shoe. An arrangement or pattern of wear characteristics that stand out against areas of relatively less or greater wear.

*Wellman outsole cutting machine* A machine which is used to cut outsoles from unvulcanized calendered outsole material. It utilizes a template that dictates the size and shape of the outsole and a sharp knife blade that runs around the template and cuts out the outsole.

*Wet origin* A footwear impression containing moisture, contributed by either the footwear and/or the surface. Although the wet impression will eventually dry, it is still an impression of wet origin.

# Appendix

Many of the successes or failures in retrieving footwear impressions from crime scenes are related to the use of proper materials or products. The following is a list of some footwear impression products and their sources. The list is not intended as an endorsement or recommendation of any particular source but is provided to those with no source information at all as assistance in locating certain products for use in the retrieval of footwear impressions.

| Company | Products |
| --- | --- |
| Dentsply/York Division<br>Dentsply International, Inc.<br>570 West College Avenue<br>P.O. Box 872<br>York, Pennsylvania 17405 | Dental Stone/Die Stone *Note:* Dental stone and die stone can be obtained from most dental supply houses. This is just one example |
| Shoe Trades Publishing Company<br>61 Massachusetts Avenue<br>Arlington, Massachusetts 02174 | Publishes "American Shoemaking Directory" (Lists Shoe Manufacturers in the U.S.) |
| Footwear News and Footwear News Magazine<br>P.O. Box 1402<br>Riverton, N.J. 08077 | Weekly newspaper and monthly magazine of the footwear industry. Includes occasional articles of interest and every other December they publish a directory of manufacturers, importers, and wholesalers |

| Company | Products |
| --- | --- |
| Poly-Shapes Converters, Inc.<br>P.O. Box 156<br>140 East End Drive<br>Gilberts, Illinois 60136<br>(312) 428-5311 | Sta-Dri Drifuss Boots (plastic boots to wear when making impressions of known shoes) |
| Eastman Kodak Company<br>343 State Street<br>Rochester, N.Y. 14650 | Roller Transport Cleanup Film #4955<br>(CAT 114 1555) 11 × 16 inches (For impressions of known shoes) |
| Sirchie Laboratories<br>P.O. Box 30576<br>Raleigh, N.C. 27622<br>1-800-356-7311 | General fingerprint supplies and powders |
| Faurot, Inc.<br>26 Nepperhan Avenue<br>Elmsford, N.Y. 10523<br>(914) 592-4604 | General fingerprint supplies and powders |
| Lightning Powder Company<br>1230 Hoyt Street S.E.<br>Salem, Oregon 97302-2121<br>1-800-852-0300 | Gelatin footprint lifters, thin rulers, fingerprint powders and supplies, physical developer chemicals |
| Foster & Freeman, Ltd.<br>25 Swan Lane, Evesham, Worcs.<br>WR11 4PE England<br>Evesham(0386)41061 | Electrostatic Lifting Kit, Electrostatic Detection Apparatus (ESDA) |
| Kinderprint Company<br>P.O. Box 16<br>Martinez, CA 94553<br>(415) 372-6667 | Electrostatic Lifting Kit, Gelatin lifting materials fingerprint powders and supplies, Snow Print Wax, clear adhesive materials |
| ODV Inc.<br>P.O. Box 305<br>South Paris, Maine 04281<br>(207) 743-7712 | Gelatin Lifting materials fingerprint powders, fixative spray |
| Identicator Corp.<br>4051 Glencoe Avenue<br>Marina Del Rey, CA 90292<br>(213) 305-8181 | Inkless fingerprint and footprint materials |
| Smithers Bio-Medical Systems<br>919 Marvin Avenue<br>P.O. Box 118<br>Kent, Ohio 44240 | Bio-Foam materials |
| Footwear Industries of America<br>1420 K Street N.W.<br>Suite 600<br>Washington, D.C. 20005 | Directory of Shoe Industry Terminology, International Directory of Footwear Brand and Trade Names, U.S. Footwear Industry Directory |

# Index